Marseille

Marseille

David Crackanthorpe

INNERCITIES
Signal Books

First published in 2012 by
Signal Books Limited
36 Minster Road
Oxford OX4 1LY
www.signalbooks.co.uk

A catalogue record for this book is available from the British Library

ISBN 978-1-908493-11-8 Paper

Cover Design: Devdan Sen
Typesetting: Devdan Sen
Cover Images: Wikipedia Commons
Illustrations: Wikipedia Commons; istockphoto.com: i, 60, 122, 174, 190,
    198; © Mary Dowey/*www.provencefoodandwine.com*
p.14 (colour section): street market Noailles

Printed in India

Contents

Preface and Acknowledgements

The fortunes of a relationship first took me from Nîmes, where I was living, to Marseille where it worked out; and so my learning of that city then was as passionately interesting as it remains, years after the personal history faded away. Marseille has the power to enlist and hold you in the long roll of its lovers, its familiars, its inhabitants even when you have left your anchorage there.

The city's fascination, which I have tried to convey through an account of its extraordinary setting and history and the streets and buildings which with the constant wash of the sea make it up, is not at once evident to the newcomer because of all the random, crowded growth spreading in disorder over a once picturesque landscape whose higher ground only survives more or less unspoiled. Yet if ever a familiar phrase was selected to match the first view from the surrounding hills of a scene so complex, ambiguous aesthetically and historically, but different from the one that inspired it, "a sight so touching in its majesty" would be the choice.

"Touching" may allow for the pathos of over two thousand years of human history, but is perhaps not the apt word for most *Marseillais* in their variety and in the shadow of the lawless reputation that has been attached to them, deservedly or not. But they appeal to the empathy of the unprejudiced (likely, in France, to come from beyond the frontiers) by what has been called their *nonchalance bavarde*, their easygoing and talkative way, friendly, open, hospitable, though essentially withdrawn. They inhabit their city like an island, and strangers can earn a reward in the process itself of growing acquainted, seeking understanding, accepting a station outside the inner ring of identity—much as the amateur of any art work can only hope to do in relation to the artist. I believe this is the right way to learn to appreciate Marseille in its beauty, eccentricity, its historical and human expression and often its manifest disfigurement.

My wife Laura first suggested I write this book to express the feeling she saw I had for the city, and so my primary debt for all is to her, and is lovingly paid.

James Ferguson welcomed the project at Signal Books, fostered it, and has my gratitude for making that ideal a reality.

I would like to pay tribute also to Jeanne Laffitte, publisher of many of the works acknowledged in the text, and whose bookshop for both new and collectors' works at Les Arcenaulx near the Vieux Port is the brilliant starting point for any appreciation of the town, its secrets, its past and future.

My thanks are due to John Murray for permission to quote from Richard Cobb's *Paris and Elsewhere*, the one work written in English to give more than a superficial account of the character of Marseille and, with its perspicacity and refusal of the received ideas which disturb and devalue so much of what is written about the city, one of the most illuminating in any language.

I am grateful to Bob Davis for drawing my attention through the report on which he collaborated, *The Making of a Ruling Class*, to the parallel between the industrial dynasties of eighteenth- and nineteenth-century Marseille and those of Tyneside with their intermarriages, cumulative economic power and self-perpetuating systems.

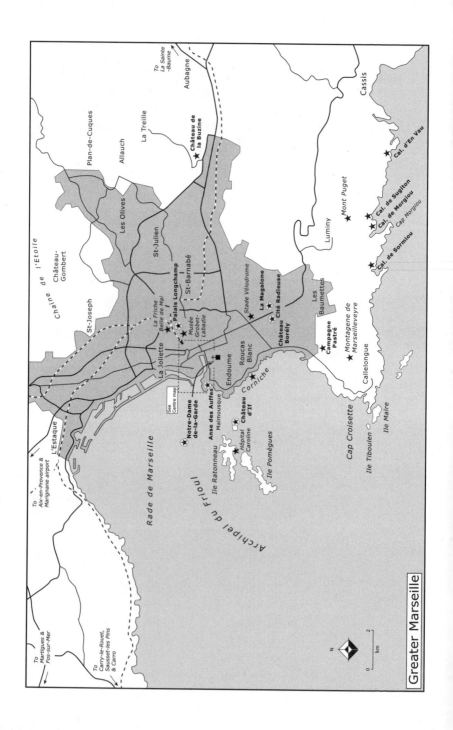

Greater Marseille

Introduction
Origins and Image

What most characterises this Mediterranean port is its secrecy.
                                                    Richard Cobb

When Paris-to-be was a riverside village of fishermen's huts, Marseille—Massalia to a Greek, Massilia to a Roman—was known over the civilized world as a stone-built maritime city with great temples dedicated to Pythian Apollo and Artemis of Ephesus, and a system of government, according to Aristotle who devoted a book to it, in which the populace shared by electing those fittest among them to rule. Of the 26 centuries of its existence, Marseille has been part of France for only six; and this truth lives on in popular awareness, undimmed by immigrant tides. Marseille belongs to whoever approaches it from the sea, wrote the novelist Blaise Cendrars, a lover who recognized the city's mystery without claiming to solve it. But it would seem too that those approaching from the sea enter the spirit of Marseille so that new arrivals from the landward side—coming out of France—meet a common front: cordial, voluble, apparently extrovert, anything but morose and designed to screen the reality of this "very complex, very hard-working, and rather austere city" (Cobb), and divert attention to other horizons.

Out of France—the phrase implies the otherness of Marseille, its setting apart within a frontier of hills (here, the sea has never been a frontier). "We are a separate republic," declared the deputy and industrialist Jules Charles-Roux in 1907, "neither national nor French." Cicero wrote of Marseille as being at the extremity of the Greek universe, surrounded by Gauls and beaten by waves of barbarism yet ruled by wisdom. Although this may seem fanciful, the *Marseillais* feel themselves to be the precipitate of the most ancient of civilizations as well as of all the migrant peoples who have constituted them since the landing of Ionian ancestors from the city of Phocaea.

Besides secrecy, an inherent taste for independence has been the essential characteristic of Marseille, if not always in its better interests. The historian and novelist Olivier Boura, writing of his native town's capacity for choosing the wrong camp ever since opting for Pompey rather than Caesar, claims that Marseille loves revolt and has a culture of sedition; she likes to pose as rival to Paris, Lyon, Barcelona. "Fundamentally," he says in one of the least explicit of the many literary feminizations which have dressed, and sometimes disfigured the image of Marseille down the ages, "she likes her solitude. To be besieged—by Caesar, Constantine, Charles Quint—to be taken, forced, humiliated, is part of her history and her being." He could have added to the list of assailants the revolutionary Convention whose repression of dissent in the town once named rebellious by Louis XIV was far more violent than his had been. Frequently sacked from end to end during its history, Marseille, according to Cendrars, remains the same—insolent, happy to be alive and more independent than ever, but the people, despite their loquacity, secretive and hard. "My God," he added, "how difficult this town is!"

Multiple Images

From Roman times this ingrained difference has marked the image of Marseille as viewed from without, and since difference is rejected by centralizing cultures, this has largely accounted for the dubious or shady reputation still attaching to its name. Athenaeus in 200 AD described the Marseillais, whom Cicero had once so much admired in the "Athens of the Gauls", as pusillanimous, effeminate and soiling themselves in shameful vices in the pursuit of pleasure. The early reputation of the city took root in moral reaction and grew, in the centuries after Marseille became incorporated into France, in a climate of increasing and increasingly imposed conformism to which Marseille remained always an exception, turned toward the outer world and corrupted by abundance.

Viewed from Paris where French perceptions have been ever more concentrated, this southern harbour stands for the geographical hexagon's nether part, an orifice by which all pollution is admitted or excreted. Yet Marseille is known for its public modesty; in 1860 there was strenuous protest against the unveiling of statues emblematic of Ocean and Mediterranean on the summit of the new stock exchange building on account of their too salient nudity, and a copy of Michelangelo's David, now displayed near the beach of the Prado, was kept out of sight for half a century for the same reason. Cobb, whose ardour for Paris became tempered by closer acquaintance, remarked that Parisians saw the Marseillais as mendacious, shallow and content to bask in the prevailing sunshine like colonial people, childlike yet cunning. But the great investigative journalist Albert Londres wrote that Marseille was a lesson in itself, a banner whipped on the wind before infinite horizons. The passionate contradiction of these views is part of the mystery of Marseille and proof of its allure.

The classical age considered the Marseillais as shrewd and temperate but quickly turned to violence and given to disrespect for the great ones of the world. Montesquieu contrasted the candour and virtue of northern people with the lively passions of the south by which the incidence of crime is multiplied. In the nineteenth century Victor Hugo and Hippolyte Taine were at one in denouncing the violence of the men of the Midi; the historian Michelet held that in a land rendered inhospitable by sun and *mistral* it was inevitable that the people should be both rough and irascible; for Balzac, they were urged on by the vice of fiery temperament. These writers formed their opinions at a time when a journey from Paris, where they lived, to Marseille took longer and was a greater undertaking than one from

Paris to Moscow; the most respectable of them worked from hearsay and drew on the great national stock of received ideas while contributing to its renewal.

In the later nineteenth century the broadcast image of Marseille began to change abruptly. The industrial revolution which transformed the docks, the arrival of the railway line from Paris in 1855, the opening of the Suez Canal and the expansion of the French overseas empire led to Marseille being looked on—often askance—as the queen of the Mediterranean and a city of mythological wealth. "They are rich and speak in patois," Hugo noted in 1847. Curiosity was attracted in greater currents, and curiosity provokes a defence in the Marseillais, still evident today, made up of an easy sociability and standard jokes designed, in Cobb's words, "to deceive the Parisian and the visitor from the north and exclude him… For generations one of the principal concerns of the Marseillais has been to keep themselves to themselves." In the service of this defence, as well for their own advancement, a number of Marseillais writers working in Paris propagated the image of their city as inhabited by grotesques whose pastime was the invention of *galéjades,* the tall stories, exaggerated and often vainglorious, which have come to be believed in as a hallmark of the Marseille spirit.

The foremost of these writers was the now forgotten Joseph Méry whose large success imposed the clichéd view of the Marseillais as boastful and neither courageous nor serious. Boura, however, points out that in Marseille as in Naples farce and buffoonery have an artistic and philosophic status. Petronius Arbiter, author of the *Satyricon* in which the amoral characters Encolpius and Ascyltus have much in common with a caricatural representation of the Marseillais, was born and educated in Marseille. The Marseillais Arnoux in Flaubert's *L'Education sentimentale* is presented as vulgar, inconsequential and unscrupulous, full of superficial obligingness. Self-mockery is not prominent in French humour and Boura suggests that there may be some perversity in the Marseillais' taste for it, a delight in seeing others take you at your word and swallow whole the ironic self-estimate you offer to the gullible.

But the handicap of all these fictions, weighted by the pervasive influence of the comedies and films of Marcel Pagnol and aggravated by social and political events between the two world wars, may never be wholly shaken off. The process has only just begun and in the minds of many from outside France and, it seems, of practically all within it, the name of Marseille still tends to signify the discreditable, the dangerous or simply the "impossible". Among the best accounts of the condition of the modern town, by the sociologist Jean Viard, is *Marseille, une ville impossible.* The critic and poet André Suarès, who led a hermit-like existence on a hillside of outlying Marseille but was widely read in his day, wrote that many Marseillais intellectuals rejected the town which had become an industrial and colonial centre: "Most often," he said, "thinking people have a horror of Marseille."

The lightweight reputation, borne ever since the slur of Athenaeus and in which the Marseillais themselves were to some extent complicit, earned for the town and its men in the army an injustice in 1914 which was never corrected. A senator attempting to cover the blunders of the military command accused the 15th army corps, composed largely of men from Marseille, of running away in the face of the enemy; the Parisian press took up the charge and kept it alive. No enquiry was made to exonerate these soldiers who, with the men who followed them to the war from Marseille during the next years, were subjected to collective military punishments, sometimes denied medical care and posted in positions of particular danger. The calumny of cowardice was not effaced by the sacrifice of more than half its officers and men by the 141st infantry regiment of Marseille, possibly in part due to envy because Marseille was far from the front; with great numbers of military passing through, prostitution had never been so flourishing, cafés and music halls were full of animation, the activity of the port and industry were known to grow during the war years, and wealth continued to accumulate—though not in the pockets of the proletariat from whose homes most of the conscripted men came.

The prejudices affecting Marseille and its perenially renewed immigrant element were part of the nationalism developing in

France after 1870, with hostility to populations considered mixed-race or *métèque*. This pejorative term is still in uninhibited use, and Marseille on the Mediterranean frontier and a short sea journey from Corsica was particularly in the sights of aggressive nationalists. Jean Viard asserts that many within Marseille, whether they were descendants of the first Greek colonists or of much more recent arrivals, connived at this denigration as they recognized in it a reflection of what they felt to be true. Unfortunately the history of the inter-war years did much to confirm them.

In Marseille, described as the crossroads of the races, Italian names often go with Corsican origins and in the mountains of Corsica the rule of law was, and may remain, a relative concept. During the 1930s the Corsican element in the mix of Marseille grew in influence; on the death of the incumbent mayor in 1931 his deputy, the communist Simon Sabiani, became temporary mayor, and after the ensuing election he acquired the real if not the nominal power in the city, backed by an obedient and active Corsican following at least ten thousand strong and aided by the gangsters Carbone and Spirito. All three moved progressively to the right and ran a regime in the streets and on the quays of threat, fear and revenge which in the press both at home and abroad earned for Marseille the name of the Chicago of France. The respectable Marseille bourgeoisie retreated in dismay to safe outlying quarters, disillusioned with politics, and Parisian journalists spoke of a lawless tribal reserve stretching from the Rue de la République to the sea. By 1939 the trio and their supporters had gravitated to fascism, and after the occupation by the Germans of the southern Free Zone in 1942 they became assistants to the Gestapo, organizers of the *milice* and complicit, if not actively involved, in the use of torture on resistant suspects. Sabiani and Spirito ended their days peacefully, the first at Barcelona in 1956, the second at Sausset-les-Pins on the coast near Marseille, where he owned a restaurant, in 1967. Carbone, at least, was blown to pieces in a trap set by the resistance before the end of the occupation.

Under this rule the security and administration of the town deteriorated drastically. In October 1934 King Alexander of Yugoslavia and the French foreign minister sent to welcome him into France on his arrival by sea at Marseille were assassinated before an enormous crowd on the Canebière; the wounded king was taken not to the hospital but to the Préfecture where he died, while the police opened fire on the crowd. The foreign minister bled to death in public for lack of a tourniquet. Although security on the day was formally the responsibility of the state, in the eyes of the world the incident helped create an enduring belief in the unsafety of the town. This impression was reinforced by a fire in 1938 in the Nouvelles Galeries, a department store on the Canebière, in which 73 people died, the fire services of the town proving inadequate or non-functional, and the hospitals unprepared. It happened that the disaster coincided with the holding in Marseille of a ruling party congress in the presence of Edouard Daladier the prime minister, who denounced the dismemberment and degradation of authority in Marseille. By decree of 20 March 1939 the council was deprived of real authority and the town placed under state tutelage, an ultimate humiliation for the city founded within two centuries of the first permanent settlement, a village inside a clay wall, on the Palatine hill in Rome. The state of tutelage remained in being until after the Liberation in 1944.

Defences

Secrecy as a general characteristic of a town or people may be as much a defence mechanism as a desire for separation and privacy. The later history of Marseille and the progressive erosion of its good name have perhaps engendered in the Marseillais a reaction of recoil from enquiry, even from any show of unusual interest where a conclusion confirming accepted prejudices is to be taken as foregone because it has so often before been reached. So in scattered texts and accounts by travellers and witnesses, allusions to the character of the Marseillais are both rare and meagre. For the most part, you have to find out for yourself and, as Richard Cobb points out, "Marseille can be, for the stranger, an extraordinarily lonely city." Stendhal claimed that the vicinity of the sea destroys small-mindedness and that unaffectedness belongs to the Midi: "It is the opposite of the politeness of Paris whose function is to remind you of the respect for himself felt by the person speaking to you and which he expects from you in return." At least in Marseille there is to be found the vibrant life of the Mediterranean street and, as the novelist Joseph Joffo discovered when as a boy during the Second World War he first came from Paris, "a sense of joy, a quick, living air that took my breath away... I learned later that the port was a centre of gangsterism but I never wanted to know. Marseille that morning was for us a great laughing fête, the most beautiful walk ever."

Every visitor is struck by the impression that in Marseille, unlike in other big towns, the proletariat seems to inhabit the centre as much as the outskirts. It is sometimes described as a plebeian city with a hint that this, together with the obvious truth that much of the *classe ouvrière* is of mixed racial origins, helps to preserve the general French habit of nervously-tinged condescension towards both town and people. But it is a mistake to suppose that the remnants of the *grande bourgeoisie,* the families who for so long profited from the fortunes of Marseille, have gone. Like the ancient Britons retreating into the Cambrian and Cumbrian mountains before tides of Saxon and other invaders, the wealthy Marseillais have taken to the hills, in their case the sunny slopes to the south of the Vieux Port where the view of the sea is spectacular and house prices guarantee exclusivity.

The *haute bourgeoisie* of Marseille, consisting of a few hundred families, is judged by its own members as one of the most closed, self-centred and interrelated in all France, and even the appointed consuls and consuls-general of the nations have difficulty in entering it (supposing they wish to). Yet Edmonde Charles-Roux, the novelist descended from one of the most prominent of these families and who was for many years the companion of the Protestant mayor and minister Gaston Defferre, could claim that in every rich Marseillais there were two dissimilar beings: one, the man of habit on whom hypocrisy imposed a morose reserve, the other a man of imagination ready to be carried away to the furthest limit of his own fantasies. The famous jurist Paul Lombard, a native of Marseille, distinguished between those Marseillais who accept and are proud of the accent they speak with, and those whose dream is to be of cured of what he describes as the "Corsican/Genoese" inflection of the heroes of Marcel Pagnol, *chantant*. Others refer to the Greek and Latin origins of the local speech. But in each case, Lombard claims, there is a vocabulary of expressions untranslatable into French which express a solidarity, consideration and tenderness foreign to northern conceit. These must be the people, all classes confounded, in whom Viard found a common memory of greatness inseparable from their image of Marseille, and a mentality of living and belonging to a capital city.

Marseille is unquestionably the most cosmopolitan city in the Mediterranean world. Fourteen per cent of its population have immediate origins overseas and a glance at the telephone directory shows the extraordinary variety of extraction of a great many more. For centuries the city, like London, has derived its power from the import and export of civilizations; it is home to every revealed religion and to men and women of all races. There is a high rate of unemployment and there always has been; in the catalogue of French towns Marseille comes in ninetieth place for the percentage of those of working age who are in work. But Jean Viard points out that here the northern and Protestant work ethic has less currency and less hold; the structuring of identity by work is weaker than in the north and the absence of work may be less destructive of family and individual fabric than elsewhere.

In the famous Marseille football stadium, the Vélodrome, populations of every origin and income level, spectators white, brown and black in the familiar local saying, are joined in a common passion and place without conflict—though as with the Roman amphitheatres of Arles and Nîmes the seating arrangements and separate exit passages are designed to avoid potentially risky encounters between classes whether defined by social category or wealth. But research shows that beyond all categories the people of Marseille esteem highest in the list of possible attributes the quality of life in their town. The apparent dilapidation which often strikes the first-time visitor counts for nothing much in the opinion of the inhabitants.

The Marseillais may be right in attempting to keep Marseille to themselves—on the whole they like it as it is, they always have, they will pull it about and demolish and rebuild, they count on the sea and the surrounding hills as a shield from interference, there is a committed loyalty easily discernible through the defences; and it is of course this that guarantees the characteristic of Marseille which the observer may feel should most of all be preserved from centralization or invasion, its non-conforming, secretive authenticity.

Euroméditerranée

In 1995 the European Union and countries around the Mediterranean set in motion a process of development of free exchange and growth in which the French state was anxious to take a leading role. Marseille was the obvious pivot and platform for this attempt—had not the poet Mistral declared long ago that the destiny of Marseille was to be the seat and capital of "Latinity"? Might Marseille, in a near or distant future, be the centre of this Mediterranean arc running from Barcelona to Milan, to reconnect it in a new perspective with past splendours? Euroméditerranée, an organism in which public money could be invested and controlled, was created with a view to pulling Marseille up in the world and rivalling Barcelona. Already a restructuring of the nineteenth-century docks and warehouses which had turned in Cobb's words "from great waterfront to a desolate industrial waste of abandonment and rusty cranes", has been carried out and these un-Mediterranean buildings, recalling the London dockland and in part designed by English architects, are being gradually and perhaps reluctantly adapted to other uses.

It is agreed that in Marseille reinvention and development have to wait on urban rehabilitation; the exception to this rule seems to be in the sphere of culture and the arts, by their nature ready to work on whatever comes to hand. The disused tobacco factory of the Belle de Mai, dating from 1860 and the days of the state monopoly created in 1674, now houses an assortment of artists' studios, film and television offices and production units, theatre, music and dance studios, and a writers' centre with workshops for the assembly and rehearsal of these projects. The election of Marseille to be European capital of culture in 2013 drew impetus from the developments at the Belle de Mai which it will also largely help to benefit.

Meanwhile, American and Dutch fund managers have invested heavily in a future commercial centre in the docks and in the renewal of the Haussmanian Rue de la République which joins the dockland to the Vieux Port. In this context, government-commissioned reports have urged, among more material projects, the promotion by the administration, the people and the cultural elite of Marseille of a better, more optimistic, perhaps more hygienic picture of their town. The long silence which followed the end of the Algerian war and the repatriation of great numbers of colonists of French origin who settled in Marseille, their port of arrival, and the consequent decline in conditions and image, were to be ended. One study concluded, "it is necessary that the Marseillais' discourse be progressively modified… since they are both vectors and producers of the image of the town." But this academic view is countered by Jean Viard: "it happens that certain of the local elites present their town, not in its complex authenticity, but in the light they believe the most seductive. Since this may not be altogether Marseille, it may not be altogether convincing either." It could seem that Euroméditerranée, before getting truly off the ground, has run up against a fixed feature of the character and history of Marseille, perenially ignored, always reemerging—a taste for independence which is seen from elsewhere as bordering on the perverse. Planners arriving from the capital point to the town's exposing of its poverty in such a way as to make a casual public show of negligence which elsewhere would be tucked away in the "ethnic" suburbs.

Nevertheless, the machinery of renewal is on the move. Investment is concentrated on a zone of 311 hectares between the docks and the railway station of Saint-Charles served, since 2006, by the new TGV line; in other words on the central area though not the historic heart of the town. Glasgow and Genoa are cited as city ports where similar operations have been carried out successfully. The Euroméditerranée vision is to consider Marseille as no longer merely itself but part of a metropolitan urban region of almost two million inhabitants though this ideal entity is as yet not well defined, lacks precise limits and whatever it may one day become, is for the time being without political cohesion. The chosen zone will, it is hoped, benefit from the installation of business centres, hotels, public and private enterprises, touristic and cultural facilities and a residential renovation (in buildings long empty of any residence at all) leading to greater social mixture.

Apart from the TGV, three motorways reach their terminus here, a new tramline is already in function, and on the waterfront a promenade of two or three miles will run alongside refashioned nineteenth-century docks for modern cruise ships, a fast growing tourist market which is an unquestioned success for Marseille among so much remaining conjectural in the ambitious campaign. In 2012 it is calculated that a million cruise passengers a year may pass through the port, and some of them through the town.

But doubting voices are raised. Marseille is the champion of inequalities between its districts, the average income is the lowest in France and certain *arrondissements* are the most poverty-stricken in the country. Doubters fear that these will be left out of range of the benefits of the Euroméditerranée project while the new apartment blocks and conversions will go to takers from outside. Between the renovated buildings of the docks and the streets to north and east of them, the aspect of urban decline is largely unchanged; the people living there maintain the unanxious, perhaps fatalistic nonchalance that characterizes populations half of whose horizon is the sea, but the sense is palpable that the inflow of capital, the propagation of grand schemes, the undoubted improvements will benefit the state and the city more than its inhabitants.

Large scale urban planning or reinvention at huge expense is unavoidably normative and prescriptive since funding must come principally from above; this is particularly true in France where assimilation directed to and from the centre is a historic concern, systematically practised. But reinventing Marseille was never going to be easy. The editors of *Marseille une métropole entre Europe et Méditerranée*, published by La Documentation Française, a publicly funded house in the capital, remind readers that history weighs heavily on the dynamics of change; and that the particularity of

Marseille is that history has been so much longer and enriched by the addition of more, and more diverse, cultures than is true of other French, European, or Mediterranean towns. Marseille, they announce, is an illustration of an urban model of which it is probably the only representative, untypical not only in avoiding the social crises of multiculturalism, but also in the constant tendency to identify its destiny with the sea and the port through which the variety of cultures has passed and which it holds so dear.

Although reinvention has started, not everyone is thought to be taking part in it. The editors warn that if Marseille has taken 2,600 years to become what it is, no one should imagine that as much time remains to bring about the changes to be negotiated or imposed. In a fine example of the psychological fracture that has always existed between the capital and Marseille, they insist that the obstacles of urban disorder and inequality must be rapidly overcome if Marseille is to cease being a commercial and harbour enclave. Will the Marseillais be wise enough for the work? is their closing question.

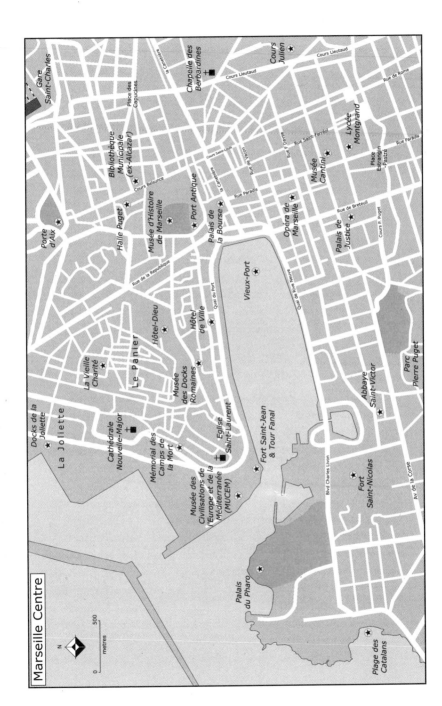

Marseille Centre

Gare Saint-Charles

Docks de la Joliette ✪

La Joliette

Cathédrale Nouvelle-Major ✚

La Vieille Charité ✪

Le Panier

Mémorial des Camps de la Mort ■

Musée des Docks Romaines ✪

Musée des Civilisations de l'Europe et de la Méditerranée (MUCEM) ✪

Eglise Saint-Laurent ✚

Fort Saint-Jean & Tour Fanal ✪

Hôtel-Dieu ✪

Hôtel de Ville ✪

Rue de la République

Porte d'Aix ✪

Halle Puget ✪

Bibliothèque Municipale (ex-Alcazar) ✪

Place des Capucines

Cours Belsunce

Musée d'Histoire de Marseille ✪

Port Antique ✪

Palais de la Bourse ✪

Quai du Port

Vieux-Port ✪

Chapelle des Berbardines ■

Cours Julien ✪

Cours Lieutaud

Cours Lieutaud

Rue de Rome

la Canebière

Cours Saint-Louis

Rue de Vacon

Rue Paradis

la Canebière

Rue Paradis

Rue F Davso

Rue Saint-Ferréol

Cours Saint-Louis

Lycée Montgrand ✪

Musée Cantini ✪

Place Estrangin -Pastré

Rue Paradis

Opéra de Marseille ✪

Palais de Justice ✪

Rue de Breteuil

Cours P. Puget

Quai de Rive Neuve

Abbaye Saint-Victor ✪

Parc Pierre Puget

Fort Saint-Nicolas ✪

Blvd Charles Livon

Av de la Corse

Palais du Pharo ✪

Plage des Catalans ✪

N

0   500
metres

1

Contours
Geography and Topography

> Marseille is washed by the sea on practically three sides; the only land access is on the fourth.
>
> Julius Caesar

Landfall

The motorway approaching the Vieux Port of Marseille from the direction of the airport rises towards the summit of the low mountain chain encircling the town and its territory, then, like the railway line before it, enters a tunnel; at the exit the whole gulf appears in one view, prodigious in sunlight, spread in an arc from north to south with hills and crowded valleys, towers and docks—and the feature that the eye first seizes, a string of islands which from this height seem to ride at anchor on the indigo surface of the sea. "The heart dilates," wrote the historian and novelist Christian Harrel-Courtès describing this view, "one becomes carefree, light, and in ecstasy at the sight of such Greek harmony."

The best way in to Marseille, that taken in 600 BC by the founding colonists from Phocaea in their fifty-oared ships, is from this arid, rocky archipelago guarding the approaches, and this is possible today for anyone who goes out into the bay and returns on the passenger launch to the Vieux Port. Seen by prospecting colonists, the vision from the islands would present the ideal site even before they found the entrance to what was to be their harbour; the topographical resemblance to the bay, islands and port of Phocaea is striking. From the shore, the land rises gradually like the tiers in an amphitheatre—now after more than two millennia largely built over—to the ring of hills enclosing it from end to end; the distance to the furthest about fifteen kilometres, and the highest rising to a height of six hundred metres, its summit rocky as the islands themselves.

The needs both of defence and cultivation seemed provided for. The swift Phocaean oarsmen would have circled the bay northwards from the cape projecting into the sea in the quarter they had sailed from. Half way round is an inlet between promontaries, narrowing to a mouth so closely set—28 metres wide—that a boom could be floated across it, and within, a deep gulf whose still water hardly shows the motion of the sea under the wind. This, which Aristotle described as the most perfect natural harbour in the universe, the Phocaeans named Lacydon, the almost unchanged anchorage now known to all the world simply as the Vieux Port.

The coast has not always followed its present line. During the last Ice Age the sea level was 130 metres lower and the tidemark fifteen to twenty kilometres farther out. Snow stood on forest-clad hills and bison grazed on the lower ground. With the melting of the ice the sea returned to invade valleys and the steep ravines of mountain sides, creating what are now the *calanques,* fjord-like inlets in some of which the land falls in cliffs to the water. Lacydon, aligned east-west and sheltered from the northern *mistral,* was the most protected and amenable of them, forty hectares of surface with a gradual sloping shore to the east and depth and width enough to shelter a fleet of ships. The Phocaeans constructed quays, built their town, Massalia, covering approximately an area equal to that of the harbour on a peninsula of twin hills to the northern side—Strabo in the first century BC described it as having the form of a theatre above the port—and for two thousand years this remained the extent of the city within the walls.

It is thought that the Phocaeans acquired the site by marriage of their leader with a daughter of the local ruler of the Segobriges, or by negotiation with this Celto-Ligurian tribe who occupied the hinterland but who are believed never to have settled on the shore and whose territory, as far as the hills, the Greeks gradually appropriated and sometimes won in battle. These hills, forming the guard and barrier of the Marseille basin and pierced only by the single narrow valley of the River Huveaune which is in turn enclosed by the Chaîne de la Sainte-Baume where it rises, delimit the Marseille *commune*, 23,000 hectares or almost three times that of Paris, and were certainly inhabited in the Palaeolithic period. In 1985 a team of divers led by Henri Cosquer, three of whom lost their lives in the exploration, discovered the entry to a rising tunnel 35 metres below the sea's surface in the cliff face of one of the calanques south of Marseille: in 1991 Cosquer finally reached the end of the tunnel, a cave largely above water level and decorated with hundreds of animal paintings, carvings and hand prints including some made by children held at the height of a man's shoulder. The entry has been permanently closed to protect the cave and its contents but this discovery seems to show how the unique beauty of the site—bay and mountain, sea and islands—have inspired human creative awe since the time of its earliest known manifestations.

Between the harbour and the hills lies the wide ascending saucer of land from which for centuries Marseille attempted to derive part of its sustenance, but from the first the climate forced the population to rely on the sea: "They occupy," said Strabo, "a territory of olive trees and vines, but too arid for cereals." Import and export became the essence and purpose of the life of Marseille, a merchant city from its beginnings, which were those of a chance trading station grown permanent. The fact that the indigenous Celto-Ligurian population soon turned hostile—Silius Italicus described the Phocaeans as surrounded by arrogant tribes and terrified by the savage rituals of their barbarous neighbours—suggests that as well as introducing the olive and the vine, the Greeks brought women with them or sent for them from their native Phocaea in order to found an expanding colony. From an early date they quarried stone—the luminous pink limestone of which the older buildings of Marseille are constructed—in excavations on the southern side of the harbour and near the Cap Couronne at the northern extremity of the Chaîne de l'Estaque, and built a quay of great limestone blocks, eleven metres long, six wide and two deep, unearthed between 1992 and 1996 on the northern shore of Lacydon. Within a century or two their town, built on rising ground above the quayside, was protected by a rampart whose remains were discovered in 1967, but the Greek colonists, "like frogs about a pond" said Plato, looked always to the sea which guaranteed their independence. The people of Massalia exchanged their highly reputed wine and oil for imported provisions, relying on commerce and on their fleet and naval skills. The rising plain, where long afterwards the wealthy class of Marseillais built their *bastides* or country houses and the poorer their *cabanons*, has been swallowed up by the spreading town, though some neglected oases of trees and fields remain, with remnants of former villages about them.

The higher slopes carried evergreen oak forests part of which, a sacred wood whose trees, according to the poet Lucan, were purified with human blood, was felled on the order of Caesar during his siege of the town for the construction of a platform and towers equal or superior in height to the stone ramparts surrounding them. Practically all the rest of the forest has been taken for shipbuilding or for burning. The historian Fernand Braudel has pointed out the connection between the slow growth of trees and the wealth of Mediterranean ports; periods of decline are needed for the trees from which good ships are built to mature, while long ages of expansion denude the neighbouring forests and drive the shipbuilders further afield for supplies of wood. The bare hills of the Marseille hinterland, now given over to walkers and to hunters in the season, testify to this; the ground vegetation is thyme, rosemary, cistus, lavender, gorse and a great wealth of wild flowers, while the remaining trees are juniper and terebinth with some Aleppo pine and wild olive.

From the highest of these hills, the Mont Puget, the entire territory of Marseille is visible, 57 kilometres of coastline from the Chaîne de l'Estaque in the north towards Martigues, where some forest survives and the calanques shelter villages and fishing ports, to the southern calanques below the Mont Puget itself, between Marseille and Cassis and mostly uninhabited and inaccessible by road. On clear days the view extends as far as the Camargue in the west to the Cap Sicié near Toulon in the east. In the centre of this incomparable seaward sweeping panorama is Marseille in the perspective of its islands, sprawling, vast, bathed in a light city haze.

Horizons: Mistral and Mountains

The city haze is hardly due to pollution, except on the stillest days. In Marseille the classic Mediterranean climate, with a yearly average of three hundred days of sun, is affected by the mistral which blows down the Rhône valley axis at all seasons and with varying strength on at least one day out of three, purifying the air and sweeping the sky of cloud. In 1828 after an outbreak of yellow fever the Hôpital Caroline, a great neoclassical group of buildings, was constructed on the Île de Ratonneau in the belief that the mistral would carry infections away to sea, and it remained in use until 1942 and the German occupation. The mistral, sometimes cold, always dry, can rise very suddenly and whip up the sea within minutes to force eight fury, shaking even the protected surface of the Vieux Port and making casual navigation along the coast dangerous or impossible; Atlantic-sized rollers hit the beaches and shipping stays in port.

Nevertheless the climate is mild with fewer than twenty days of frost which seldom goes below minus five, although in 1506 and again in 1709 even the salt water of the Vieux Port froze hard. The winds of Marseille, like most local climactic peculiarites, inspire in the population both fear and love; Harrel-Courtès describes the mistral as "sovereign, tempestuous and at times terrible", but goes on to say that on summer afternoons a movement of air off the sea tempers the heat which in towns away from the coast can become stifling, while at evening a breeze from inland, by definition northerly, is deliciously reinvigorating. Another Marseille novelist, Yann de l'Ecotais, recounts that from the end of 1769 the mistral blew for fourteen consecutive months; but without the mistral, he says, Marseille would be unimaginable, it would be like Paris with no grey skies, no pollution, no din.

In autumn between days of serene limpidity the rain is brought by the south wind, with violent storms and chaotic downpours but from which some zones such as the islands and the calanques from Marseille to Cassis are practically exempt, counting as the driest areas of France. The winter is brief and often sunny: the novelist Madeleine de Scudéry noted in 1645 that "in high winter you make calls without the need of a fire, and you walk round the port as if you were in the Tuileries in July." In summer the aridity renders the hill-sides above the building line especially vulnerable to wildfires spread by the prevailing winds, with pine trees blazing like torches and the desiccated undergrowth of herbs and shrubs fast burning out of control. In 1998 4,000 hectares were destroyed and draconian regulations introduced, including a ban on access to the massif of the calanques when conditions are extreme—a prohibition hard to enforce in an area largely without roads but approached by innumerable former goat tracks and erratic paths that die out perversely among the trees or in waist-high scrub.

The hills or mountains of Marseille—taken from west to east, the massifs of la Nerthe, l'Etoile, Garlaban, Saint-Cyr and Marseilleveyre (the highest)—rise to between three and six hundred metres; they are composed of calcareous rock raised in the pre-Tertiary Era leaving basin floors filled during the Tertiary with a conglomerate called in French *poudingue,* from puddingstone, and in the valleys with alluvial deposits dating from the Quaternary. On these foundations, between hillocks and low-lying plateaux cut by streams, the city is built. The most prominent of the hills within the present town is the Massif de la Garde, 162 metres in height and crowned by the Basilica of Notre-Dame, the emblematic church of Marseille though not the largest. The hill has always been used for keeping watch over the sea approaches not visible from the harbour; from the tower of the Fort Saint-Jean at the entrance to the port the view is limited to a distance of sixteen kilometres against the radius of fifty within sight of la Garde, which has therefore served across the millennia as far more than a feature of the landscape to be carried in the memories of seamen and ships' passengers, or recorded by writers such as Madeleine de Scudéry: "It is the most beautiful place in nature... on one side you have the port at your feet and so close that you can hear the galley pipes played. On another you have more than twelve thousand bastides and on the third, the islands and sea as far as the eye can reach... on the fourth side you see a great desert bristling with outcrops of rock... where the sterility and solitude are as awful as the abundance on the others is delightful."

Water: Aqueducts and Sewers

In the climate of Marseille, both civic amenity and natural abundance must depend on the reliable presence of fresh water. From the beginning this was a problem that increased with the town's growth. The great rivers flowing to the Golfe du Lion from the Alps—Rhône and Durance—run on the far side of the enclosing hills. The only substantial streams crossing the territory of Marseille are the Huveaune and the Jarret, the first rising on the northern side of the Massif de la Sainte-Baume and the second in the Chaîne de l'Etoile within sight of the sea, and turning to rivers in their relatively brief course only in the two seasons of generous rain, spring and autumn. The antique city on its hill was endowed with springs and wells, perhaps enough for the first population, but karstic fountains in or beneath limestone hills fail in times of drought unless their source is a multiple reservoir deep below the surface; even the apparently inexhaustible Fontaine d'Eure upstream from the Pont du Gard and captured by Roman engineers to take its pure water fifty kilometres across country to Nîmes, has an irregular seasonal flow varying between 150 and 1,300 litres a second.

In the old town of Marseille deep underground cisterns called the Caves Saint-Sauveur, subject of much legend and built of the same pink limestone as that used for the ramparts, have been found beneath the Place de Lenche, and another, dated to the third century BC, near the line of the walls. The Saint-Sauveur cisterns have a capacity of at least 3,000 cubic metres, are composed of seven chambers measuring ten metres by five with a height of approximately eight metres to the vault and were fed by stone galleries receiving water from an aqueduct and from rain water drains, of which a large quantity have been discovered. Outside the rampart and in proximity to the Greek quayside and the later Roman docks was a huge well six metres in diameter by ten deep, which is thought to have been used to replenish docked vessels with fresh water.

As the population grew in the Middle Ages an aqueduct was built from the Jarret, and later from the Huveaune, to the city and completed in 1318. Each quarter of the town was made responsible for providing fountains, wash places and drinking troughs. The aqueduct remained in use until the mid-nineteenth century and was protected by summary measures that show the vital importance of water supply; the Swiss Thomas Platter recorded in 1605: "I passed an aqueduct of seventeen arches… which is uncovered, but if anyone damages it he is taken up… and without more ado the hand that committed the offence is cut off."

Until recently most towns and cities, whatever their water supply, lived with conditions of hygiene that even hardened inhabitants of the time found difficult to bear. Marseille had the sea which was believed to purify anything put in it, as everything was, but on the way the Vieux Port, now so scintillating, received the discharge of every street and gutter of the town above it. The cry of *passarès!* from the upper window of an alleyway would be heard as the package or pot of refuse and its content, wrapped or not, fell to the ground at the feet of passers-by lucky enough to avoid it. In 1323 a piece of machinery called a *marie-salope* with wheel and buckets, still in use in 1654, was installed to drag the bottom of the port, operated by galley slaves who then carried the dredged matter to be thrown further off into the sea. Medieval statutes attempted to control the habits of the populace: "It seems to us easier to contain the filth before it falls into the port than to get it out once it has," they stated hopefully. The yellow *torpilleurs* or torpedo boats for collecting the contents of latrines from such houses as possessed them continued to pass in some steep and narrow streets until the middle of the twentieth century, and the sea continued to serve as before. Thomas Platter wrote of the port that in summer it smelled so strongly as to make it impossible to approach on an empty stomach; but, he added, one gets used to it in the end. Stendhal in 1837 remarked to his boatman, with whom until then he had been on good terms, that the port smelled terrible. "He denied brusquely and rather impolitely that his harbour smelled bad. Maybe the Marseillais are insensible to a certain stench—luckily for them!"

In 1870 there were no more than forty kilometres of underground sewers, the discharge of the old town and of the Canebière ran directly into the port and that of the southern parts of the town into the mouth of the Huveaune. A succession of cholera epidemics culminating in those of 1884 and 1885 at last convinced the municipality under the mayor Félix Baret, and in 1891 work began. A 220-kilometre network of sewers was built to cross under the town from north to south, ending its journey in a calanque far from the nearest habitation, while elevating machinery was put in place to raise the effluent of low-lying streets so that at last Lacydon was freed of what the historian Raoul Busquet remembered from his youth as "a perpetual pestilential afflux... which on fine August afternoons perfumed the Vieux-Port".

For more than another eighty years the belief held that the sea would take care of everything, with the result that the coast around Marseille became progressively polluted, the fauna and flora suffered and retreated, and between the growth of the town, the sea currents and the prevailing winds the whole gulf was brought to the edge of asphyxia. The Huveaune, formerly used by the town's launderers for its clean water, became an open sewer. Pressure from ecologists and hygienists finally resulted in the creation of a filtering plant for a population of more than a million so that today Marseille has one of the most advanced cleansing systems in the world, further modernized in 2006, whose outflow of water is said to be the purest of any French city. The observant Platter described the methods available in his day: "Infection is combated by the smell of every sort of spice and by the daily application of tar to the ships which are so tightly packed... that one hardly sees the water under them."

By the sixteenth century the water sources under the town, augmented by the aqueduct of 1318, were already inadequate in dry summers, and the extensions of the seventeenth century, with the building of new streets and squares on the nearest adjoining land, made for a growth of population continuing throughout the eighteenth, while shortage of water worsened the chronic problem of hygiene. A drought in 1834, when there were riots around the heads of exhausted springs and wells was followed by a cholera outbreak in December, originating from India and reaching Marseille via Paris, which caused panic in a population born to folk memory of the great plague of 1720. By the end of 1834 the municipality, led by the mayor Dominique Consolat, had determined to bring to Marseille at whatever cost the water of the River Durance, a decision which would in the end transform the town and the countryside around it. Work began in 1837, financed with the backing of local industrialists who were among the first to benefit, and continued for more than ten years under the direction of a Swiss engineer, Franz Mayor de Montrichet. The water was captured near Pertuis in the Vaucluse and carried 84 kilometres by canal, over bridges, passing through 17 kilometres of tunnel and crossing the valley of the Arc on the aqueduct of Roquefavour, modelled on the Roman Pont du Gard though nearly twice its size.

The water of Durance was finally released at an initial rate of six cubic metres a second into reservoirs and cascades in November 1849, to the sound of cannon fire and church bells, and continues to supply the town whose houses were slowly adapted to more or less modern plumbing systems. The day of the kitchen water tank and the sand filter was past. The giant reservoir constructed under the Plâteau Longchamp, later to carry what must be the most triumphant, or vainglorious, water tower in Europe, continued in service until 1996. Filtering plants were installed and branches of the canal encircled the town, following the contours of the ground to end at its southernmost extremity, feeding fountains, gardens and fields along the way as well as houses and street hydrants; not least of the effects, once the sewage system was installed, was to prevent the Vieux Port from becoming a silted cesspool by pouring into it the flow of fresh water that now allows a view to the depths in spaces between yachts, launches and fishing boats. Between 1850 and 1938 the population increased, thanks to the water supply as well as to continuing migration, from 195,000 to 650,000 inhabitants. Future needs have been provided for by the building of a huge reservoir in the hills, fed from the River Verdon, which holds fifteen days supply of water for the entire area of Marseille.

Bastides: Secondary Residences, Grand or Modest

Industrial installations, particularly soap manufacturing whose odour, "insinuating, acrid, sickly with castor oil" according to Harrel-Courtès, pervaded the area behind the ports, and the tile factories for which Marseille was famous, benefited from the permanent water supply to continue functioning during the dry season. Moreover, all the cultivated territory below the level of the canal at its entry into the town between the Chaîne de l'Estaque and the Chaîne de l'Etoile at Saint-Antoine became agricultural and market garden land, orchard and meadow where before it had grown only vines and olives. Owners of bastides who possessed also—though in modest amounts, often no more than ten or twenty hectares—much of the farmland which for long provided for the town, ornamented their grounds with fountains, cascades, pools and canals. "Anyone lucky enough to own a couple of Italian pines is as proud of himself as an English lord in his park," wrote Frédéric Bernard in his travel book of 1855, *De Lyon à la Méditeranée*.

The bastides, whose number varies according to accounts, were a particular feature of the landscape of the Marseille hinterland. "I have never seen," Thomas Platter wrote, "any town surrounded by so many country houses." The first of them were supposedly built as refuges from plague epidemics by families of the Marseille nobility, old or new, and their proliferation was due to the increase during the eighteenth and nineteenth centuries of the bourgeois merchant class, often Protestant, that created, preserved and stored much of the wealth of the community. Even in the seventeenth century there were complaints that the families enriched by the sea lost their sense of mercantile adventure and preferred the life of the landed gentry. Nicolas Arnoul, intendant of the galleys, calculated there were 9,000 houses in Marseille and 9,000 bastides in the country, and wrote to Colbert his master in 1668: "The Marseillais are so degenerate on account of their bastides, wretched holes of houses which they have out in the country, that they will turn down the best piece of business in the world rather than miss a party there." Stendhal wrote nearly two centuries later that "the bastides are the dominant passion of the Marseillais, which is why there are no entertainments on Saturdays."

This way of life drew to a close during the first half of the twentieth century as the spreading town encroached and owners took advantage of offers to demolish and rebuild. Harrel-Courtès gives an account of the process: "These vast villas rivalled with one another in ugliness, but an ugliness that one regrets now… how far away they seem, those days of the triumphant bourgeoisie… my mother and aunts sold off their seven hectares and hurried to abandon that ravishing property to acquire, each of them, a secondary residence by the sea." A few hundred of these buildings remain, many ruinous, some converted to clinics and convalescent homes, some to house the town hall of one or other of 110 villages spread about the amphitheatre or *couronne des saints,* so called for its many saints' names; some splendid examples—the Château Borély of 1767 and the Château Pastré of 1860, both at the town's southern end between Mazargues and the sea, and La Magalone on the Boulevard Michelet—are now the property of the town and can be visited, while 212 bastides are registered in the town development plan of 1991, giving some degree of temporary protection. The Château de la Buzine, built in 1867 in the style of Louis XIII, is a monument to Harrel-Courtès' "triumphant bourgeoisie" in its grandiose pretention and figured in Marcel Pagnol's *Le Château de ma mère.* Pagnol bought it when he became rich and successful in the hope of creating there a *cinecittà* of Marseille, but the war interrupted a metamorphosis which has finally, in the ownership of the town, been completed for the purpose.

The economy as well as the appearance of the communes was transformed by the arrival of the canal; above the irrigation line smallholdings remained poor and arid and for more than a hundred years peasant occupiers found work in the season of drought in farms attached to châteaux or bastides below the line, or as part-time workers in soap and other factories. This social and economic formation continued much as it had been until the growth of the post-war years and the profit-taking by owners selling land for housing development, including the construction of tower blocks where bastides had formerly stood. Some parts of the old villages—Château Gombert, Plan de Cuques, Allauch, La Treille—survive above the level of these scattered suburbs while the rim of the amphitheatre behind them remains almost untouched; the commune of Marseille has 9,000 hectares of open natural space supporting a wide range of life including wild boar, and standing on this high ground with immense views over the territory from mountain to sea, the historic delight of the Marseillais in their country retreats, whether bastides or cabanons or farms, is easy to imagine and the sense of living in a land apart, unmindful of a centralized culture of imperatives, seems within reach and easily shared. But the amphitheatre's bowl, a continuum of hillocks and valleys still decorated with patches of woodland, fields and olive groves, is for the most part an example of large-scale anarchic urban growth and haphazard design, the spread of concrete and the hurried creation of housing for a population which increased by 300,000 between 1945 and 1975, with little of the directing control that a planning imperative might have given.

The Etang de Berre

At the northern extremity of Marseille is the former fishing village of l'Estaque, now endowed with a marina and appearing as more of a picturesque preserve and extension of the town than do the villages higher in the hills. The numerous tile factories, using locally quarried clay, whose chimney stacks figure in the foregorund of some of the great paintings by Cézanne and Braque of the Gulf of Marseille from l'Estaque have almost disappeared; the tiles, with a characteristic widening funnel-like form imparted to them by women workers who rolled up their skirts to model the clay against their thighs, were shipped from the docks to many parts of the world including Mexico and Sydney. A single factory remains, belonging to a large French construction group using less homely techniques.

The Chaîne de l'Estaque shelters the village from the mistral; beyond it to the north is the inland sea of the Etang de Berre, and still further, the Rhône delta. Marseille was a great port without a river, and historically the main trade route between the Mediterranean and northern Europe was the Rhône to which Marseille had no direct access. The dream of successive nineteenth-century Chambers of Commerce was to join Marseille to the Rhône and eventually the Rhine by a canal from the sea to Arles, 81 kilometres away, passing by the Etang de Berre, and in April 1911 work on a shipping tunnel began on the seaward side at L'Estaque, carried on by the firm which had taken the Paris Metro under the Seine. Two and a half million cubic metres of rock were extracted from the mountain by a workforce of thousands, largely recruited overseas, using smokeless compressed air engines to haul the truckloads. In January 1915 work was started on the side of the Etang de Berre and the two arms of the Tunnel du Rove met in February 1916. The vault was completed in 1923 and by 1927 three thousand vessels a year were passing under the mountain by this rapid short cut, 22 metres wide to allow barges to pass, fifteen metres high on a four-metre draught, to reach the growing industrial zone around the Etang. The tunnel had every expectation of indefinite, useful life. But before dawn one morning of June 1963 the captain of the barge *Storm*, navigating with lights, met a thickening cloud of dust and a fall of huge rocks blocking the water ahead. When the hillside was inspected it was found that a funnel-like chasm 45 metres wide had opened in the limestone to the depth of the water surface. The Tunnel du Rove had caved in as if its spine was broken, and it has never been mended.

The development of Fos-sur-Mer as a tanker terminal and re-finery between the Rhône delta and the Etang de Berre brought an end to the importance of Marseille as an outlet to the sea with its back turned to the continent, an importance already diminished by the winding-down of the French colonial empire, the repatriation of the *pieds noirs* or Algerian colonists and the growth of nationalism in southern Mediterranean countries. Seventy per cent of the port ac-tivity of Marseille-Fos consists of petroleum of which a large part is carried by pipeline for refining at Lyon; this may be some economic loss to the Marseille region, but not a great loss of potential em-ployment since oil refineries are not labour intensive. The investment in the development of Fos of funds derived from the sale of their bastides and surrounding land by many of the Marseille bourgeoisie, some of whom also filled important posts there after the collapse of family-owned industries, did little for the social problems of the town or the conversion to new uses of former industrial sites within the Marseille commune.

The Etang de Berre, the largest inland sea in Europe, has lost much of its salinity due to derivation into it of fresh water from the Durance used for hydroelectric purposes, and it is heavily damaged by industrial pollution and domestic effluent from rapid urban development in the region of Marignane airport. The petrochemical miasma associated with oil refineries hangs over the 155 square kilometres of water once famous for its fish population. Advocacy of a re-opening of the Tunnel du Rove as the only hope of rescuing the Etang de Berre by allowing the sea to surge in and refresh it, is countered by the fear that what might actually happen would be an outflow of polluted water from the Etang into the Gulf of Marseille close to the very site from which Cézanne first portrayed its splendour.

Dynamiting by the Germans in 1943 left the upper part of *le Panier* fortunately intact

2 | **The Urban Map**
Growth and Development

The house doors remind me of those in London. They are of polished wood with brass knockers, and raised by two steps off the pavement which is separated from the street by a running stream of clear water. Of course, I am speaking of the new town... you only enter the old one if you are in love and want to hide.

Stendhal

For me, the Canebière was a street leading to the unknown.

Joseph Conrad

Le Panier: Heart of Marseille

The popular name for the old town is of uncertain origin but there are several theories. One is that the name came from a statue of the Virgin which held on one arm a basket (*panier*) in which offerings for divine intervention were left by the optimistic: another is that it referred to a house where women were available and clients placed the price in a basket in the window before entering. Each seems plausible since the Panier had a higher concentration of churches than any other quarter of the town, and was for long reputed to be the greatest centre of prostitution on the Mediterranean coast. A third theory derives the name from an inn whose painted sign depicted a fish basket (*panier à poissons*), and perhaps this metonymic turn identifying a Greek city two thousand years old with a perishable item of working life is apt enough for a town described by Victor Hugo as an antique city without monuments, and by Joseph Méry as being without antiquities. The Marseillais have always rebuilt on the demolished ruins of what stood before, preserving little and careless of architectural prestige and often of history as if their vitality were too great to need antecedents.

Another explanation of this disregard for buildings could be that the structure and character of the site itself are so potent that changes within it counted little to inhabitants whose outlook went always seaward. The deep rectangle of water and Lacydon's narrow mouth, the backdrop of mountains, the open hill of la Garde and the lower hills built over with streets and houses make the spirit of the place; they constitute and identify it so strongly that the burial of antique ruins under the foundations of new building, destined to ruin in its turn, may seem less regrettable. From the quayside of the Vieux Port and looking northward, imagination can replace the Greek town, of which nothing visible but a few metres of stone wall remains, onto its small defended founding hill directly above the water with more ease than it can reconstruct the Roman cities of the plain, Nîmes and Arles, from among the surviving beauty of their monuments. A museum stands still while a hush, favourable to study, falls over its relics; it is enough to walk the streets of Marseille like the seventeen-year-old Conrad to know that hush never falls here.

Lacydon to this day is the core and heart of Marseille. All roads and channels of desire flow towards the quays and their forty hectares of contained water. Originally the area was greater; at the eastern end the inlet curved northward like a horn for three or four hundred metres more and it was here that in Roman times the docks, whose remains are visible in the Jardin des Vestiges, were built outside the ramparts, while the northern shore, where the Phocaeans landed and later constructed their first harbour installation, discovered below the Place Villeneuve-Bargemon at the foot of the Hôtel-Dieu in 2004, was both irregular and nearer to the foot of the hill than the straight-sided modern quay, realigned in 1855. From the Greek landing stage it can be taken that Pytheas the astronomer and navigator set sail in the fourth century BC to find a sea route to the sources of tin and amber. On his return he recounted to a sceptical audience of his compatriots the journey he had made; Strabo the geographer dismissed his account and he became known as the Liar but now, resuscitated by later scholars, he has his statue in a niche on the first floor of the imposing nineteenth-century Palais de la Bourse beside the nude figures of Ocean and Mediterranean.

Massalia evolved by stages over four hundred years, first on the promontory where since 1660 the Fort Saint-Jean stands guard over the port, and eventually comprising the three hillocks of the ancient town, protected on the landward side by the massive rampart of which a section can be seen in the Jardin des Vestiges, and covering approximately fifty hectares or an area roughly equal to the surface of Lacydon itself. On the highest point, the Butte des Moulins, 42 metres above sea level and which has never been systematically explored by archaeologists, was the Temple of Artemis, and below it, on the site of the Place de Lenche, the *agora* of the Greek city. A second temple, dedicated to Pythian Apollo, is thought to have surmounted the Butte Saint-Laurent whose seaward slope was built with terraced houses and later a Roman theatre near its foot. But no evidence has been found of any grid or regular planning in the construction of the town which continued its development in the more or less haphazard fashion still evident, with narrow steep streets and flights of stairs, unexpected turns, dark alleyways and sudden openings where distant views of water or hillside appear between the banks of houses.

By the second century BC, with the completion of the wall, the town had taken the form in which it remained for almost two thousand years, with rich and poor, patrician and plebeian side by side, regularly devastated by epidemics of plague but renewed by autogenesis and immigration, exporting and importing through the Roman epoch, the Middle Ages, the Renaissance, sustained by the fruit of a wide agricultural basin and the product of the sea, watered by wells and streams feeding the great reservoir below the Place de Lenche, and surviving with its independent proclivities siege, subjugation, sack and even, at last, incorporation into France in 1481.

A History of Demolition

A series of more or less dramatic changes, mostly imposed from outside, eventually fell on the original city though without altogether obliterating its streets or extinguishing its character. The first was the demolition of the walls by order of Louis XIV after his triumphant visit of 1660, and the laying out and construction of a new town to the east with avenues and squares of aligned mansions into which the nobility and wealthy bourgeoisie removed, leaving the ancient town to the poorer part of the population to live on in neglect and growing insalubrity. Nearly two hundred years later a second upheaval followed the building of the new docks to the north of the Panier at La Joliette and Arenc, destined to serve the expanding French colonial empire and exploit the advantage of the Suez Canal. This involved straightening and extending the shoreline further westward into the bay, destroying coves and beaches that had been a popular pleasure ground in times of peace for as far as memory reached, and replacing them with dockyards and buildings inspired by, and rivalling for the first time on the continent, the London dockland.

The Romanesque cathedral, of which less than a third survives, stood on a bluff directly overlooking the sea; the extension of the shoreline created a platform on which the nineteenth-century cathedral in Byzantine style was built. Then in 1864, in the full hubristic period of the Second Empire, it was decided to cut through a part of the Butte des Carmes, demolishing streets of houses in the poorest quarter to build a wide, straight thoroughfare connecting the Vieux Port to the complex of new docks and warehouses. A large slice of hillside, 25 metres deep and 250 long, was amputated as if by crude surgery on the battlefield, and nearly a thousand houses destroyed with the disappearance of forty streets, picturesque but dark, overcrowded, steep, allegedly malodorous and unpassable by any vehicle for cleansing or evacuation of waste. At least 16,000 people were evicted under a system giving little help even to the poorest of them beyond the authorities' hope that the exiles "find lodging with air and light and appropriate to their condition", and most had no choice but to settle where they could reach work and pay rent, near villages on the outskirts or in cheaply thrown-up rows of houses around and beyond the hill of la Garde, in Endoume and Bompard where their descendants still live in what is now among the most unchanged and unambiguously Marseillais quarters of the town, secretive, exclusive and sought after.

If the clearance and destruction needed to bring into being the "Haussmanian" and un-Mediterranean Rue Impériale (nowadays called the Rue de la République), "monumental and monstrous" according to Hippolyte Taine, constructed by the Compagnie Immobilière de Paris and a financial failure because the Marseillais were never reconciled to it, seem socially and architecturally brutal they were modest by comparison with the unrealized project that preceded them. In 1858 a plan for levelling and redeveloping the old town proposed the razing of the hills of the Panier, the eviction of sixty thousand inhabitants or a quarter of the entire population of Marseille and the construction on level ground of a modern, perpendicularly laid out residential district. The municipal councillors of the time took fright, whether because of the social problems involved, for financial reasons, or due to the fact that the hills above and to the north of the Vieux Port sheltered shipping within it from the mistral, is uncertain. "Let us not disturb the poor in their humble domicile," the town council concluded.

But it is apparent that by the mid-nineteenth century the existence of the Panier with all its wanton and insanitary character as the ages of neglect and the constant flux of migrants had left it, with its population of proletarian and ethnically mixed communities, and with the possibilities of a site so magnificent and historically vital, was already a magnet for the covetous and a focus of attention for social, and probably political reformism. In 1932 plans were produced for the demolition and renewal of the old streets nearest the port, and in 1941 the idea was adopted by the municipality and the project put in the hands of the Vichy government's chief architect. These interests were to be spectacularly served in 1943 with no more, perhaps, than indirect participation of the local authorities, by the Germans who had moved south the year before to occupy the Free Zone of which Marseille was part.

The German operation may be considered as an act of war, though without causing direct loss of life. In January 1943 a number of attacks on German soldiers seemed to confirm the Nazi authorities' belief that the maze of dark streets of the Panier with inextricably connected decrepit houses, alleged secret tunnels, hiding places below ground and within walls made a nest for resistants, spies and Jews and was no doubt packed with arms and explosives. Moreover,

Hitler is said to have had an obsessive loathing for the supposed degeneracy and miscegenation of the inhabitants. This prejudice, far from being peculiar to Hitler, was fuelled by literary accounts of life in the quarter between the wars. "This bastard population... fruit of who knows what baroque and impure couplings... the one corner of France where racial decadence by cross-breeding is a fact," wrote the journalist and music critic Lucien Rebatet in 1941; and the academician Louis Gillet asked, "this empire of sin and death, these once patrician *quartiers* abandoned to the rabble and to their shame, what means are there to void their pus and regenerate them?" André Suarès wrote of the streets of prostitutes in picturesque fashion but vividly enough to confirm any fascinated horror there may have been in the mind of others: "This site of magnificent obscenity is no more in my eyes, to my senses, than a giant sexual organ, gaping, unique... its alleys are folds, its houses swellings... it is the pounding blood, the strong pulse of the vulva of earth stretched out to the port..." Christian Harrel-Courtès, Marseillais from a long-established bourgeois family, took a less inflamed view. As a boy, he was forbidden to enter the tangle of streets between the Hôtel-Dieu and the quays, supposedly the haunt of criminals and footloose sailors ashore, but he became familiar with them in wartime for their black market restaurants: "In fact, there was a population of modest Marseille born people there who were quite comfortable with the promiscuous mix of girls and their hundred brothels."

The order to destroy the *vieux quartiers* of Marseille is said to have come directly from Hitler, and on 23 January the area was surrounded by a regiment of SS, and by elements of local police and mobile reserve groups. The population was commanded by French speakers on loudhailers to leave at once, taking only what they could carry. Forty thousand people were evicted, six thousand arrested, sixteen hundred deported of whom none returned. The others were temporarily housed in camps, some in the seventeenth-century workhouse of the Vieille Charité, some in warehouses and disused factories. The explosions began on 24 January and continued for seventeen days, spreading thick clouds of dust over the town and creating fourteen hectares of ruin among the streets nearest to the quay of the Vieux Port. The eighty-year-old curé of Saint-Laurent refused to leave and rang the bells of his church throughout in protest against the crime and the lies surrounding it, defending his parishioners many of whom were families of fishermen and dock labourers, their parents and children: "Apart from certain physically or morally insalubrious streets, the forty streets of my parish were inhabited by a working population... of how many ancient respectable families, worthy of regard!" The only buildings spared were the historic Hôtel de Ville, the Hôtel-Dieu, the Church of Saint-Laurent and a few ancient houses which had figured on a list of monuments to be preserved in the execution of the plan drawn up in 1941 for demolition and restructuring of the area.

In the days following the explosions a company with both French and German capital was created for building developments in Marseille. The question of complicity by local financial interests in the operation has been left, and will probably remain, unanswered though often posed; notably by Paul Lombard, one of many whose concern would be rather to exonerate than indict his fellow Marseillais. The area of former run-down streets was replaced after the war and the tragic *faits accomplis* by alignments of apartment blocks, expensive, socially safe and banal in character but not disfiguring, although their facing in ochre-coloured stone from the quarries near the Pont du Gard seems anomalous in a city with a coastline of beautiful and accessible pink limestone. There is no doubt that fortunes in iconoclastic outlay and rehousing expense were saved thanks to the Nazi clearance, and more fortunes cashed in its peacetime aftermath.

What remained of the Panier, streets and squares covering the higher ground, was for long afterwards left in darkness and decay while the new buildings went up around the Hôtel de Ville. Even the seventeenth-century Vieille Charité, blackened with neglect and squatted in by generations of the homeless, was threatened with demolition until acclaimed for the masterpiece it is by the Swiss architect Le Corbusier and was later magnificently restored. The process of restoring houses in the Panier and rehabilitating of streets, with some local demolition to create open spaces and admit light, have been part of the ongoing project to bring a new lease of life to the founding quarter of the most ancient town in France.

The charm of small squares and well proportioned houses can be seen in the Place des Moulins where the Temple of Artemis once stood, and in the Place de Lenche on the site of the *agora*. An influx of artists, students and young couples come to share the quarter with the migrants and the original Marseillais has to some extent created an atmosphere deliberately reminiscent of Montmartre, with the municipality buying properties to house these socially desirable elements. But the Panier, says Harrel-Cortès, "though a bit tamed and made up, has not lost all its former allure," and the strength of Marseille, according to Jean Viard, lies in its immense disorder so that even if some ethnologists and other intellectuals (perhaps in about the same proportion as in London's Soho) have attempted to settle here the mix is much as before, of Africans, foreigners, indigenous Marseillais and a shifting populace of no fixed abode. This seems one more example of how Marseille resists the changes that far-seeing and sometimes impatient planners try to propagate here, in order to go on keeping itself to itself. Such tidy functional projects, says Viard, fit badly into the intrinsic untidiness that Marseille has always lived with and which its long history has engendered.

Without the Walls: Louis XIV and the Baroque

The age of Louis XIV, however, brought every effort to the work of architectural and schematic order. The medieval walls were swept away by command of the *roi soleil*, opening the enclave of the ancient city to the land eastward of it where spacious dwellings for the wealthy were to be built. The image of the great Mediterranean port would be redrawn and the prestige of the monarchic state enhanced by the creation of a baroque, aristocratic city. The Intendant of the Galleys, Arnoul, was charged by Colbert with the work of extension and beautification which, as in other seventeenth-century cities, was motivated by propaganda as well as aesthetic and social interests. In 1668 the municipality was granted direction of the work and immediately extended the project to take in the area surrounding the southern quays of the port. An extraordinary opportunity to create the first modern city among the still medieval townships of France was offered and the first to recognize it was the great Marseille architect and sculptor Pierre Puget before whom, in his own words "the marble trembled" into life. His designs for the Cours and Place Royale and streets around them were everywhere acclaimed, admired by Colbert and the king, became the model for the creation of *cours* in other baroque cities, but were finally rejected by the town authorities on grounds of expense. Regret for what might have been may be tempered by asking whether Marseille would have preserved much or anything of this baroque masterpiece had it been realized. In the event, the work was given to the two municipal architects one of whom was Puget's cousin, and the result, five hundred metres long by 39 wide, owed much if not all to the design of Pierre though it represented no more than a small part of it.

For the first time patrician and plebeian would be housed in different quarters and Marseille would build a new town of ideal beauty and cleanliness fit to be compared with Italian cities. The separation of classes in a society constantly affected by immigrant shifts and population increase was to be a continuing feature of Marseille life, and of the growth of residential districts for the well-off preferring to escape the neighbourhood of a proletariat of mixed origin; a choice which helped determine the self-centred and endogamous character of the bourgeoisie noted by Harrel-Courtès.

Aix-en-Provence, often in rivalry with Marseille since its foundation in 122 BC, had its famous cours, now the Cours Mirabeau; the rulers of Marseille built a thoroughfare of mansions which would be—as it was described in 1682—the most beautiful place in Europe, wide, tree-lined, symmetrical and elegant. The Cours de Marseille, reaching north to south from the Porte d'Aix to the Rue de Rome, was completed in 1687 and remained for more than two hundred years the principal place of "promenade" of the town, the avenues and pavements where it was appropriate to be seen, the popular class at the northern end, the well-heeled and the pickpockets traditionally following them in the middle and southern parts on either side of the crossing with the Canebière. Stendhal admired the Cours de Marseille but noted a disadvantage: "There can be no deceived husbands in Marseille on account of the streets drawn in straight lines. When you are in the rue Paradis you can be seen from as far as the Canebière... everyone sees everything. In Marseille all is calculated for husbands, they lay down the law and their wives are their humble servants." Very little remains of the seventeenth- and eighteenth-century houses of the Cours, a few disfigured façades above shops in the Cours Saint-Louis, a monumental doorway at the northern end of the Cours Belsunce whose entire western side, behind the nineteenth-century Palais de la Bourse, was demolished in 1913, leaving a desolation of three and a half hectares which remained undeveloped and without even a public garden until 1967. But the Cours Belsunce, the Cours Saint-Louis and the Rue de Rome, rebuilt like many parts of eighteenth-century London without architectural discipline or discernment during the nineteenth and early twentieth centuries, are still streets for promenade and for all varieties of comopolitan urban experience, while Pierre Puget's own house, designed by himself and modestly placed at the acute angle formed by the division of two streets, giving it the form of a slice of cake, is preserved by chance at 25 Rue de Rome.

Lacydon, Canebière and Bourse

The earliest cartographical drawings of Lacydon show its southern shore as swampy ground, presumably watered by streams, at the foot of the hill. By the end of the fourteenth century when galleys were first introduced into the armament of the fishing fleet of Marseille to repel corsairs, this shore supported buildings and boatyards which were later to be known as the Arsenal. The word "galley" comes from the Greek word for cat; "Did not this ship... fast, cunning, subtle, treacherous... have something in common with the cat?" asked the author of *Archéologie Navale*. In 1488 the first Arsenal was built on the order of Charles VIII and by 1564 the galleys were manned by slaves, mostly Turkish, and condemned criminals who lived and worked under a régime of extreme harshness, chained day and night and considered simply as a moving force without human claim. Louis XIV added recalcitrant Protestants, including pastors, to their number after the Revocation of the Edict of Nantes, and in 1687 caused the Arsenal to be greatly enlarged and its shipbuilding capacity inflated to match the pretentions of the state, bringing to the heart of the new town created at his command and with a population, including Le Panier, of seventy to eighty thousand, a prison and military town of twenty thousand men to whose misery not all free consciences were closed, particularly when side by side with it. To add to the anomaly, by the late seventeenth century the galley was a naval anachronism, fast but fragile and outgunned by English and Dutch ships sailing the Mediterranean. Its role had become largely decorative: Madeleine de Scudéry wrote, "I can tell you that the most beautiful sight of all is that of the galleys in the port on Christmas Day, lit by a countless multitude of paper lanterns, and to the sound of the cries of sixteen thousand men." Eight hundred vessels were sunk during the Seven Years' War with a loss of two thousand Marseillais lives, while with the inexorable population growth the area occupied by the Arsenal, the space-consuming rope-making and timber yards in parallel streets mounting the hill behind, was covetously regarded by the town authorities.

The Arsenal was finally sold by the state to the town in 1781, the remaining fleet removed to Toulon and the royal shipyards demolished. Their place was taken by the ranks of somewhat forbidding warehouse-like buildings variously filled by dwellings, storehouses, offices and more recently artisans' and artists' workshops, amply supplied with windows but as plain and denuded of ornament as if designed by Huguenot Calvinists commemorating the wretchedness of their ancestors' fate (the novelist André Chamson was one of several who wrote gruelling fictional accounts of it), which still stand between the quay and the Cours d'Estienne d'Orves. These buildings, allowed to fall into decay, surrounded the Place Thiars, a zone now restored and almost entirely occupied by restaurants, and an ancient canal where small haulage vessels continued to tie up and masts were seen as a natural feature, swaying and rattling, between house walls. "The bowsprits of ships sailing from America," said Stendhal, "smash the panes of first floor windows."

The canal was filled in 1927 with rubble taken from the demolition of the west side of the Cours Belsunce—how many cubic metres of seventeenth-century dressed stone, plinth, cornice, pilaster?—and a multi-storey car park took its place; after years of protests this was at last removed in 1987 leaving the Cours d'Estienne d'Orves as it is, rather bare and echoing between high buildings and with no central focus, but popular night and day as a pedestrian extension from the quays of the Vieux Port.

The Canebière, running eastward at right angles to the Cours, was also first created after the subjection of Marseille by Louis XIV. The name derives from the Provençal *canebe* signifying hemp, the street being built on the site of a rope making and trading centre. The etymology seems apt to Conrad's sense of the Canebière as a highroad to the unknown, and to the history of almost hallucinatory exhilaration always associated with it as the threshold of a wider world and a freer life for which it became famous. "If Paris had a Canebière," says Edmond Dantès in *The Count of Monte-Cristo*, "it would be a little Marseille." At first, the Canebière occupied a relatively short space between the wall of the Arsenal which shut it off from the port, and the narrow Rue de Noailles, coming to a dead end in the new town wall built after the demolition of the old. But with the late seventeenth- and eighteenth-century aggrandisement of Marseille, the growth of seaborne trade and the accompanying further enrichment of the plutocratic families whose ambitions, predilections, fears and migrations have so greatly influenced the development of the town and its quarters, a far grander approach from the fashionable quarters to the port was desired. From its eastern extremity to the sea which, whatever the apparent social detachment of the wealthy remained the source of their fortunes for more than two thousand years, the Canebière measured over a kilometre in length after incorporating the Rue de Noailles and the elegant triangle of avenues and mansions of the Allées de Meilhan. Although it still has its original dimensions the glamour is not easy to restore to the imagination in its present state. In Marseille, the movement of history and the changes of middle-class habitat leave fields of the historic patrimony to lie neglected as if the supply of fresh ground to build on was inexhaustible, as it may have seemed when the 101 villages of the *couronne des saints* still stood among farms reaching to the town walls.

But in the nineteenth and for a large part of the twentieth centuries the name of the Canebière as a fashionable and vibrant prolongation of the quaysides where, by 1840, at least 9,000 ships a year tied up, was to carry its fame across the world. "They speak of it in the sands of the desert and the snows of Lapland," claimed a local newspaper in 1841, and this was no doubt why Marseille was the chosen starting point for the seafaring career of the young Josef Konrad Korzeniowski, later British Master Mariner. Hotels and luxurious shops lined the street, the best dressed women paraded in it and Stendhal compared it favourably to the Rue de le Paix in Paris. With the completion of the Palais de la Bourse, "a temple to the age of capital", in 1860, the Canebière became the hub of financial and shipping activity between France, the Mediterranean and the overseas world, as well as the central artery of the life of Marseille; the cafés were famous, their activity non-stop so that Horace Bertin in *Les heures marseillaises* described the best known of them, aptly called the Café de l'Univers, as "a dazzling sight recalling the Thousand and One Nights".

The Canebière's progressive deterioration can be dated to the Second World War which put an end to the practice of long sea voyages, and from the growth of air traffic; then the shifts of economic power deprived the Bourse of its widely influential role, the luxurious shops and providers of services followed the exodus of rich inhabitants further south towards the Rue Paradis and the Prado as their fine town houses became offices, and later on, locations for new modern hotels were chosen away from the congested centre. The Grand Hôtel de Noailles, built in 1679 for a constructor of galleys and turned in the nineteenth century into Marseille's most opulent hotel and social centre, was abandoned for thirty years and is now a police headquarters.

At the end of the war, the Canebière was still an international throughfare, however much reduced. Peggy Guggenheim wrote of her husband Max Ernst "often meeting on the Canebière old friends he had known in the internment camps. They looked like ghosts but for him they were living beings who called up common memories. To me it was a strange new world where one cited the names of the camps as if they were Saint-Moritz, or Deauville." Harrel-Courtès described the street, although less alluring, dirty and dangerous at night time, as retaining a certain aura still attractive to bands of young people from outlying parts of the town, and to tourists slightly lost who put their faith more in the legend than the reality. With the ending of the Algerian war and massive repatriation of ex-colonists, followed by an influx of Algerians expelled from their native land, and more recently with the arrival of African and other immigrants, the Canebière became increasingly a frontier between the north and south of the town and deserted by wealthier Marseillais who began to find the population of the northern en-croaching on the southern side. An attempted process of cleaning up, of investment and reclamation, is still in the early stage, and it is already clear that the result, as far as the Canebière itself is concerned, can only be the spread of a tidier, uglier popular commercialism as evident in the crowded Centre Bourse, built on the abandoned ground of the Cours Belsunce.

Belsunce epitomizes some of the paradoxes and dilemmas of the old centre of Marseille, away both from the rich residential areas around the Prado and Corniche, and from the socially and racially disadvantaged zone north of the docks. The first building operation of the Centre Bourse in 1967 revealed, under the accumulated rubble of centuries, unsuspected remains of the Roman dockyard and the Greek ramparts; the municipality was with difficulty persuaded of the inestimable value of these discoveries, the best conserved port installation of the ancient world, and of the need to delay the build-ing to allow archaeological work to be finished. The end result was the creation of the Jardin des Vestiges where the quay of the ancient dockyard, a length of the wall and other foundations can be seen in the open air, and of a museum of the town's history as part of the Centre Bourse.

But overlooking the garden and dominating the area of the former Cours Belsunce, three eighteen-storey tower blocks were erected, their architecture designated as part of the patrimony of the twentieth century but execrated by many as an intrusion in a histor-ically sensitive setting. These buildings are part of an ongoing social policy aimed at what has been called a "reconquest" of Belsunce, the reclaiming from a population of immigrants of a part of the town which the more prosperous element had long since deserted. "In Belsunce," a journalist wrote in the 1940s, "there are cafés, tarts, pimps, Greeks, Jews, Arabs… narrow, crooked streets, mysterious doorways yawning on dark corridors… and a smell of cats and un-washed sheets."

A complex procedure of repossession and evacuation was aimed at achieving an upwardly mobile social mixture and perhaps an ef-fective exclusion from these quarters of the town of a by then largely Arab population, thought to provoke political extremism which would earn for Marseille, in common with other southern towns, a bad name to further harm its reputation. Landlords were allowed to understand that the municipality would buy their properties if empty; they proceeded to issue repossession notices which the immigrant oc-cupiers were either too poor, too intimidated, too illicit or too igno-rant of the law to contest, and the town sold the buildings on at low prices to developers who would attract another social level of tenant. Even in French this process is known as gentrification, and was to be backed up by financial inducements in the form of easy terms of pur-chase and modest rentals. The ironical outcome is said by Jean Viard and other sociologists to be that many of the incoming tenants, some of bohemian tendency with means and bourgeois origins from else-where, soon departed and the original families began to return to ren-ovated homes vastly superior to those they had left.

The process was nothing new: in 1870 Antoine Olivesi in his *Marseille au xix siècle* wrote that the people were reconquering the centre of the town from which they had been driven by the great building works of the imperial period. Marseille resists social engi-neering; the old town, the seventeenth-century new town and its once elegant neighbouring streets built in the eighteenth and early nineteenth centuries have all in turn acquired their present charac-ter, which impresses the unfamiliar visitor as an example of relative urban decay and social decline, thanks to their progressive and ap-parently irreversible abandonment by the bourgeoisie. This is what is meant by the observation of planners that Marseille is a popular city because ordinary people still want to live there. The Intendant Arnoul wrote to Colbert in 1666, "If the gentlemen of Marseille had in view... obedience and the good of their town, we would all be agreed, but private interest and mutual distrust so divides them that I can say I have never met such people."

South: Prado, Corniche and the Hills Between

The long, straight, north-south axis of the Rue de Rome, built along the line of the Roman road to Italy, runs behind the hill of la Garde so that the surrounding streets, mostly constructed in the eighteenth and early nineteenth centuries, seem divorced from the sea and give the impression of belonging to an inland town. Many of these streets, such as the Rue Saint-Ferréol, the Rue Paradis, the Cours Lieutaud and the Rue de Rome itself, are still lined with houses of architectural distinction, or at least harmony with the characteristic to be seen everywhere in Marseille of three windows to each floor whether in houses occupied as a unit by well-to-do families, or by humbler families with one floor each, but for the most part these buildings, many with gardens behind them, appear as if conceived for a more distinguished life than their rather forlorn present state allows. Shops, cinema entrances and offices untidily and sometimes damagingly occupy many of the ground floors, tides of pedestrian and motor traffic wash constantly around them and the attentions of designers for the care and improvement of urban environment which may embellish the streets of old towns, or denature them with anachronistic re-styling, seem to have been denied or avoided. An exception to the rule of neglect is the beautiful and pampered Cours Pierre Puget whose steep avenues and regular line of façades convey the spirit as well as the features of their age, even if the houses behind them are mainly used as expensive office space.

The Rue Paradis, built in two stages in 1849 and 1862 and three kilometres long, leads in a straight line uphill and down from the Bourse to the Avenue du Prado, in whose vicinity many of the wealthy bourgeois families built their refuge from the overcrowded centre, emphasizing the process of separation between the place of work and residence which by the twentieth century was believed to be one source of the problems of Marseille. The separation is now even more complete, and the quiet streets and handsome tree-clothed hillsides in the districts of Perier and Saint-Giniez on either side of the Prado are the quarters of the rich, the secret, or simply the fortunate classes of Marseillais, as well as of consulates and banks.

The Prado, an extension of the Rue de Rome and once lined with centuries-old plane trees killed by a disease emanating, it is said, from infested packing boxes belonging to the American army, runs in parallel to the Rue Paradis and then turns at a near-right angle towards the sea; the continuation of the first part of the dogleg being the Boulevard Michelet which leads past the famous football stadium, the Vélodrome, and between well-off residential streets as far as the former village of Mazargues and the hills lying directly behind the southern calanques. Mazargues and the Prado were transformed by the arrival of the Canal de Marseille bringing the water of the Durance in 1850, and became dotted with bastides, sumptuous villas and houses surrounded by gardens, encouraging the exodus of those who could afford it from the centre.

On the further slopes of one of the hills lies the Domaine de Luminy, once an estate of the Abbaye de Saint-Victor, the most powerful and ancient of the Marseille monastic communities, where the university has built the new faculty of science and the school of architecture among woods and at the end of an approach road going no further, with student residences and more suburban extensions nearby at the south-eastern extremity of the town in the direction of Cassis and La Ciotat. The Avenue du Prado reaches the sea near the outflow of the Huveaune beside whose channelled and filtered bed a tree-lined walkway has been laid out, and close to the racecourse and the superb Château Borély which is now the property of the town. Southward from this meeting point are the former fishing villages, still peopled by Marseillais of long-established stock, la Pointe Rouge, la Madrague, and les Goudes where the coastline turns eastward and the calanques begin, while at the foot of the Prado a beach covering forty-two hectares was created in 1976 by filling in the shoreline with rubble extracted from under the town in the building of the Metro.

Between the Prado and the Vieux Port is the Corniche winding beside the sea and along coves and over ravines descending from the hill above, and overlooked by many of the most expensive and sought-after villas and apartments of Marseille. The Corniche was first created in the mid-nineteenth century, giving work to the great wave of unemployed in the financial crisis of the Second Empire, as a scenic drive for those who possessed a calèche, or a promenade on foot for those who did not, and was doubled in width between 1957 and 1969 to become probably the most congested of the roads in and out of the centre at peak hours. It encircles, on the seaward side, the hill of la Garde and the rocky eminences of Roucas Blanc, Bompard and Endoume, and returns, eventually, to the western end of the Vieux Port by way of the Malmousque peninsula.

Roucas Blanc is said to be the costliest district of Marseille and has within it many of the most extravagant seaside mansions and villas of the nineteenth century. A steep valley divides it from Bompard and Endoume, more modest but still privileged localities unknown to most passing visitors and inhabited by families who consider themselves among the most authentic of Marseillais. In 1941 Louis Blin wrote in *Marseille inconnu*, "This, and not the centre, is Marseille! The Canebière, the rue Saint-Ferréol, the Bourse, the Prado, all that is the town of foreigners, travel agents and guides. But this corner... is Marseille." Many of the families are descended from those displaced from the Panier by the building of the Rue Impériale and the predilection of the Marseillais for keeping themselves to themselves is here served by the character of the area, with streets leading nowhere, alleys and precipitous stairways on hillsides, houses and cabanons built in any style and on any irregular plot and often reached only by steps cut into the rock, but bathed like the hill and gardens and patches of woodland in the brilliant liquid maritime light, and for the luckiest with views over the bay. The contrast between this charmed, architecturally anarchic but secretive reserve, and the more uniform, rectilinear, darker streets excluded from the sea by the hill between, seems not merely of different towns, but of worlds apart.

East: Longchamp and Plaine

Rectilinear streets continue eastward around the extension of the Canebière, the Rue de la Libération and the Boulevard Longchamp with at its end the Palais Longchamp, where the waters of the Durance were finally delivered in cascades into the heart of Marseille. These streets have a population similar and related to that inhabiting the quarter of Périer, an example, says Jean Viard, of successful "Haussmanization", in other words of settled middle-class society, old and new, living sheltered from the human traffic of the centre. A perfectly preserved illustration of the setting for this life is found at the Musée Grobet-Labadie on the Boulevard Longchamp, built in 1873 as the home of the family of that name and containing the furnishings and collections of a rich Marseille industrialist whose only daughter married a musician, painter, and patron of the arts.

To the east of Longchamp is spread out in successive waves the broadening restless tide of building growth, reaching into and submerging the farms and the hundred villages of the *couronne des saints*, creating new streets of villas, gardens and apartment blocks mercilessly raised in exposed positions to tower over the surroundings, and extending southward as far as the industrialized valley of the Huveaune. Walter Benjamin, who spent his last days as a fugitive in Marseille before his suicide in 1940, described the process then in pessimistic terms: "The suburbs... tell a story of the close combat between telegraph poles and agaves, of barbed wire against palm fronds, of gas fumes in reeking corridors against humid shade of the plane trees..." Nevertheless, certain villages partially survive as recognizable entities, of which Saint-Barnabé with a strong Armenian colony is one example among many. And scattered about the entire area of the amphitheatre are the remains of bastides, ruinous or sometimes put to other uses, and cabanons still serving their original purpose of allowing a foothold in the hinterland to townspeople, not all of them now from the former *classe ouvrière*. Of this region a German traveller wrote in the early nineteenth century, "All the suburb of Marseille is covered with thousands of country houses which from a distance resemble a second town strewn with trees." With an effort of the imagination it is possible, here and there, to revive this impression and to see, with the town in the distance, an idyllic region of self-sufficiency and independence which preceded the current sprawling, voracious, urban increase.

The highest part of the town, apart from the hill of la Garde, is a plateau lying to the east of the angle formed by the Rue de Rome and the Canebière, and known as the Plaine. What was historically a military terrain, the Champ de Mars—the Crusaders encamped here before embarking—and a parade ground for troop reviews is now the Place Jean Jaurès, a bourgeois enclave favoured by Marseille intellectuals but where prices have risen vertiginously due to the arrival of immigrants not from the sea, but from the north. Since 1892 the Place Jean Jaurès has been the site of a great daily market, while the nearby Cours Julien, which was also a market place until 1972, with plunging views towards the hill of la Garde and the Vieux Port, has been landscaped, pedestrianized, repainted, given cultural ambitions and has become the focus of a movement of return to the centre, mostly on the part of a section of the population which had probably never lived there: "It's a village where the people are far more open than in the old quarters of the town... it is a quarter which is à la mode," claims an inhabitant come from Paris.

The Cours Julien was built in 1785 on the site of the tournament lists outside the ramparts, and was given the name of Cours des Citoyens; a curiously Marseillais presage, at a time when absolute monarchy still reigned, of the revolutionary appellation of a few years later.

North: Belle de Mai and Dockland

The railway station of Saint-Charles, on a high plateau and with a long stone stairway overlooking the roofs of the town and often likened to the Odessa steps, was the entrance to and from a changed world; it anchored Marseille to northern France as never before. The opening of a tunnel under the Masssif de la Nerthe brought the first trains in 1848, and a line to Paris in 1855. Since 2006 there has been a second revolution. Until the creation of the new TGV line, the journey from Paris took ten hours; now it takes three and by bringing Paris to the doorstep in the age of the 35-hour week it has made of some parts of Marseille an outlying settlement of weekend homes for Parisians, and brought a doubling of house prices as a consequence. "The Marseillais," says Yann de l'Ecotais, "feels himself dispossessed... hardly at home any more. His town is opening itself to France... France is invading it."

Yet accompanying the invasion is investment. The quarter closest to Saint-Charles on the northern side and historically tied to it is the Belle de Mai, until 1848 a famous wine producing area with a population of barely six hundred. The arrival of the railway brought industries—chemical, sugar refining, soap making, alcohol and tobacco—and the construction of working-class housing on a large scale with anarchic siting and random design, tall blocks of social housing in the grounds of abandoned bastides, making Marseille, with a population of half a million by the end of the nineteenth century, a fifty per cent working-class town with a one in five immigrant workforce. Two-thirds of the town's stock of social housing is situated in the northern sector, which is also where the North African immigrant community is largely concentrated. Jean Viard has suggested that the heterogeneous and incoherent character of the outlying town is due both to the diversified ethnic origins of the population it housed, and to the fact that within the commune of Marseille there was little pressure on space; "hence a greater individual liberty to developers than in a denser city".

But between 1970 and 1980 the industrial installations closed one after another, leaving the Belle de Mai among the most rundown quarters of Marseille which Euroméditerranée is attempting to revive. The huge factory complex once belonging to the nationalized tobacco industry, the Seita, has been converted to become the centre of modern cultural activity; it houses the archives and the department of conservation, has brought work and will, it is hoped, act as a lever for the regeneration, as part of the Euroméditerranée project, of a section of the town with a twenty per cent unemployment rate and six or seven hundred hectares of abandoned sites which for long attracted no speculative interest, and showed little sign of life other than the *puces* or flea market in the former Alsthom factory, known as the market of the poor and swarming every day with crowds. Yet despite the appearance in some quarters of the town of a degree of segregation, Viard points out that the overlapping in the centre of sectors of population which further afield are separated, creates part of the charm of Marseille and its great urban difference from Lyon or Paris and at the same time gives a sense of permanent instability, and therefore of life.

The earliest and visually dramatic evidence of the Euroméditerranée operations is in the dockland of La Joliette and Arenc, constructed after 1853 and fallen into neglect and disuse from the end of the colonial empire, the development of air traffic to the Mediterranean ports it served and the installation of the tanker terminals at Fos-sur-Mer. To build the docks, the hillside overlooking the coves of the Lazaret and the Ourse was razed and they, with the beach of Arenc, made way for an artificial port fronted with brick and stone built warehouses and offices. Of Arenc as it was, Flaubert wrote, "When I was there... I had the whole sea to myself... sometimes I spread out my limbs and remained suspended on the water doing nothing, looking down at the sea floor carpeted with wrack..."

The Marseillais of the time were not all happy with the great changes brought about by developers and architects from outside and taking inspiration, in the case of the engineer Gustave Desplaces, fom the London docks and warehouses. The poet Victor Gelu complained of the speculators that "they know nothing of our pleasures, our needs, our climate... they would cut away the hill that protects us from the ravages of the wind... and fill up Lacydon with the rubble of the old town," while for Taine "the vast port and the constructions that go with it make of Marseille a Liverpool of the Midi."

The world-renowned Marseille docks from which in their heyday every adventurer set out and where hundreds of thousands of tons of merchandise a year were passed, became a sad sight in their long, rusting, empty decline, abandoned in 1980 and practically deserted except by fishermen off the monumental, seven kilometrelong stone protective dyke which was built in 1844 at least in part to give the townspeople a promenade by the sea to replace the coves and beaches they had lost. Now the dyke, for security reasons, is forbidden territory, the warehouses have been magnificently rehabilitated and contain as well as office space, apartments, art galleries, restaurants and bars, while cruise ships and ferries to Corsica and North Africa bring new activity, with three quarters of a million tourists passing through in 2010.

To the north of the docks an attempt has been made to return access to the sea to local people, and this culminates in the marina and beach at l'Estaque from where the bay and islands can be seen, as far as their elemental features are concerned, just as Cézanne saw them. Near the furthest northern boundary of the commune of Marseille is the village of Château-Gombert below the Massif de l'Etoile. Here in the 1980s, at the end of the period of building academic centres at the periphery of which Luminy at the other extremity of the town is the shining example, the Technopôle de Château-Gombert was created on some of the last open fields and endowed with a totemic status as centre of scientific research. Jean Viard suggests, with perhaps characteristic Marseillais dissidence, that had the *technopôle* been installed in the disused docklands their rehabilitation would have begun ten years earlier and some open country space preserved, but he grants that Château-Gombert, linked by the Metro to the hospital and faculty of medecine at La Timone at the other end of Line 1, is more than merely totemic since it functions with growing success and repute.

Also spared death by dynamite, the hôtel de Cabre was revolved through 90 degrees by an engineering feat in 1954

3 | Landmarks
Buildings and Styles

Of the Greek town, nothing remains; of the Roman town, nothing...
Marseille is a pile of houses under a beautiful sky, that's all.

Victor Hugo

Marseille... is the only antique capital that doesn't crush us with the
monuments of its past.

Blaise Cendrars

Pagan: Docks and Walls

Systematic archaeological research below construction sites in historic towns was unknown in Hugo's time. The survival of so many
Roman monuments at Nîmes and Arles is due to the chance that
they became backwaters after the decline of the empire, never disturbed by the political and demographic turbulence or, above all, the
commercial ferment of Marseille where, at best, amateur antiquari-
ans collected curiosities, noted, preserved and sometimes donated
them. Most of the collections made in the seventeenth and eighteenth centuries were dispersed either on discovery or by later par-
tition. During the "devastating blast" of the nineteenth-century
rebuilding in which dozens of hectares of the town were razed
without any vestige left in sight, an inventory of findings, *Catalogue
des antiquités grecques et romaines*, was prepared and stored in the
Musée Borély by Wilhelm Froehner, who witnessed the destruction.
In the absence of an organized archaeological museum, most of the
more spectacular discoveries were spirited away into private hands.
The German dynamiting of part of the old town in 1943 left the site
of the earliest occupation and building in Marseille temporarily open
to the sky; in 1945, under pressure from the developers, a rapid in-

vestigation was carried out and the configuration of the Greek and Roman port was established. It was only from 1953 that archaeological work before reconstruction became a general rule, sometimes honoured, and it is from the start of excavations behind the Bourse in 1967 on three hectares of the demolished Cours Belsunce that the beginnings of urban archaeology in Marseille can be reckoned.

The negligent indifference and late awakening of the town authorities can be gauged from the fact that even in 1982, when an urgent dig was carried out on ten hectares of the northernmost part of the old city within the walls, all the discovered remains from a zone of housing and ancient artisan workshops disappeared and were said to have been destroyed. In 1985 the municipality finally created an archaeological service with two permanent archaeologists, now increased to eight.

In the Jardin des Vestiges behind the Bourse are almost the only unearthed traces of ancient Marseille left above ground and now visible, in a setting among lawns beneath the windows of the Musée d'Histoire de la Ville de Marseille, thanks to a press campaign and the locally unwelcome intervention of the Ministry of Culture; the municipality of the day under the respected Gaston Defferre was at first in favour of reburial, as was done with part of the Roman rampart of Nîmes in 2005 allegedly to preserve it, but according to dissident opinion for mainly economic reasons. In the end, the Defferre municipality created a small-scale landscape which, being so near the Vieux Port and in the sea perspective that nothing changes, moves the visitor by its effect not so much of an exposed foundational site which it is, but of an unageing physical memory within the incessant shift and densely built environment of a modern town.

This was the first large archaeological rescue operation in a town centre in France. The Greek and Roman vestiges brought to light are unique as the monumental remnant of an ancient harbour installation, including a staircase down to the former level of the sea and a 500 cubic-metre stone reservoir of fresh water for the revictualling of ships, and as an integral part of the founding work of the city—for that reason, and with the submerged finds preserved in the Musée des Docks Romains behind the Hôtel de Ville, even more redolent of its early life than is the circular stone Castellum at Nîmes where the water carried by the Roman aqueduct poured after its fifty-kilo-metre run over hill and gorge. Remains of a series of ramparts have been discovered in the precinct of the gardens, the oldest dating to the sixth century BC, the most visible, known as the wall of Crinas and built of the rosy limestone cut from the Cap Couronne and transported by water, to the second century BC. The blocks of stone, meticulously dressed, measure a metre in length by a half in height, the rampart has at its base a depth of three metres and it is thought that the height was not less than six, surmounted by a parapet; this was the rampart, with a gateway protected by two towers of ten metres depth, that withstood the siege of Caesar, and whose line the medieval walls followed, enclosing the old town from Lacydon to the narrow mouth of the open sea, with the entry to the port secured in medieval times, and probably also in antiquity, by a chain or boom.

Sacred and Military: Saint-Victor, the Forts and Churches

The Abbaye de Saint-Victor towers over the Vieux Port from the south, and for as long as Marseille subsisted within the walls on the northern side of the water it stood fortress-like and independent, the capital of its own landed realm. The monastery accumulated wealth and power for thirteen hundred years from its first foundation by a Coptic monk arrived from Egypt in the fifth century, and grew to become one of the most influential in the Christian Mediterranean world until dissolved during the revolution. The wider community ruled by the monastery numbered up to five thousand monks, and the abbots, one of whom became pope as Urban V and rebuilt part of the upper church and fortified the building in 1363, came often from the same family dynasties as those that ruled the town. The abbey was constructed above the quarry which had been the first source of building stone of the Greek settlers, producing a limestone to which later on the pink stone from Cap Couronne was preferred; but the earliest Christian basilica was cut into the rock and its remains form part of the enormous crypt below the present church. At the revolution the monastic buildings were destroyed, the abbey church owing its survival to use during the years of revolutionary

nominal atheism as a barracks and prison until returned to ecclesiastical function as a parish church by Napoleon in 1804. Entry is
through the Tour d'Isarn, named after the Catalan monk who
revived the fortunes of the monastery in the eleventh century and
whose tomb and effigy are in the crypt; above the entrance door to
the tower is a carved stone tablet depicting the legendary figure of
Saint Victor slaying a dragon in one of the *calanques*. The naves of the
upper church are largely Romanesque but the transept and choir, the
work of Urban V, are gothic and of an austere, dark simplicity despite
the addition of baroque side altars in exuberant taste. The original
stained glass of the few windows was destroyed in the Allied
bombing of Marseille in 1944. The combination of a Romanesque
body of the church with a gothic apse is reminiscent of Vézelay in
Burgundy, but Saint-Victor lacks Vézelay's light and sculptures and
falls short of its supreme achievement of architectural union: it is a
fine religious building of which there are so many in France, but
unlike Vézelay, not uniquely admirable as an abbey church of the
later Middle Ages.

What is unique in Saint-Victor is the crypt. This immense ex-
cavation in the rock of the hillside, carved on a north south axis at
ninety degrees to the church above it, is more than a catacomb,
evoking the life of the early Christian Church as no masterpiece of
medieval sacred architecture could. With the cathedral-like height of
one of its underground chambers, the burrowing humility of others
and the arbitrariness of the space it has cut from the hillside, the
crypt exemplifies the persuasive power of primal authenticity. The
most hardened sceptic leaves it with a new perception, seeing the
baroque side-altars above as debased precursors of a questionable en-
lightenment.

The military look of Saint-Victor is matched by the two
fortresses guarding the entrance to the Vieux Port, the Forts Saint-
Jean and Saint-Nicolas. Both were built in the reign of Louis XIV,
designed by de Clerville the rival of Vauban whom he had taught,
and both intended as much to intimidate the rebellious, dissidence-
prone town behind them as to protect it from naval invasion. Earlier,
Thomas Platter had described the fourteen pieces of artillery com-

manding the entry to Lacydon as the longest he had ever seen, and able to throw cannon-balls the size of a man's head; after the building of the fortresses at least half of the armament was trained inwards onto the port and town, and in 1790 a commando of the National Guard attacked and demolished the "Bastille of Marseille", the part of the fortification of Saint-Nicolas turned against the city.

The Fort Saint-Jean stands on the foundations of a building of the Knights Hospitaller of Saint John, and is dominated by the Tour Carrée built by King René in 1447, and the Tour du Fanal of 1644, a columnar watchtower of distinctive and affectionately regarded phallic outline, a resemblance which in the nineteenth century an attempt was made to reduce by the addition of a corbelled stone ring that in effect underlines it. Round the foot of the Tour Carrée is a terrace broadening out to an esplanade between the walls and quays on which the Euroméditerranée project of a Cité de la Méditerranée is to be built, while on the other side of the tower is the entry to the Mémorial des Camps de la Mort, constructed within a blockhouse left by the Germans and housing, among other documents and photographs, an archive relating to the destruction of the old quarter of the town in 1943. In 1844 the moat of Saint-Jean was opened to allow a canal to pass from the Vieux Port to the new dock at La Joliette, and the fort became an island; the canal was filled in to make the road tunnel under the Vieux Port and the present approach road in 1967.

The defences of Marseille have never, since Caesar's successful siege, prevented an invasion despite the lie of land and islands which at first sight seems so favourable to the defender. At the time of the construction of the Château d'If by François I, between 1527 and 1529, the late medieval castle plan had already become anachronistic because naval guns were by then heavy enough to neutralize it. It is also thought that the range of the artillery of the château was too short to command the full width of sea between the island it stands on and the harbour. The fortress, the last of its kind to be built in France, nevertheless gives an ideal theatrical effect of its intended purpose as an armed and impregnable lock to the chain made up of the towers and ramparts of the town. The three round corner towers, one higher and deeper in circumference than the others, are so proportioned as to cover the flanking walls by fire from splayed embrasures, and the platform running the length of the walls is continued at the same level within the flat circular summits of the towers, imparting to the whole building at night the appearance, in the words of Alexandre Dumas in *The Count of Monte-Cristo*, of "a granite giant, blacker than the sea, blacker than the sky, rising like a threatening ghost". Though militarily archaic, until 1880 the Château d'If had a long use as a sure place of incarceration for state prisoners with a list of illustrious names—Mirabeau, de Sade, the man in the iron mask among them, legendary or not—as well as Protestant dissenters after the revocation of the Edict of Nantes; the cells were arranged on three levels, the most fortunate receiving some light from the inner courtyard but none with any sight of the sea which Dumas described as "the cemetery of the château d'If".

The eleventh-century cathedral of Marseille and the fifth-century baptistery, one of the largest in Christendom, disappeared except for the apse and octagonal cupola still awaiting restoration with the construction between 1852 and 1893 of the new Eglise Notre-Dame-de-la-Major overlooking the nineteenth-century docks. The Romanesque building stood on the edge of a cliff above the sea at the northern extremity of the walled town and had been adorned with a magnificent baroque portico of which nothing remains; because of this unusual position of the cathedral at the limit of the town, where it still perches uneasily between docks and highways, Marseille seems to lack a central focus of religious practice as if the sea has always been its hemisphere and the surface of Lacydon, reflecting the sky, both temple floor and roof.

On the northern side of the Vieux Port is the severely simple and sober Provençal Romanesque Saint-Laurent, the fishermen's church, and with Saint-Victor the only entire remaining medieval church in Marseille; badly shaken by the explosion of the Panier in 1943 it remained closed for fifty years. Formerly surrounded by parishioners' houses, it now stands in isolation on its promontory, with an air of austerity and purity reinforced in the interior by the removal from the three naves during restoration of the accumulated decorative additions of the centuries, leaving the beauty of the Cap Couronne stone unobstructed, but bare.

As well as Saint-Laurent, the explosions around the Vieux Port spared with near-surgical precision the seventeenth-century Hôtel de Ville and the Hôtel-Dieu, and in the vicinity of the quays the two most ancient remaining houses of Marseille, the only relics of the patrician dwellings of the old city to survive while the destruction of others continued in the speculative rebuilding of the post-war years. The Hôtel de Cabre is now the oldest house in the town, dating from 1535 and showing the persistence of the gothic style long after the Renaissance was in the ascendant. In 1954 the house was again saved from demolition, when the Grand-Rue was widened, by the engineering exploit of raising it bodily on jacks, turning it through ninety degrees and settling it without damage on a new foundation. The Maison Diamantée, so called on account of its outer walls closely set with stone bosses formed in the conventional representation of cut diamonds, was built at the end of the sixteenth century and in spite of the probably unique appearance of its façade which has puzzled art historians down the ages, is otherwise in an orthodox early Renaissance idiom. It houses the Musée du Vieux-Marseille and has a staircase whose rising ceilings are elaborately decorated with plaster work based on drawings in the architectural treatise of Sebestiano Serlio, an employee of François I at Fontainebleau and specialist in theatre design.

Enlightened: Town Offices, Vieille Charité, Bastides

The Hôtel de Ville, now somewhat dwarfed by the modern apartment blocks around it though less so than was at first planned, with towers of fourteen storeys mercifully reduced, is the work of Gaspard Puget (brother or cousin of Pierre) and Mathieu Portal between 1653 and 1673 in a style echoing the patrician villas of Genoa. The appearance of the building, surprisingly modest when compared to the town halls of Aix, Lyon or Toulouse, has been affected by changes to the double slope of the original mansard roof, but thanks perhaps to that modesty and to its position looking onto the Vieux Port it has kept its charm and the affection of the generations. The original design left no room for an internal staircase and access to the council chamber on the first floor was by a wooden bridge at the rear of the building, replaced in the eighteenth century by the existing stone gallery, and the monumental staircase of 1816.

Close to the quayside, and between the Hôtel de Ville and the Fort Saint-Jean, is the elegant single-storey building of 1719 housing the sanitary office where the declarations of ships' captains were presented while the ships waited in the quarantine area of the Île de Ratonneau for permission to sail into the port. In the year after its construction Marseille suffered the most disastrous plague in its history. The building was doubled by the erection beside it of an exact replica in the late nineteenth century.

The Hôtel-Dieu on the hill behind the Hôtel de Ville stands on the site of the twelfth-century hospital and was built in its present form in 1753 to a design of a member of the Hardouin-Mansart family, and modified during the Second Empire by the addition of symmetrical pavilions to the wings containing the staircases. The hospital of Marseille abandoned the building in 1993 and its conversion to a hotel and apartments is to be completed in 2013.

High in the Panier and set back from the sea and the port is what is beyond all doubt the finest building in Marseille and in scale the most important, the Vieille Charité by Pierre Puget. This baroque workhouse, built from 1671 in the beautiful rose and ochre stone of La Couronne, was rescued from neglect and threatened demolition by the intervention of the Swiss architect Le Corbusier who recognized it as a work of genius when planning his own building, the Cité Radieuse at Mazargues, and it is now magnificently restored. Built in collegiate form around an immense quadrangle, it turns three of its walls almost blindly onto the outer world while the fourth, enclosing the gated entrance, is a storey lower than the others and provided with plain, domestic-scale windows. It is from within the quadrangle that the splendour of the building is apparent. The three taller sides present a uniform aspect of triple superimposed and arcaded galleries throughout their length, the delicately emphasized horizontal and vertical lines of masonry uninterrupted and bare of decoration other than by the deep shadows of the arcades, varying only with the height of the sun and the orientation of the wall. The impression of severity, order, enclosure is complete and appropriate to the building's purpose which was to house, or imprison, the indigent, the lesser delinquent, the prostitutes and beggars and aged human refuse of the seventeenth century become at last objectionable to the city rulers in the formal and perhaps pharisaical age of Louis XIV's embellishment of the town.

The austerity of the enclosing quadrangle, unrelieved except by the warmth of the stone, is the dramatic contrasting framework for the chapel at its centre. This, which is the chief evidence in Marseille of the genius of Puget (who was born in a nearby street in 1620 to a family of master builders) is a baroque building of complex design with an oval and elongated dome and an interior in which colonnades and galleries, staircases and passages create a maze-like effect under the illumination of the dome and windows. The design, like a Roman amphitheatre, allowed for separate access and evacuation of poor and rich, inhabitants of the workhouse and their governors. In 1861 the Ionic façade of the chapel was replaced, in the more grandiose Second Empire taste, by a pediment and Corinthian portico which though ponderous in comparison with the building behind it, is as impressive as it was meant to be when the deep perspective of the court is first seen through the entrance gates from the exterior, where clearance and restoration of the surrounding area are in progress.

In the Charité's long history it has been used as hospital for the plague-stricken in 1720, as barracks, refuge for displaced families after the destruction of the old quarters of the town in 1943, then as an unregulated squat until 1962 when the remaining occupiers were evacuated and Puget's masterpiece threatened with demolition. André Malraux is given, or claimed, credit for its rescue after 1968 and the intervention of Le Corbusier. Since their restoration and reopening with a famous surrealist exhibition in 1986, the buildings house, as well as offices of the town's department of culture and exhibition spaces, the Musée d'Arts Africains, Océaniens et Amérindiens, and the Musée d'Archéologie Méditerranénne.

Apart from his own house in the Rue de Rome, Puget left only one other architectural legacy in Marseille, the small, covered, open-sided market building called the Halle Puget whose lightness and grace may be due to the unusual distance between the twenty supporting columns in relation to their weight, and to their uneven number on each side, five by five if the first and fifth columns on the shorter sides are excluded from the count on the longer. It is ironical that Marseille, of whose native artists Pierre Puget was the best endowed with the combination of panache and austerity which is characteristic of both people and landscape, should have preserved of his work only a magnificent poorhouse and an ethereal fish market, both now essential to the city's spirit in their aesthetic finish and conviction.

The Cours Saint-Louis, once considered among the most splendid streets in Europe, has retained some of its original façades not easily discernible among the careless reconstructions and conversions. The most striking relic of the days of its glory is the entrance to the Hôtel de Pesciolini near the Porte d'Aix, with giant *atlantes* supporting the balcony above. In Aix-en-Provence this doorway would be prized by the city's conservation department and admired by well guided visitors and tourists; in Marseille it is perhaps valued but blackened by traffic fumes and disfigured by shops occupying the ground floor on either side, with their display of cheap and cheerful household goods such as offered in the famous *marché aux puces* at Arenc. The nearby Porte d'Aix from which for centuries the visitor from the north first viewed the long plunging perspective of the cours as far as the Rue de Rome and beyond, was adorned with a triumphal arch in 1825 to the glory of the armies of the revolution and Empire, seven years before completion of the work on the Arc de l'Etoile in Paris; both are examples of a neoclassical attempt to borrow the splendour of Roman triumphs, and that of Marseille is the less convincing due to the town's temperamental antipathy to Bonaparte, and because it is built in a white stone which pales beside the sensuous pink limestone of the Marseille hills. The arch stands isolated near the exit of the *autoroute*, emphasizing by its formal self-sufficiency and irrelevance to everyday purposes the inhabited urban disarray around it.

Buildings in the classical style of the seventeenth to nineteenth centuries are widely spread about the town, often overwhelmed by surroundings of indiscriminate addition and change. The Eglise des Chartreux of 1680 to 1702 is distinguished by its relatively unspoilt context as well as its great purity of composition of superimposed orders, Ionic and Corinthian with an eight-column peristyle. The neoclassical chapel of the Couvent des Bernardines near the Cours Julien, with an elegant shallow dome, is now a theatre for experimental productions. In the Rue Grignan are two notable buildings: the Musée Cantini in the town house of 1694 erected as the home of a family whose fortune was derived from coral fishing off the Algerian coast, and which now houses a collection of paintings of the period 1900 to 1960; and the Protestant *temple* of 1825 with a Doric colonnade, the first non-Catholic church to be built in Marseille. In a courtyard of the neighbouring Rue Montgrand is the town house, considered to be the finest in Marseille and now the Lycée Montgrand, built in 1745 by the shipbuilder André Roux who sent his personal fleet to war against the English during the Seven Years' War, and was eventually ruined as ship by ship went to the bottom.

A great neoclassical ruin, the Hôpital Caroline on the Île de Ratonneau, built between 1823 and 1828 as a "sanitary utopia" or quarantine for sufferers from yellow fever, was the work of Robert Penchaud who was also responsible for the Porte d'Aix. Designed in an epoch when the virtues of fresh air were believed to be enough to blow infections away, its small window openings were intended for ventilation rather than light, and the central chapel, reproducing with its Doric order the extreme simplicity of a Greek temple, allowed the sick to attend religious services in an open-sided church. The Hôpital Caroline was occupied by the German army during the Second World War and heavily bombed by the American air force on 27 August 1944, leaving it entirely in ruins where each year a music, dance and theatre festival is organized, *les Nuits Caroline*. Also on the island is another simulacrum of a Greek temple, the Chapel of Port-Frioul standing on a bluff above the landing stage and village.

A great part of the architectural heritage of Marseille lay in the bastides, which the twentieth century roughly swept away in face of urgent housing needs and in the interests of rapid road building, leaving of the thousands (no one is any longer sure of the number) scattered about the countryside only an estimated two hundred in varying states of decrepitude, with here and there, as if by accident, a gateway, the remnants of a bridge over an irrigation canal or an avenue ornamented with broken statues. A surviving example of this race of historic *résidences secondaires*, with superbly restored interior and much of its original furniture, is the famous Château Borély near Mazargues, built in 1768 for a family of merchants ennobled by Louis XV which had the ambition to create the most sumptuous and elegant country house of the Marseille region. Borély and its contents were saved from the twentieth century by becoming a museum in 1863; it is now the property of the town and with its formal gardens, remodelled during the Second Empire, is certainly the prime illustration of the habitat and way of life of the Marseille élite which endured for at least four hundred years on the modest and economically unprofitable acreage of farmlands which had been their patrimony. The formal simplicity, balance and proportions of the building and its pediment, and the restrained moulding of its stone surfaces appear vividly contrasted with the fierce profile of the Mont Marseilleveyre rising behind it, and the sea visible across the racecourse from the terraces of the garden. Another example which can be visited is La Magalone on the Boulevard Michelet, built in the late seventeenth century but altered in the nineteenth and now carefully restored. La Magalone stood in a *domaine* of thirteen hectares, an illustration of the thesis that the paucity of land holdings surrounding these architecturally and socially ambitious bastides was one cause of their ready abandonment in face of twentieth-century urbanizing pressure.

The Château Pastré near La Pointe Rouge, a short distance to the south of Borély had, exceptionally, a domain of 125 hectares, now a public park. The house, built in 1860 for a family originally of Languedoc shepherds arrived in Marseille before the revolution, and which went on to enrich itself in the wool trade with Egypt and

North Africa and become one of the wealthiest in Marseille, is in a Louis XIII style using Marseille brick and pale stone from Arles, its gardens irrigated by water from the canal created in 1849. The château, relatively modest in size, houses a museum of the *faïence* for which Marseille and Moustiers were famous, but its place in history depends more on the courage of the last private owner, the Comtesse Lily Pastré who sheltered there musicians, artists and academics attempting to reach safety overseas during the early years of the Vichy regime.

Sacred and Imperial: the Era of the Grandiose

As happened elsewhere in industrial Europe, nineteenth-century expansion and commercial ambitions began the break up of the territory of Marseille that the twentieth century completed. This process altered for ever the townscape and left many of the most familiar and monumentally inflated buildings that characterize it in the popular view and are recognizable from afar, nowadays usually with patient and affectionate suspension of criticism. But first, in the romanticizing reaction of the early part of the century, a number of neo-gothic churches appeared. French architects, particularly those from the south, seem not to have worked with entire conviction in the neo-gothic style, perhaps because the great northern cathedrals of the twelfth and thirteenth centuries were felt to have exhausted the imaginative possibilities of the genre; but in Marseille the Eglise Saint-Vincent-de-Paul of 1855 to 1888 (also known as the Eglise des Réformés), at the head of the Allées Gambetta and the Canebière, is a graceful reproduction of northern architecture designed with fidelity to period detail and with spires at whose base the elongated window openings, without tracery or glass, transpierce the masonry of the towers on both axes like a double arch, giving an aerial lightness of effect.

It is about the steps of the Eglise des Réformés and the pavements and streets in its neighbourhood that the annual festival of *santons* is held in the weeks before Christmas. Santons (from the Provençal *saintoun*, little saint) are a show of piety now honoured more perhaps for its festive than its religious aspect, particularly in a widespread community of varying ethnic origins and faiths. The tradition of the santon dates from the time of the Revolution when churches were closed and nativity scenes banned. A Marseillais, Jean-Louis Lagnel, conceived and realized the idea of figurines modelled in clay, painted in lively colours and dressed in local peasant costume to represent inhabitants of the town and personalities of the tradesmen and artisans of old Marseille, for display in homes and shops. The tradition spread and santons now appear in churches (and souvenir outlets) throughout France and particularly in the south as a *manifestation folklorique*. There is a Musée des Santons behind the Théâtre de la Criée on the Vieux Port where the techniques involved in manufacturing santons from all over the world are displayed.

Another parish church, Saint-Michel, has an interior of exceptional purity and great height but lacks the towers intended for it as it was never completed. It was only with the arrival on the scene of Jacques Henri Espérandieu that the ecclesiastical architecture of Marseille made a new departure, and then it was the Romanesque, perceived as more native to the Mediterranean world, which was taken as inspiration, the neo-Byzantine as its particular variant, and under the permanent influence of the sea, Venice as its distant source. The construction of the new dockyards brought shipping towards that part of the old town where the ancient cathedral lay humble and half hidden among buildings demolished to make way for access to the extended shoreline, and to provide rubble to force the sea further out. Marseille was the only big town in France to lack a vast cathedral and the ambition was conceived early in the nineteenth century to build a new one that would rise up high above the quays and impose itself from far off on the vision from the sea. The Bishop of Marseille convinced Napoleon III of the desirability of the work which was begun in 1852, at first to the design of Léon Vaudoyer but later by Espérandieu, and intended, in a phrase echoing the vainglory of the Second Empire, as a "Christian triumphal arch raised up at the gateway to the Orient".

The result, the Cathédrale Sainte-Marie-Majeure de Marseille, is a building which has never been kindly received by the Marseillais, despite its undoubted originality and the impressive effect it makes, particularly from a distance, across the water. The twin towers fit incongruously with the several domes, large and small, which owe little either to the Renaissance or to Saint Mark's in Venice but have an oriental air uncomfortable in the context of European medieval city remains; the polychrome masonry is in strongly marked horizontal bands of green Florentine and white Calissane stone, with pink marble pillars under the portico. The more recognizably Romanesque interior is majestic and the polychrome of ochre, porphyry, red marble and gold mosaic makes a ceremonial and less eccentric impression. The roofs of the octagonal central and three smaller circular domes are painted largely in blue with gilded ribs and generously lit with windows. If the overall effect of the interior, though gorgeous in its profusion, seems also frigid it may be that any resurrection, however enthusiastic, of bygone architectural style seems often more moribund than newborn.

Espérandieu was born in Nîmes in 1839, an abandoned child adopted by a rich family of Protestant millers who gave him his Bunyanesque and appropriate name and sent him to study in Italy. His other work in Marseille endowed the town with at least two of its great landmarks, Notre-Dame-de-la-Garde on its hill, and the Palais Longchamp. It is the triumph of Notre-Dame-de-la-Garde to be dominantly visible from almost everywhere, and above all from far out at sea. The sanctuary is among the icons of Catholicism in France, like the Sacré Coeur in Paris, and is the most visited Marseille monument, exuberant within and without, "romanobyzantine" in style and decoration but also, fittingly for a building erected on a site owned by the Ministry of War, fortress-like in its high tower and in some architectural details such as gun emplacements and bartizan turrets. The hill of la Garde was the last stronghold to be surrendered by the German army at the Liberation, after fierce fighting which left the building almost undamaged. The interior, composed of the upper basilica and a huge vaulted crypt, is brilliant with mosaics and, being a famous place of pilgrimage, is charged with innumerable ex-votos of which many are appreciated as examples of naïve art. One of them, carved in the marble, expresses her appreciation to the almighty of Queen Alexandra, who visited the basilica in 1905, for his goodness to her family.

The Palais Longchamp deserves a high place among the nineteenth century's grandiose public monuments of Europe, celebrating not a bygone victory or a dead leader, but the living flow of water from the Durance brought by the Canal de Marseille and delivered in fountains and cascades, amid abundant animal and human statuary and staircases, to a flight of pools at the foot of this elaborate and striking temple-like construction on the hillside beyond the Canebière. From the central pavilion, built like a helmeted arch, semi-circular double Ionic colonnades lead to wings, in one of which is the Musée des Beaux-Arts and in the other, the Muséum d'Histoire Naturelle. With the other Second Empire monuments of Marseille, the Palais Longchamp expresses the power and confidence of the growing and prospering commercial and imperial centre that Marseille became in the second half of the nineteenth century, while its imaginative vigour and fluent invention of play with stone from the nearby mountain quarries are baroque characteristics in the wide sense. A more severe, neoclassical though still relatively exuberant building is the Palais de la Bourse of 1852 to 1860, formerly home of the most ancient chamber of commerce in France which dates from 1599. The exterior overlooking the Canebière is imposing and handsome, with a gallery of Corinthian columns thirteen metres high above the main entrance. But the hall, once the central enclosure of the stock exchange and the heart of Marseille's financial activity, with a black and white marble floor, is a magnificent arcaded space of double height under a coved ceiling and long central skylight, powerfully conveying the sense of its historic purpose.

A far less architecturally successful and historically significant Second Empire building is the Palais du Pharo, sited on a bluff previously used for military executions and overlooking the mouth of the Vieux Port which with the forts of Saint-Jean and Saint-Nicholas it combines to dominate. Constructed by Napoleon III as a gift for Eugénie, his empress, this rather bland and lifeless seaside palace was never occupied but was returned to the ownership of the town by Eugénie from her eventual exile in England, and is now used for congresses and official ceremonies.

Among other notable buildings which adorn the streets, or in some cases are half-hidden away from the main currents of traffic, are the Préfecture, the Palais de Justice and the Caisse d'Epargne in the nearby Place Estrangin-Pastré, all of the nineteenth century, and the Opéra in the Rue Molière, first opened in 1787, much loved by the Marseille public, damaged by fire in 1913 and reconstructed in 1924 in Art Deco style though retaining the neoclassical façade above which the sculptor Antoine Sartorio added a series of allegorical stone figures.

Fountains and statues, carvings and columns abound in the squares and streets of Marseille, largely invisible in the rush of traffic and the undisciplined urban developments around them. An exception is the ornate Fontaine Cantini on the Place Castellane, displacing the obelisk of 1811 by Penchaud which had previously occupied the space and was removed to the Rond-point de Mazargues; both stand in the long perspective of the Rue de Rome and the ancient road to Italy, visible in its length from the height of the Porte d'Aix.

Radiant: Le Corbusier

For engineering reasons the railway station of Saint-Charles was built, in 1848, on a hilltop plateau so the lines approaching it would remain near the level of the Tunnel de la Nerthe, for many years the longest in Europe. It was not until 1927 that the monumental staircase from the station down to the Place des Marseillaises and the Boulevard d'Athènes was added, with its commanding view over the town and ornamented with statuary evoking the French colonial empire. Simone de Beauvoir described her experience as a young woman first arriving at Saint-Charles in 1931: "I stood still at the top of the great staircase. 'Marseille,' I exclaimed to myself. Under the blue sky, sunlit tiles, wells of shadow, autumnal plane trees; in the distance, the hills and the blue of the sea… the odour of burnt grasses… it was love at first sight."

In the same year of 1927 the reinforced concrete towers, fifty metres high, of the great silo for treatment and storage of grain were built at Arenc; this familiar building at the entry to the docks is now converted to house an auditorium, a restaurant, offices and a *café-musique*. The rehabilitation of the warehouses and dockyard offices, designed between 1858 and 1863 by the engineer Gustave Desplaces under the influence of those in London, has brought to public attention a group of exceptionally fine nineteenth-century industrial buildings at the water's edge, converted to new uses by the architect Eric Castaldi and greatly admired. Antoine Sartorio (sculptor of the figures on the opera house), who was born in Menton but studied and worked most of his life in Marseille, was also responsible for the low-relief carvings of the Seven Deadly Sins which somewhat ironically decorate the stark and bare outer wall of the Prison des Baumettes, a name translating as "little caves" such as the many tunnelling the rock where the prison stands, on the road towards the Calanque de Morgiou.

The best-known and most influential of the modern buildings in Marseille is Le Corbusier's Cité Radieuse at Mazargues, commissioned by the state, constructed between 1945 and 1952, more reproduced in international architectural manuals than any other monument in Marseille and expressive of Le Corbusier's utopian vision of a "community" or vertical garden city, the new model of urban habitation. Raised on concrete pillars, each of the building's eighteen floors is conceived as a street in itself, some with shops, and on the roof are a gymnasium, a running track and a swimming pool installed in a 500-square-metre space originally intended as a chapel. Of the 337 apartments, most are duplex in design and there were, in the early days, a hotel and an infant school. The original object was purportedly to house disadvantaged families displaced by the destruction of the old town but the Cité Radieuse failed to appeal to this sector of Marseillais, and before long it became clear that its real target was a sophisticated, upwardly mobile and professional urban middle class looking for a self-contained and serviced environment; from 1954 the apartments were made commercially available to this group which now constitutes the entire population of a thousand occupants.

Richard Cobb, a violent critic of Le Corbusier's proposed Parisian tower blocks, described the architect as doggedly determined to line both banks of the Seine with a barrier of dragon's teeth, and as perpetrator of *la maison du fada,* a "blot on the Marseille horizon and the object of much popular derision". The nickname signifies the "crackpot's house" and was instantly given to Le Corbusier's invention. "To sign up for one of these places," wrote a journalist at the time, "you would have to be more *fada* than the *fada en chef,* who himself is the most *fada* of all the *fadas* from end to end of Marseille." But the architectural manuals continue to feature it as prominently and as often as ever.

Arch of Triumph, Marseilles

Erected to celebrate the Victories of the Empire.

The Porte d'Aix, monumental and generally ignored by passers-by

4 | **Rulers and Ruled**
      A Brief Social and Political History

> The inhabitants of Marseille show a serious and disciplined charac-
> ter... A supply of hemlock is conserved by the public services for
> those who can satisfy the Six Hundred of the reasons for their desire
> to die... so a means to this end can be offered to whoever, having
> known enough either of happiness or of unhappiness, wishes to avoid
> that the one should cease or the other continue.
>
> Valerius Maximus

> The Marseillais consider Mirabeau simply as a politician of great
> ability whose principles agree with their own; as for his private char-
> acter... they say... that they would rather trust a capable rascal than
> an honest man without talent.
>
> Arthur Young

Foundation and Prosperity

The historian Fernand Braudel wrote that Marseille "looked seaward
and could thus be unusually independent of central authority". With
its concomitant, the general acceptance of incomers from the sea by
founders and predecessors who had arrived in the same way—in
1869 Léon Gambetta compared Marseille to New York—this seems
the most enduring characteristic evidenced by the history of the
Greek colony which was to become the oldest and the second city of
France. Both independence and constant traffic with the sea can
make for a reality and a realistic sense different from those perceived
in the mainland mass, and this may be the second stable and lasting
characteristic of Marseille. Jean Viard points out that political unity
is terrestrial: "At sea, risk and discontinuity are omnipresent; piracy
continued longer and religious unity never came. This dangerous and

violent world was far removed from that of harvests and ordered successions… hence the ceaseless renewal of the people of Marseille… and an old dissentient background more radical than in the rest of the Midi." In 1862 a minister of finance wrote that "everything about this city seems out of all ordinary proportion… reality overtakes any forecast and every hope."

Herodotus claimed that the Phocaeans were the first Greeks to make long voyages on the high seas, that they sailed beyond the Pillars of Hercules and discovered Tartessos at the mouth of the Guadalquivir in Andalucía. The twelve Greek cities of Ionia, founded in the eighth century BC, suffered from chronic food shortage for growing populations and from the dominance of a caste that prevented redistribution of land. By the time the Phocaean expedition set out, the nearest new territories were already colonized from the city of Miletus, and the colonists from Phocaea, the most northerly of the Ionian cities, looked further westward in the direction their forebears had travelled. Etruscans and Carthaginians occupied much of the accessible coast but the region which was to become Massalia was uncultivated and relatively unsettled and the site itself, two thousand kilometres rowing distance from Phocaea, was, in spite of its topographical advantages, apparently deserted. The stream named Lacydon, running into the eastern arm of the *calanque*, provided for centuries an adequate water supply for the town and its population which before long, and with a second immigrant flow including women after the destruction of Phocaea by the Persians in 540 BC, reached the census figure of ten thousand. Stone for building was abundant, close at hand and accessible, the law allowed marriage with local women as well as Greek, and once their first city was built the new Massaliots ruled themselves in political independence from their Ionian origins, conserving in autonomy only cultural, legal and theological systems linked to those of the motherland.

The Massaliots became known for their relatively strict morals. The executioner's sword rusted in its scabbard for want of use; mime in the theatre, usually concerned with illicit sexual relations, was banned for fear of bad example; luxury was forbidden, the law put a limit on the value of dowries and of the jewellery to be worn by women; no armed man was allowed entry to the city. Tacitus claimed that Massalia harmoniously combined Greek manners and provincial austerity, and that those arriving from the sea quickly conformed to the prevailing customs. For centuries, Massalia remained a piece of Ionia implanted in foreign soil; its political system, for which Strabo is the chief authority since Aristotle's book on the subject is lost, was universally admired, and is strongly reminiscent of the Venetian constitution that endured for more than a thousand years. "The Massaliots have the best regulated political regime of all aristocratic systems. They set up a college, or timocracy, of six hundred members appointed for life and who choose a superior council of fifteen to control the execution of current affairs; three of these have considerable powers and one of them presides. No one can become a member who has no children, or less than three generations of citizenship behind him. The laws are Ionian laws." Cicero pointed out, however, that "although the Massaliots are governed with the most perfect justice... there remains in the position occupied by the people something like servitude."

Concurrently with the building and expansion of their walled city to cover the area of fifty hectares which remained its limit for two thousand years, and the plantation of vine and olive in the countryside around, the Phocaeans cultivated those trade connections which, with their knowledge of the ways of the sea and the power of a fleet able in the sixth century BC to defeat that of the Carthaginians and Etruscans combined, was to be the permanent basis of the economy. Diodorus of Sicily and Fernand Braudel gave accounts of the tin route from Britain along the Saône and the Rhône valley, with minerals brought in large quantities by merchants on horseback, and M.-C. Amouretti mentions the extraordinary speed with which commerce was developed in the western Mediterranean during the first two generations from the founding of Marseille. "In the west-east direction went tin from Brittany and Wales, gold from Spain and copper from the Languedoc mines, cattle, probably slaves, wheat, silver, perhaps amber from the northern lands... bound for the Italian and Greek cities... while in the opposite direction came wine, oil (both much consumed in Massalia and which the Greeks introduced to and traded with their Celto-Ligurian neighbours), decorated ceramic ware, bronze vases…"

Aristotle noted that the founders of Massalia practised a system of *emporia*, otherwise an export-import trade in the interface between two areas of unequal cultural and economic development. This reliance on traffic and exchange rather than on production whether industrial or agricultural, with the exception of local wine exported northwards and for which Marseille became highly reputed, was to be the hallmark of the prosperity and development of the city down the ages, and the economic characteristic governing its outlook, habits and oligarchic interests running to the present day. And as Massalia gradually and by a defensive reaction against hostile neighbours expanded its territory to include, eventually, all the coast between Cap Couronne and the Rhône delta, so it established other, subsidiary colonial settlements and trading posts further afield, maintained under its rule but later to become the famous towns of Nice, Antibes, Hyères, Agde, Arles and Ampurias in Spain. From a simple Greek town in exile Massalia became a potent ruling city state with wealthy colonies and trade links throughout the known world, whose limits Massaliot sailors continued to explore and surpass.

The best known of these adventurers were Euthymenes in the fifth century BC and Pytheas in the fourth. Euthymenes, in search of gold, sailed down the Atlantic coast as far, perhaps, as Sierra Leone but without knowing quite where he was. He found the mouth of a powerful river, probably the Senegal, with crocodiles and hippopotamuses, which he took for the Nile, and was later subjected by Seneca, who confused mistakes with fabrications, to a sarcastic geographical correction. Pytheas was even worse treated by Strabo although his accounts of northern journeys were credited by Diodorus and Pliny the younger, and have been supported by later scholars. The narrative of Pytheas, who was financed by merchants of Massalia hoping for the discovery of a sea route for imports of tin and amber, was destroyed in the fire of the library of Alexandria but extracts have survived in the books of others. His itinerary took him through the straits of Gibraltar and northward along the coast of Gaul as far as the Channel which he crossed to Britain, a land he claimed to have traversed from end to end on foot; he journeyed on to Ireland and from Shetland northward to an unknown island which he named Ultima Thule, where the night lasted two hours and "there was neither earth, nor sea, nor air but a Medusa-like mixture of these elements". He reported on the ways of the population he met: "It is said that the manners of the natives of the great island of Britain are old-fashioned... and in fact their character is very simple and far removed from the cunning and wickedness of people nowadays..."

Even the sceptical Strabo admitted that Pytheas was a respectable mathematician and astronomer, and by the sixteenth century his observations on the tides and the influence of the moon, on eclipses from which he deduced the rotundity of the earth whose circumference he estimated with a margin of error of ten per cent, and his precise calculation of the latitude of Marseille with the aid of a gnomon, were recognized and his reputation as the first teller of *galéjades* was cleared away once and for all. Amouretti suggests that one reason for the long lack of belief in Pytheas and his journey was the Mediterranean-centred outlook of the Roman epoch which discredited the possibility of any inhabited world beyond the forty-fifth parallel north or south, whereas Pytheas had demonstrated its existence beyond the sixtieth. Far ahead of his times, he was known by the name Strabo gave him, the Liar, and the Marseillais who came after him have often borne the same slander.

With the growth of Roman power the independence of Massilia (the Latin version of the city's name) was bound to be overshadowed. The relationship with Rome was long valued on both sides; during the First Punic War the Phocaeans, living in competition with Carthage though formally neutral in the war, supported the Romans in Sicily and gave helpful guidance in the relatively unknown Iberia where they had established trading posts. Montesquieu stated that the ruin of Carthage and Corinth increased the wealth and glory of Marseille. In the Second Punic War Marseille was allied to Rome and by the presence of its forces along the coast obliged Hannibal to enter Italy through the Alps. In the years after the Carthaginian defeat, the Romans several times came to the aid of their Massiliot allies against Ligurians, Cimbri and

Teuton barbarians; the territory of Massilia was protected and increased but by degrees the orbit of Roman power and permanence spread; Aquae Sextiae (Aix-en-Provence), close to Marseille itself, was founded in 122 and Narbonne in 118 BC.

Independence in face of irresistible republican hegemony became a jealously guarded but more and more illusory ideal, while Roman rule extended throughout the surrounding regions of Gaul and northward, opposition being surmounted by Caesar's armies. In the rivalry between Caesar and Pompey, Marseille attempted to establish a position of neutrality in which Caesar, by his own account, did not believe. "The deputies replied to Caesar, 'With the services rendered to Marseille equally by Caesar and by Pompey our duty is to give neither of them any aid against the other, and to receive neither of them in the town or port.' Meanwhile Domitius [partisan of Pompey] arrived with his fleet and the inhabitants of Marseille welcomed him and put him at the head of the city. Caesar, outraged, advanced three legions…"

The courage of the Marseillais during the ensuing siege and naval battles of 49 BC was praised by Caesar himself: "They showed a gallantry which lacked nothing… and which was hardly inferior to that of our own troops." On land there was a sacred wood which Lucan described as very dense among the naked hills, not occupied by nymphs but containing sanctuaries where barbarian rites were practised, and as never having been profaned before: "Caesar ordered this forest to be cut down… and two assault towers equal in height to the ramparts to be built." These appear to have stood on mounds made by filling the hollow between the hill of Saint-Charles and the Carmes with felled trees from the forest, creating a platform of trunks on which the siege engines could be operated and the towers advanced into position. The siege lasted several months but Caesar's victory at sea, the flight of Pompey's fleet when failure seemed certain and the Roman occupation of the mainland prevented any revictualling of the town; epidemics raged, and on Caesar's return from the completion of his Spanish victories, the Massiliots surrendered, gave up their arms, sailed their ships out of the port and made over their funds. The occupation by Roman forces symbolized the final loss of the city's full independence and the start of a new era, still continuing in reduced and disguised form, in which dissidence, perennial revolt and cultivation of an unspoken but persistent separatism took the place of the original Greek pride in sovereignty.

Nevertheless, Caesar showed himself generous in victory, allowing the Massiliots their lives and liberty. There was no massacre or sale into slavery and the ramparts were left intact, if damaged. Marseille, retaining its government by the Six Hundred at least until the end of the second century AD, became a federated city tied to Rome by a treaty setting out both privileges and duties. The port was able to resume trading activity and many of the richer inhabitants became Roman citizens. But the colonies of Massilia were confiscated for the benefit of Narbonne and Arles, and Marseille, though possibly retaining a coastal band including Nice until the third century, was reduced to the approximate size of the present *commune*. In his own words, "Caesar permitted the town to subsist, considering its name and antiquity rather than its conduct towards him. He placed in it two legions as garrison, and departed for Italy."

In spite of defeat and the loss of political independence, or thanks to it, Marseille became a town whose culture and reputation entered into fashion as a symbol of resistance. "While other peoples trembled at the mention of Caesar's name, the Phocaean youth had the courage not to submit to destiny," Lucan noted. Rich Roman families took to sending their sons to Marseille in preference to Athens to learn Greek, and the famous medical school flourished, producing doctors whose names such as Crinas, who was also an astronomer and according to the elder Pliny prescribed dietary regimes varying with the movement of the stars, and Charmis, whom we know from the same source to have forbidden hot baths and prescribed cold at all seasons, are still remembered. Economic prosperity returned and the port installation and warehouses were rebuilt and expanded.

Massiliots were to be found in the Middle East and in Egypt, and in Marseille itself there were communities of Jews and Syrians belonging to the trading community. The school of rhetoric was mentioned by Strabo: "All citizens of good family are well acquainted with philosophy and the art of speaking and the city has served as a school for barbarians… And the taste for culture is not for the few but for all; the Marseillais welcome teachers and pay them, some privately, some by the town, and it is the same with doctors." Marseille, without political influence unless as a city to which exiles were sometimes sent, remained for several hundred years a cultural centre of the first importance and a town where life was agreeable and the search for pleasure continuous.

Gradually, however, the town was Romanized. Rule by duumvirs replaced the ancient timocratic constitution and Latin became the language of administration, and side by side with Greek, of culture and teaching, while Marseille profited as a centre of Hellenism, at least until the fourth century, from the long Roman peace. The ancient authors were read and reread during the ages that followed, and their eulogies of Marseille, its constitution and cultural brilliance fixed a certain image of the Phocaean town until the time of the revolution. For the Marseillais themselves, as for other cities and peoples of the empire, the golden age lasted until the advent of the two influences coincident with its gradual end: the spread and adoption of Christianity and the barbarian invasions.

As a city in the Greco-Roman intellectual tradition, Marseille did not readily turn to new religions, merely adding from time to time a Gaulish or eastern god to the pantheon. The artistic and intellectual flowering benefited from the arrival of exiles retreating from the advancing invasions, as was to be repeated in Marseille in the early years of the Second World War until the German occupation of the Free Zone in 1942. The earliest evidence of an active Christian community dates to the fourth century; not until the fifth did John Cassian, a native of the Black Sea region, found the first religious houses in Provence and the monastery of Saint-Victor in Marseille. In 476 the town fell to the Visigoth invaders, and as elsewhere in Provence, the first wave of barbarians was followed by others. Yet in spite of this succession of military and political disturbances, of theological quarrels among Christians with their accompanying bloodshed, Marseille seems to have remained a haven of relative peace, the last bastion of *romanité*, an urbane centre of cultural life and host to a surviving tolerant paganism, until the Frankish invasion under Charles Martel and the first sack of the town in 739 put an end to a process of civilizing expansion and prosperity that had lasted since the city's foundation thirteen hundred years earlier.

Medieval Adversities

As a hub of sea and land traffic Marseille was vulnerable to epidemics, particularly of bubonic plague; from the seventh century onwards they became endemic, though after each decimation life and sea trade were gradually renewed. But there were other dangers. Mediterranean commerce fell more and more under Arab control; "Saracens" from North Africa or Spain regularly attacked the port and in 838 they pillaged and sacked the town. Marseille, with Provence, was politically divided from France from 843 until the fifteenth century, and little protection was given by distant Carolingian sovereigns who had neither the means to defend the coast nor great interest in the Mediterranean. Fernand Braudel pointed out that the principal trade route northward from Italy, and therefore the development of European capitalism, passed increasingly through the "German isthmus" via Strasbourg, Frankfurt and Cologne to Antwerp, the North Sea and London. The Rhône was a frontier and the Alps were less an obstacle than a stimulus. "That is why, compared to Genoa... a town like Marseille was not, in those days, in the same league." Historians have also suggested that the long survival in Provence, and especially in Marseille, of modes of thought and belief from the ancient world was a factor in their missing the cultural and religious renaissance of northern France and Germany before and after the millennium.

In 948 the first Viscount of Marseille, ancestor of a long-ruling dynasty, was named, and for two centuries both the bishopric and the abbacy of Saint-Victor were shared among members of the same family, while a degree of independence from Provence and the remote imperial authority was established. However, the three powers of the town—abbacy, episcopacy and viscounty—became progressively separated due to internecine rivalries, and by the twelfth century the leading merchant families had set up a Confrérie du Saint-Esprit, theoretically open to all, which functioned as a sovereign body to create an effective republic, until this was brought to heel by a violent repression under the first Angevin ruler in 1264. Thereafter, Marseille and its dominant mercantile caste shared in the Angevin adventure in Italy, as in the previous century they had shared in that of the Crusades (Richard Coeur de Lion anchored with the Anglo-Norman fleet in 1199). They also benefited from shipbuilding and the grant of commercial advantages, particularly in the Levant—there were merchants and consuls from Marseille in Cyprus in 1302 and trading in North Africa in the thirteenth century—serving to restore the town's prosperity; but illusions of independence were lost. Difference, however, remained. An example is that whereas at Arles the *chevaliers* had their council and the bourgeois theirs, and at Montpellier there were only bourgeois, in Marseille the frontiers of caste were less distinct, the people were "citizens" and this dissimilarity became an enduring mark of the town's character and history. "All classes," wrote the local historian and journalist Jean Boissieu, "are singularly dignified in their inequalities."

With the Sicilian Vespers of 1282 and the decline of Angevin power in the Mediterranean, Marseille was exposed to the rivalry and piratical incursions of Catalans culminating in an attack by the Aragonese fleet in 1423. The Aragonese landed to the south of Lacydon, smashed the chain which was floated on beams across the sea entry, sailed their fleet into the port and proceeded to sack and burn the town whose population, it is estimated, was reduced by two thirds in the fighting and by further outbreaks of plague, leaving perhaps ten thousand inhabitants. From these disasters, by the date of the death of the "good" King René in 1480 which bequeathed Provence to the French crown, Marseille had begun a slow and modest recovery with improvement in transport to the interior along the Rhône valley and some pacification of the seas allowing a development of *cabotage* or coastal navigation and trade, both of these elements lying beyond the control or even influence of a town which once had dominated them. On 11 December 1481 Marseille once and for all became, with Provence, part of France.

The Royal Will

The acquisition of Provence by the crown was not an annexation, and in 1486 an act set out terms of union after negotiation which were henceforth respected, or ignored, by the central government according to the balance of powers prevailing. Marseille in particular remained a distinct entity preserving liberties and franchises at least in name. The process of uniformity of the state was gradual and still incomplete at the time of the revolution. But Marseille was not hostile to the union, whatever taste for independence may have lingered on. In the words of Braudel, "In France, the seaward periphery was a ready focus for dissidence... unmistakable to the point of being spectacular in the case of Marseille... having well-established liberties and clans... and coming late into the French complex." But under the act of union considerable advantages were won: the freedom allowed to foreign shipping to use the port and exoneration from export and import taxes made of Marseille the bonded warehouse between Western Europe and the East.

During François I's confrontation with the Habsburgs and his adventures in Italy, the Marseillais remained faithful to the king and contributed largely to the ransom demanded for the liberation of his sons, held captive in Madrid after the Battle of Pavia. And when, to the scandal of Christian Europe, François allied himself with the Turks, it was in the port of Marseille that in 1543 the Turkish galleys of Barbarossa were officially received. The alliance and its treaties brought serious trade advantages to the Marseillais and a privileged relationship with the Ottoman Empire which supported both the prosperity of the town and its continuing bias toward autonomy in relation to the central power. In 1569 the reigning sultan granted "capitulations" by which all Europeans, with the single exception of Venice, entering his territory had to do so under the French flag, a settlement of which Marseille was the exclusive beneficiary. In the same period and under the same aegis, the sea coral company of Bône was founded and with participation of Marseillais capital funds obtained a monopoly of the coral trade on the Algerian coast; coral was then exchanged in Egypt for spices from India which Marseille merchants sold at the Lyon trade fairs, buying linen and textiles for export to the Levant. The example illustrates the development of Marseille as a transit centre for trade between continental Europe and the Mediterranean countries which was to have decisive economic consequences in the long term for the town and its people.

In the wars of religion Provence was divided, Languedoc still more so, but in Marseille the Catholic party predominated and with growing obduracy rejected the claims of the Protestant Henri of Navarre; after his accession, the ultra-Catholic Charles de Casaulx, one of the leaders of the League and a former Intendant of the port of Marseille, provoked riots and assumed power in the town, naming himself "first consul" as Bonaparte would later do. In an episode which was not the least extraordinary in the history of Marseille, Casaulx refused to recognize Henri IV as King of France after his conversion to Catholicism and erected a dictatorship in Marseille whose administration combined good works such as the creation of the Hôtel-Dieu and improvement in the town's hygiene with a permanent state of siege and an increasingly despotic personal rule. He was assassinated in 1595, the population rallied to the royalist troops and Henri IV was reported to have declared "Now I am king of France!"

Marseille was allowed comparative autonomy, power being exercised by three consuls elected from a council of 72 co-opted members, with a sovereign chamber of justice independent from the *parlement* of Aix. In 1599 the first chamber of commerce was founded in Marseille, a century before any other in France, "to oversee business concerning trade and restore it to its first condition of splendour". To the renewal and confirmation of the town's rights was added the designation of Catholicism as the sole authorized religion, a privilege that lasted to the end of the eighteenth century. Marseille always refused to apply or record any royal edict of tolerance, including that of Nantes, and declared by a new regulation in 1585, never abrogated and clearly intended to reinforce the oligarchic ruling element in the town, that "no one may enter or take any office whatsoever in the house of Marseille who is not of the Catholic, apostolic and Roman religion." How this apparently inflexible Catholicism came into being in a city which for so long had preserved the relative suppleness of ancient practices, historians do not say; but in spite of the rule of exclusion the Marseillais seem easily to have accommodated Protestant financiers and merchants who by the eighteenth century made up more than fifty per cent of the numbers of this rich and powerful body in the town's affairs.

The scene of jubilation, real or assumed, in the port of Marseille celebrating the disembarkation in France of Marie de' Medici for her marriage to Henri IV is portrayed by Rubens in a spectacular painting now in the Louvre; the rapport of Marseille with the king remained warm and appreciative on both sides. But this good relationship was not repeated with his grandson, Louis XIV, with whose centralizing policy, as well as his pride, the independent leanings of the city lay ill at ease. The strategic position of Marseille as a great Mediterranean port was too critical to be left to the political whim of local rulers corrupted by a taste for dissidence, and the formal plan of absolute monarchy left no room for any peripheral inclination towards autonomy. Matters came to a head in 1660, the pretext being an illegal seizure of power in the town in 1650 by a family of the nobility dominant since 1610, and a subsequent refusal of tax demands. Louis arrived with an army at Aix-en-Provence and sent a force of seven thousand men to breach the walls of Marseille and reduce the city to submission. This done, he entered the city himself, not through the royal gate according to protocol, but by the breach in the rampart to signify, contemptuously, that he came as to a conquest.

The humiliation of the Marseillais was completed by the imposition of a new constitution abolishing the consulate and excluding the nobility from the administration, the construction of the forts of Saint-Nicolas and Saint-Jean to maintain obedience in a population "too often the prey of criminal agitation", and the demolition of the major part of the walls. Paul Lombard expresses the sorrowful regret of the Marseillais which many other writers also suggest is still alive: "When Louis XIV departed never to return, he left behind him a garrison of three regiments. The Marseillais wished him adieu. Adieu their franchises. Adieu liberty. Ever since, Marseille mourns its ancient regime."

Yet the ambitions of the *roi soleil* and his ministers had other, less negative consequences for Marseille which owed to them its first great enlargement and embellishment. Much of the aligned layout of the central plan of the town, though not for the most part its present buildings, is the result of this operation. The Canebière and its neighbouring streets became the fashionable quarter, new walls were constructed embracing this far wider space and the old city was left to the poor, the mariners and their families, the bars, cafés and brothels providing for the needs of seamen and soldiery, the indigent and homeless until the day they were shut up in the Vieille Charité. The swampy southern shore of Lacydon was drained, the quays of the Rive-Neuve constructed and a monumental arsenal for the king's fleet of 42 imposing, swift but soon anachronistic galleys was built as a town within the town including a hospital; this enclave was peopled by galley slaves, shipbuilders and soldiers who made up more than a quarter, 20,000 men, of the total population estimated in 1660 at 65,000. The fleet of galleys and the men were transferred to Toulon in 1748 and the arsenal with its workshops and shipyards was finally demolished in the 1780s, to be replaced by warehouses which still stand, converted to other uses.

The subjection of the city to the royal will was not meant to impoverish it, the minister Colbert attaching great importance to the development of commerce by sea and its resulting influence, as well as to defence. The early years of the eighteenth century saw the beginning of the major period of expansion of Marseille's trade, and the building of fortunes by dynastic families of merchants and entrepreneurs. In particular, an edict of 1669 gave privileges amounting to monopoly to the chamber of commerce, which received power to appoint consuls and authorize French subjects to set themselves up in the eastern Mediterranean and North African ports of transit of the Ottoman Empire. These appointments were known as *les Echelles du Levant* (the term *échelle* derived from the Turkish *iskele* denoting a jetty built on piles for embarking and disembarking merchandise). At the same time, customs barriers were withdrawn to the exterior of the town, creating a free trade zone, and Colbert established a school of oriental languages, financed by the Marseille chamber of commerce, whose aim was the training of interpreters, the *drogmans*, for work in the Echelles. Marseille had benefited from the wars between Venice and Constantinople to become dominant in Mediterranean trade, and that of the Levant represented almost half of the commercial revenue of town and port by the time of the revolution, when it was interrupted by the suppression of the chambers of commerce in 1791, and later progressively replaced by British interests.

Exports consisted mainly of textiles from the Languedoc, paper, hardware, silver and coral, while imports were of silk and spices, precious stones, drugs, skins, wheat, coffee and oil used in the manufacture of the famous *savon* (soap) *de Marseille*. Alexandria was the port most frequented by Marseillais and the greatest of Marseille fortunes—those of the Pastré, Borély, Roux and Fabre families, for example—were founded on Egyptian trade, much of it in cotton. The numbers of large ships sailing out of the harbour increased tenfold over the eighteenth century, and trade routes to the West Indies, the Americas and the Indian Ocean were explored, making of Marseille a world port. In 1790, the *Solide,* belonging to a Marseille shipbuilder, was the first French vessel to circumnavigate the globe. Coffee and sugar from the lands of cheap labour and silver coinage in contraband from South America, much in demand in the Far East, swelled many fortunes but the slave trade was not, it seems, practised by what became known as the Marseille aristocracy of commerce. This important, self-interested segment of the population, the *négociants*, was no more than forty per cent of Marseillais origin; some came from the Alps or from the Languedoc, others, as world trade grew, from Italy, Britain, Switzerland, the Levant, Germany or Scandinavia and many of these, including Protestants, remained to put down roots and breed native Marseillais to succeeding generations.

Marseille continued to live overwhelmingly from the sea but some industrialization developed in the eighteenth century: sugar refining, soap manufacture, glass making, tobacco and textile works and for a time the most famous of all, the *faïenceries* producing the fine porcelain of Moustiers and other factories. But from the wealth created and multiplied in this age of commercial adventure the proletariat benefited little, and the injustice of the system of indirect taxes, all others being refused by the ruling oligarchy, prepared the ground for revolution in Marseille as elsewhere. The register of grievances of 1789 stated that Marseille was "the town where the people are the most impoverished by the vice of administration and the odious manner of demanding taxes..." Nevertheless, the exceptional economic vitality of the city was demonstrated in the aftermath of the last great plague epidemic of 1720, which killed 40,000 out of 75,000 inhabitants. "God declared war on his people," wrote the parish priest of Saint-Laurent. But contemporaries were struck by the speed of recovery in population numbers, both from an extraordinary rise in the marriage rate as soon as the plague died away, and by immigration from neighbouring territories—Provence, Italy, Spain—as people came to fill vacancies in the ranks of poor labour in a city whose prosperity in the upper social reaches at that period nothing could stop. And by 1789 the population was estimated, perhaps with slight exaggeration, at 120,000.

Revolution and Empire

The name given to the French national hymn, the *Marseillaise*, makes for a misleading impression of Marseille as a centre of revolutionary fervour. Certainly in the early stages Marseille was among the first cities to see uprisings of "patriots", who were perhaps no more than a minority of activists moving against a mercantile community unwilling to commit its wealth to the patriotic struggle, just as it had left the majority to struggle with poverty. And the forts guarding the harbour, and that of Notre-Dame dominating the town, were seized in a symbolic action against the centralizing power, never accepted, as much as against despotic monarchy. Then in the general enthusiasm the Marseille deputies voted with others, in the name of the "new ideals", for abolition of privileges including those, centuries-old, of their own city which they had been sent to Paris to defend. Marseille now became a French town, no longer an adjacent territory, and this change was often to be regretted. The verses of Rouget de Lisle and their music were sung along the roads to the capital by the five hundred volunteers of the Marseille battalion of the National Guard on its way to Paris: "The little band of Marseillais, crossing through villages and towns, both exalted and frightened France by the frenzied ardour with which they sang the new song. In their mouths, it took on a wild and murderous accent..." wrote Jules Michelet, and their name became attached to it.

But this revolutionary energy did not run for long in the same direction. Soon the federalist tendency was opposed to the centralizing forces of the Convention and in June 1793 Marseille, rejecting the authority of the Assembly, raised an insurrectionary force to capture Avignon, declared itself "in a legal state of resistance against oppression" and announced the formation of an army to march on Paris under the slogan, "One and indivisible republic; respect for persons and properties." Marseille, says the historian of the revolution William Doyle, was now a byword for political turbulence. The response of the Convention was swift; Marseille was invaded in August, given the title "town without name" and between that month and April 1794 351 dissident heads fell to the guillotine on the Canebière. Bonaparte had no liking for a city which he considered counter-revolutionary; "You are naturally lively," he told the Marseillais, "and you have been led to your downfall in the way that has ruined so many people, by the exaltation of your vanity." In 1797 Paris accused Marseille of an ardent love of the *ancien régime*; the city's antipathy to the Empire was reinforced by the consequences of the British blockade which put an end to prosperity. In 1811 there were 20,000 fewer inhabitants than in 1789 and 30,000 to 40,000 were said to be indigent.

After the downfall in his turn of Napoleon there was an explosion of delight in the streets, the population destroyed the monuments erected to his glory and sent a delegation to Paris demanding the restoration of traditional franchises. Marseille gave a cold reception to the emissaries sent by Napoleon on his return from Elba and after the hundred days a number of summary executions took place, followed by a massacre of oriental refugees who had followed the emperor from Egypt and been installed with their families in Marseille. The restoration of the Bourbons was enthusiastically received in the same way as the rule of Henri IV after the adventure of the "dictator" Casaulx who for a time had been as ardently supported by the people. Braudel and Cobb have both pointed to the waywardness of the Marseillais in political matters, sometimes approaching caprice; this characteristic of behaviour, perhaps to be understood as a defence of jeopardized independence, later showed itself during the Second World War when at the end of 1940 Marshal Pétain was acclaimed in thronged streets which after the Liberation in August 1944 were filled by crowds frenzied with joy.

However, attachment to the restoration was sincere and lasting and above all, it was formed "as to a fecund source of industry and riches" (Braudel), though this did not flow at once. The blockade had ruined many hopes and the Echelles had been disorganized if not dismantled. English, Genoese and even Austrians had taken advantage of the absence of France from its privileged embrace with the Ottoman Empire, which was displeased also by the formation in Marseille of a philhellenic committee active in the Greek insurrection against Ottoman rule. Nevertheless, after 1820 there was a revival of traffic from the port in the direction notably of Egypt, the Black Sea and the Arab countries of North Africa. The French expedition to Algeria, which became a colony in 1830, aroused greater enthusiasm in Marseille than in any other part of France, and was the beginning of a momentous relationship whose consequences are still not played out either in the city, the suburbs or in newly developed towns of the hinterland where far right-wing politicians cultivate their constituency.

The town itself changed little in the first decades of the nineteenth century; but the arrival in 1849 of the canal from the Durance to supply the land, houses and industries with an inexhaustible flow of water, and that of the first railway line to reach the plateau of Saint-Charles in 1848, revolutionized the commercial and industrial future of the ancient port and town. Railway tunnels and immense construction works to create the new docklands were undertaken with the help of English engineers, Belgian technicians and a cheap Italian workforce. From 1855 the new port of Marseille, designed to accommodate steam ships constructed—often by English engineers—in the neighbouring naval shipyards of La Ciotat, could compete with those of London and Liverpool, on which it was modelled, in the scale of worldwide navigation and shipping operations. In 1822 there had been an influx of Greek shipbuilders after the massacres of the isle of Chios during the Greek War of Independence, and in 1840 the English engineer Philip Taylor acquired land on which the steelworks Les Forges de la Méditerranée was created, but the extraordinary development of Marseille in the nineteenth century was not only the work of enterprising foreigners; by the end of the restoration there were over 9,000 establishments of different kinds of industry, many (though not all of them) small workshops, and this base allowed Marseille to participate fully in the first movement of continental industrialization. "The Mediterranean dream carried by Marseille in these triumphant years… was a dream of reconciliation and prosperity of the peoples by the opening of frontiers and commercial development." (Emile Témime). Despite this, the main economic activity remained speculative, and profit in the hands of the bourgeoisie was more often ploughed into land and property than into industrial investment, a preference that had important consequences for the town when, in the twentieth century, the traditional role of exchange and transit, which Aristotle named *emporia*, began to fail.

The opening of the Suez Canal in 1869 was an epiphany, in the Joycean sense, for the adventure of the Second Empire in which hubris, colonial ambition and profit-seeking were served by spectacular technological initiative and capitalist audacity. Marseille came to be known as the gateway to the Orient and the queen of the Mediterranean, the "centre of relations between Europe and Asia" proclaimed a minister, while the journalist Edmond About wrote that "if one is interested in the future of France, one watches this living town with passionate curiosity to see it visibly growing like a tropical plant." In the years that followed, however, the canal was found to be less an advantage than had been expected when Marseille capital was poured into it, principally because the drastic reduction in the cost of transporting goods to and from the east reduced the flow of profit into the Marseille economy. But during these years of capitalist expertise, when the banking sector expanded along with the armament industry and steamship lines such as the Messageries Maritimes, the population continued to increase; between 1851 and 1873 by 120,000 of whom 100,000 were immigrants from other parts of the Mediterranean: Greeks, Levantines and above all Italians. And around the middle of the century the town began for the first time to invade its countryside over twenty thousand hectares, the largest city commune in France, where the population doubled in a few years against a fifty per cent increase in the city itself. The sprawl, which to many visitors is the most disconcerting element of the town's personality, preventing a perception of the whole on account of the incoherent disorder of its parts, is an inheritance of the industrial revolution as much as in any English Midland or northern city.

Antipathetic to Bonapartism and true to historic form, Marseille erupted in riots at the first sign of defeat of the imperial armies during the Franco-Prussian War, and after the disaster of Sedan the population occupied the Préfecture as the seat of centralizing power. On 23 March 1871 the town preceded Paris in declaring the Commune de Marseille under the presidency of the young "advocate of the poor", freemason and utopian socialist Gaston Crémieux. The *commune* lasted until the army invaded the city on 4 April. The leaders were tried in military courts and Crémieux was executed six months later, occasioning Georges Clemenceau's ironic remark that "military justice is to justice as military music is to music". Marseille was again placed under state supervision and the condition of siege endured until 1876. Radicalism, freemasonry and socialism continued to make progress, however, and in 1892 for the first time in a large French town a socialist, the Protestant doctor from Languedoc, Siméon Flaissières, was elected mayor, remaining in office with a break between 1902 and 1919 until his death in 1931. During this long reign he introduced many social reforms to benefit the underprivileged part of an electorate in which the suicide rate by the late nineteenth century had reached three or four per day.

At the same time social conflict increased and political division between left and right hardened until forces became equally balanced by the outbreak of the First World War, with a population of half a million, fifty per cent of them industrial working class of whom a fifth were of foreign origin. There were increasingly frequent strikes from 1903, culminating in a dock strike of 23,000 workers in 1919. In June 1881 nationalist fervour had led to an attack on Italian workmen accused of demonstrating against a military and patriotic parade of troops returning from Tunisia where French and Italian interests were opposed; during this so-called "Marseille Vespers", a running riot lasting four days with the encouragement of the nationalist Parisian press, three were killed and hundreds wounded in an outbreak of xenophobia in which it seems that all social classes of whatever political allegiance shared. In the long history of Marseille, a town where, as Braudel pointed out, "all... are the children of immigrants", this seems an isolated incident, perhaps provoked by an element in the population attracted to the street violence which was to add so much to the bad name of their city in the twentieth century.

Wartime

As though a prelude to a war of empires, the first great French colonial exhibition was organized in Marseille in 1906, led by the principal families of ship owners and merchants in the chamber of commerce and under the leadership of one of them, the parliamentarian Jules Charles-Roux. Marseille was at the centre of the colonial adventure of France and of its commercial development. "The ambience of Marseille," it was said, "is colonial." The exhibition, with at its centre the *grand palais* rivalling that of Paris but to the glory of Marseille alone, was a huge popular success, thanks largely to the colonial pavilions with two million visitors by the time the exhibition ended, and it served to fashion a grandiose image of the colonial empire which was preserved in Marseille until close to the Second World War. And with this connection came new immigrant waves, at first from Algeria and then, during the war of 1914 to 1918, a passage of four million men of the Allied armies through the port and town from departure points in different quarters of the globe, or towards them.

Distance from the battlefields spared Marseille some of the impact of the tragedy of the war; the activity of the port was swollen by movement of men and armaments, and war industry works, including shipbuilding, replaced the loss of some markets. The departure of men to the front, the death roll and the recall to Italy of reservists created a shortage of labour, particularly for the great undertaking of the shipping Tunnel du Rove to the Etang de Berre, which was made up by immigrant workers many of whom settled in Marseille when the war was over or returned to it later with their families. Another effect on the population, which had doubled between 1850 and 1914, was the arrival of at least 100,000 civilian refugees from the battle grounds. But the atmosphere of Marseille during these years often seemed to those arriving from the war-torn north comparatively recreational and prosperous, and this contrast between the city on the Mediterranean and the towns and country nearer to the scene of fighting created an envious resentment, contributing to the reputation for separatism and non-solidarity which already weighed on the town and its people. The cheerful spirit of Albert Londres, who remarked that if you hoped to find someone lost to sight at the other end of the world it was enough to sit at a café table on the Canebière and wait because sooner or later they would turn up, was not shared by those French who had suffered privations; this opened another fault-line in the relationship between the city and the mainland beyond the surrounding hills which was to have drastic consequences in the period between the world wars when "Marseille was not forgiven its prosperity" (Boissieu).

Siméon Flaissières, by now aged 68, was re-elected mayor in 1919 at a time of widespread strikes and with the support of the communist and pacifist Simon Sabiani, who became increasingly influential in the town's affairs while he swung continuously further to the right; Flaissières, whose earlier period of administration had been more noted for philanthropic reforms than financial grasp, faced in his own last years a decline in the city's fortunes and growing economic challenges. A second colonial exhibition in 1922 celebrated an empire which had become a haven of protectionism for trade, particularly from Marseille, after the loss of markets in Turkey and the

Black Sea, and the doctrine of economic liberalism was soon forgotten. Nevertheless, traditional industry in Marseille fell into more and more difficulties. As examples among many others, in 1922 the oil industry functioned at a little over half its capacity, and by 1930 there remained only a single sugar refinery. If the activity of the port survived the world economic crisis, it was thanks to its imperial near-monopoly; "Firm and reasonable in our confidence and hope," declared the newspaper *Le Sémaphore* on 31 December 1935, "let us hail the colonial year about to start."

The purpose of the Tunnel du Rove was to create a link by water to the Rhône and to foster the industrial development of the Etang de Berre and, eventually, of Fos-sur-Mer. In 1890 the visionary Marseille shipbuilder Cyprien Fabre imagined a canal of 84 kilometres, a spinal column extending the port of Marseille towards the great European rivers: "There exist marvellous sites for factories on the Etang de Berre... which will become the industrial port of Marseille... we must join Marseille to the centre of France and of Europe." Much of this process of spreading industrialization, which has contributed to the atrophy of the docks of Marseille and led to the lethal pollution of the *étang*, was financed by the rich bourgeoisie transferring funds from the sale of their bastides and land: "Colbert would have been delighted," says Jean Viard, who suggests also that part of the motive at the time was to displace from the town centre towards the new areas of employment a part of the communist-voting electorate. The first oil refineries were constructed on the Etang de Berre in 1933 and others followed in the years to the Second World War, creating some impression of economic fair weather while the politics of the town went badly adrift.

Marseille had become more than ever a crossroads or destination for people of many origins, notable among them Armenians after the massacres of 1915. The disarray of the ageing and revered philanthropist Flaissières can be measured by his letter in the press in 1923: "Forty thousand more of these guests are on their way, which is to say, smallpox, typhus, the plague are coming... the population of Marseille demands that the government repatriate these lamentable human herds... a public danger." Infinitely more dangerous to the wholesomeness of the body politic than these peaceful and homeless refugees, who demanded little of France and received next to nothing, surviving for years in shanty towns on deserted sites, was the arrival from Corsica of the shadowy bands who were to make up Sabiani's personal guard and army of supporters numbering, it has been calculated, at least 10,000. After Siméon Flaissières' death in 1931 an election followed in which Ribot, a second rank politician quickly passing into the background became mayor while Sabiani emerged as the real power in the city, with a regime of clans, clients and enforcers led by the gangsters Spirito and Carbone to do their business in streets, bars, clubs and on quaysides.

Sabiani, who was not unpopular in the well-off quarters of the town, was an admirer of Mussolini whose precept, "don't overthrow a feeble power, reinforce it", he put into practice in Marseille. It was in this atmosphere that the assassination in 1934 of the King of Yugoslavia by Croat terrorists and the disastrous burning in 1938 of the department store of the Nouvelles Galeries took place, both on the Canebière, marking the reputation of Marseille for years to come. Prime Minister Daladier was in Marseille attending a conference on the day of the fire; there was no pressure in the fire-engine hoses and Lombard describes the living torches hurling themselves from upper windows, watched by the crowds below. Daladier was heard to cry, "Is there no one here who can bring about the reign of order in this town?" The outcome, in practice if not principle, was to leave the city still more in the hands of Sabiani and without a political direction to check the anarchic working of those speculative interests which played a part in the destruction of a large part of the old town in 1943, and the neglect of much of the rest. Jean Boissieu states that Sabiani did the dirty work of certain "men of business" and was responsible for encouraging the Nazis to blow up the Panier, although it had for long been his power base.

Marseille was put under state tutelage on 20 March 1939, but within six months the state itself was on its way to dissolution and the problems of Marseille were left, as indeed the Marseillais have always wished it, to see to themselves. Yet in 1994, with the cloud of prejudice still hanging over the city's name, Harrel-Courtès claimed, perhaps with a note of irony, that "the good people of Marseille were no more contaminated by all this than the worthy bourgeois of Hamburg who never put a foot in San Pauli... or the wily Neapolitan worker who has never dirtied his hands with shady fiddles."

Occupation

At the approach of war the political right in Marseille showed a marked pacifism; *Le Sémaphore,* organ of the business community, advocated an alignment with fascist Italy while the far right, to which by this time Sabiani had migrated, was successful in a partial election of 1939. The historian Julian Jackson asserts that in 1940 Marseille was not chosen as seat of the Free Zone government under Philippe Pétain because its "unsavoury reputation rendered it an unsuitable location from which to launch a moral renewal of France". If so, Marseille was spared the discredit of seeing its name linked to the regime for ever associated with Vichy, and if the history of the town in the Second World War includes the noble private actions of a majority with the ignoble work of a few well-placed opportunists, this is a record not unlike that of most French towns, large or small.

The first and most striking consequence for Marseille of the German occupation of northern France was the arrival of thousands of Jewish and other refugees in search of a passage out of the port and over the Channel or the Atlantic. From 1941, says Jackson, "Marseille was culturally vibrant thanks to the presence of so many French and European intellectuals, waiting to escape"; and the novelist and academician Roland Dorgelès declared that "Paris melted into Marseille like a piece of ice in a glass of pastis." In the summer of 1941 Jean-Paul Sartre and Simone de Beauvoir made a recreational trip from Paris to watch American films in Marseille: "We decided to go to three a day," they recorded as Europe struggled. In the relations between *Vichyssois* and the local bands of resistants, Richard Cobb detected a deliberate parochialism quite consistent with Marseillais separatist traditions: "no one is really entirely villainous (Carbone and Spirito are but they are expendable because they are Corsican immigrants)... no breach seems to have been irreparable, no channel of communication completely cut off... 'let's arrange things among ourselves.'"The enthusiastic welcome given to Pétain in December 1940 no doubt in part at least expressed this tendency to reconciliation. But there could be no illusion about the plight of refugees, some penniless, waiting to get on ships. Religious organizations—Jewish, Protestant, Catholic—worked both openly and clandestinely to help those in danger, and an American Quaker, Varian Fry, set up a rescue committee which aided more than a thousand writers, anti-Nazi politicians and artists to escape either by sea or through networks leading to Spain and Portugal, many, including Walter Benjamin, after failing to obtain a visa. Fry himself was expelled on 4 August 1941, as the resistance became more organized with Marseille as its centre. In the Château Pastré at Montredon under the hill of Marseilleveyre, Comtesse Lily Pastré sheltered many more refugees, including particularly musicians, gave subsidies and took part in the risky operation of obtaining passports, official or not.

Active resistants were everywhere a minority; the general populace waited in resignation for whatever else the tragedy might bring them. But this attitude changed with the occupation of the Free Zone by the Germans in November 1942, and as the rounding-up of Jews and foreigners, a process already started by the French police in July and August, increased in frequency and above all in visibility. Guy Brochier, whose parents kept a hotel in the Rue Consolat near the Eglise des Réformés, recalls in childhood hearing cries and shouts in the night as clients of hotels further up the street were driven into lorries and taken away. In January 1943 there were six thousand arrests and eight hundred Jews were deported on the eve of the destruction of parts of the old town. In the course of that operation, announced as an "act of moral cleansing" when streets of houses were emptied of their occupants (see Chapter 3), 1,600 more victims were deported. Jean Cocteau described (or imagined) the scene: "The amazed Germans saw emerging whole farms with cows and dairies. When they threw in tear gas bombs out appeared Chinese with tons of opium, intoxicated blacks, forgers of dollars, queers, lepers, and a camp of English aviators." At the same time, rationing became stricter and goods fewer; communications with

North Africa were interrupted by movement of armies, ships rusted at the quayside and factories closed for want of supplies. The war became part of the daily life of the town and attacks by resistant groups more frequent. In the spring of 1944 there were marches of hungry women unable to feed their households, and a strike which by March had become a general insurrection was only interrupted by the Allied air bombing campaign, generally judged unnecessary and ineffective, in which two thousand Marseillais lost their lives.

On 20 August began the Battle of Marseille which lasted a week. With a garrison of fifteen thousand men, the Germans fell back on the ports much of whose installations they destroyed. On the 28th the defences of Notre-Dame de la Garde fell to French forces aided by resistant groups, one of which was commanded by Gaston Defferre, destined for a historic term of office as Mayor of Marseille; and on that day the garrison surrendered. Two hundred boats and ships had been sunk to block the channels and the railway line was cut. In conditions of anarchy, revulsion and vengeance thousands of arrests were made and an uncertain number of summary executions carried out. On 5 September a court of justice was put in place, restoring some legality to trials which still remained expeditious to perfunctory, and were without appeal.

On 15 September, a day of great heat, and in the presence of a "numberless crowd, frenzied, shouting with joy" (Matthew Cobb), General De Gaulle, the personification of northern French rigour, attended a victory parade in the streets of the town. Heroine of the Resistance Lucie Aubrac described the "maquisards in tattered clothes... they had flowers in the barrels of their rifles. They were pulling a German armoured car on which were perched some young women in skimpy dresses. They were shouting and waving flags. De Gaulle sat there in his uniform murmuring, 'what a farce. What a farce.'"

Defferre and Reform

The far left groundswell affecting the political life of France in 1944-45 was particularly evident in Marseille, with communist control of the unions in the docks and the requisition of a number of industrial enterprises. Gaston Defferre, a socialist of a new generation who directed the first municipal body put in place after the Liberation, attempted a coalition with the communists but soon made way for them. The work of reconstruction was impeded by social and industrial confrontation which culminated in violent strikes in October 1947 putting an end to collaboration between socialists and communists. Finally in May 1953 Defferre was elected mayor at the head of a coalition of centre and left parties and remained in office until his death in 1986, dominating local politics with the support of the newspaper *Le Provençal*, which he owned, eliminating all possible political rivals and leaving a permanent mark on the city both physically and morally.

Defferre was a Protestant like Siméon Flaissières and a lawyer by training. It has been pointed out that Marseille has often had recourse to rulers from outside, and that this is logical for a city of immigrants. In character Deferre was, some said, a complex mixture of pride and modesty, puritanism and extravagance, severity and wiliness, but all agree that in his time everything that happened in Marseille, particularly in the cultural sphere, or that did not happen, passed through him. The city's budget during his long term was multiplied by seven and Lombard credits him with remodelling the face of Marseille, its coast and most of all its reputation; the Marseillais remained faithful to him while he lived and in the collective memory he is the arbiter evoked at every turning point, even if in 1983 he was elected for the last time with communist support. He died in 1986, unexpectedly in an accident, and his funeral was attended by vast throngs of Marseillais.

The long process of renewal and redress coincided with the decline of the ports, the end of many industries, the loss of empire and the close of the Algerian war which brought home a flood of repatriated colonists. At the Liberation there were already almost 100,000 homeless or precariously housed people and three thousand families were lodged in empty bastides and certain châteaux whose owners were suspected of collaboration. The high price demanded for land caused much new housing built on these occupied domains to be densely concentrated on the horizontal plane but invasive in the vertical, with damaging consequences socially and aesthetically. But new roads, a tunnel under the Vieux Port, a Metro, new hospitals, university departments, cultural centres and theatres were constructed; and the finances of the town were reformed and purged. The efforts, and strains, of reform continue under an administration of the centre right and in an atmosphere of relative though not invariable social and political appeasement, and largely aided by funding, and planning, from the Euroméditerranée project.

The irreversible development that has had a deep effect on the life of Marseille is that of the industrial port at Fos-sur-Mer and its equipment for docking giant oil tankers and container carriers. The port is designated as Marseille-Fos under largely state control and with the mission to become the Europort of the Mediterranean as Rotterdam is that of the Atlantic. Harrel-Courtès believes that Marseille, as a town, was short-circuited by this operation since industrial activity was promoted far from the traditional centre and the international companies deal directly with banks and headquarters in Paris. The centuries-old aspiration to create a link with the Rhône valley and the north has been realized, but at the expense of the docks and port of the centre and the industries with which they had a symbiotic relation, and of the ancient city itself whose air of abandonment in some quarters is hardly tempered by the sight of cruise ships where ceaseless ocean going traffic once sailed.

GAUMONT S.A.B. présente une co-production FILMS JEAN-JACQUES VITAL•FILMS RENÉ MODIANO•S.N.E.G. (Paris)•CINERIZ-ROYAL-FILM (Rome)

LOUIS JOURDAN
YVONNE FURNEAUX
PIERRE MONDY
FRANCO SILVA
dans une réalisation de
CLAUDE AUTANT-LARA

d'après le célèbre roman
d'Alexandre Dumas

LE COMTE DE MONTE-CRISTO

Adaptation et dialogues de JEAN HALAIN
avec BERNARD DHERAN (Sociétaire de la Comédie Française)
JEAN-CLAUDE MICHEL
JEAN MARTINELLI
CLAUDINE COSTER
RONALDO LUPI
HENRI GUISOL

Musique de
RENÉ CLOEREC

EASTMANCOLOR
DYALISCOPE

5 | The Written Word
The City in Literature

Such literature as concerns Marseille has been written by strangers
and travellers whose only reason to be in the city would be to get out
of it... All that Evelyn Waugh could retain of the place was the
cheekiness of the prostitutes, as they leant out of windows to deprive
his leading character of his hat... A genuinely Marseillais literature...
might give too much away, so better not to write it down.

Richard Cobb

Marseille... beautiful in its humanity.

Jean-Claude Izzo

Marseille was more alive in the perceptions of the young
Joseph Conrad in 1874 than, apparently, in those of
Evelyn Waugh who spent an evening in 1927 with his
brother Alec, "beginning decorously at Basso's with caviare and
Meursault and ending less creditably in the slums", as he designated
the historic ancient city. Conrad was sixteen when he left Poland to
go to sea, with his uncle and guardian Thaddeus' permission and an
allowance "modest but sufficient", which he soon overspent.
Marseille may have been chosen because Thaddeus had acquain-
tances there, and Conrad arrived with introductions, particularly to
the *Marseillais* Baptistin Solary:

This Solary (Baptistin), when I beheld him in the flesh, turned out a
quite young man, very good-looking, with a fine black, short beard, a
fresh complexion, and soft, merry black eyes... I was still asleep in
my room in a modest hotel near the quays of the old port, after the
fatigues of the journey via Vienna, Zurich, Lyons, when he burst in

flinging the shutters open to the sun... How pleasantly he startled me by his noisy objurgations to be up and off instantly for a "three years" campaign in the South Seas.

The pilots of the Vieux Port were to be Conrad's instructors in the science of navigation:

The very first whole day I ever spent on salt water was by invitation, in a big half-decked pilot-boat, cruising under close reefs on the lookout, in misty, blowing weather, for the sails of ships and the smoke of steamers rising out there, beyond the slim and tall Planier light-house cutting the line of the windswept horizon with a white per-pendicular stroke... or dodging at night under the lee of Château d'If on the watch for the lights of ships... and I have been invited to sit in more than one tall, dark house of the old town... had the bouilla-baisse ladled out into a thick plate... by thickset girls, with pure pro-files, glorious masses of black hair arranged with complicated art, dark eyes, and dazzlingly white teeth.

Until Conrad joined his first British ship, the *Mavis*, in 1878, Marseille remained the home port from which he sailed across the Atlantic and Pacific; it is probable though unproven that he became involved in smuggling for which Marseille was a centre, and possibly in gun-running missions into Colombia. During periods on land he lived at 18 Rue Sainte near the Opera and moved, an excitable, spend-thrift, romantic youth, on the perimeter of bohemian circles and among journalists congregating in cafés on the Canebière. In January 1878 he was present when Henry Morton Stanley arrived in triumph in Marseille after his reception by the Prince of Wales in Cannes; the *Gazette du Midi* described Stanley's meeting with Livingstone and the presentation to the "Master of African Exploration" of three medals of honour by the town in its colonizing mode. In *Heart of Darkness* Marlow says of Kurtz that "he desired to have kings meet him at railway stations on his return from some ghastly nowhere".

Three weeks after Stanley's visit to Marseille, Conrad's life took a dramatic turn in circumstances of which contradictory accounts exist and which he left unexplained, like an event in a novel offered neat to the reader's imagination. While on business at the Kiev Fair in February, Thaddeus received a telegram: "Conrad wounded, send money—come." He reached Marseille on 27 February, stayed two weeks, settled Conrad's debts and apparently concocted with him the tale, elaborated in later fictions, which for long was believed in as explanation of the wound. Caught in a romantic entanglement of love, smuggling and Spanish royalist politics, Conrad in this version had fought a duel, receiving a bullet which passed near the heart; by the account he gave his uncle, he had lost a large amount of borrowed money at Monte Carlo and had shot himself in the chest. "I took an oath that even if I knew he would shoot himself again, he could not count on a repetition of my weakness," Thaddeus wrote, and at this point Conrad abandoned the idea of joining the French merchant marine and began the process leading, eventually, to a place in the English literary canon. Experience of Marseille, highway to the sea, had ignited a ready imagination: "I was feeling a little lonely… the carnival time was drawing to an end. Everybody, high and low, was anxious to have the last fling. Companies of masks with linked arms and whooping like red Indians swept the streets in crazy rushes while gusts of cold mistral swayed the gas lights as far as the eye could reach. There was a touch of bedlam in all this."

City of Anarchy

Anarchy is a recurring theme in literary references to Marseille, the attention of writers being drawn to conditions of supposed chaos from which order must be shaped. The young Flaubert wrote:

> Marseille is now what Persia must have been in antiquity, Alexandria in the middle ages: a capharnaüm, a babel of all the nations, where you see close-cropped blond hair, great black beards, white skin striped with blue veins, sallow Asian complexions, blue eyes, black… You hear a hundred unknown languages…

For the poet André Suarès, the images of chaos and its antidote were personified: "Anarchy is the tide of Marseille; the flood of races, wave on wave, seems to submerge the antique Phocaea. But in vain; Marseille, ancient and young, a female lair of energy and joy, regains its balance. The life instinct… more potent than anarchy… drives back the swell of chaos." Agostini and Forno point out how writers, mostly coming from outside, describe above all the agitation of a swarming populace and its unexpected well-being, due not to mastery of the urban environment, far from it, but simply to the good fortune of the site. Reading them, say these authors, one feels already abroad, though whereabouts abroad is never defined; and it is never the same Marseille they write of since the descriptions date from any time between the Middle Ages and the colonial era. Only with the novels of the romantic age does the image of a Babylonian port, a provincial curiosity, begin to recede into myth, with its place taken by a new mythical image, even wider of the mark, of a sun-drenched, *farniente*, sentimental, maritime proletariat overseen from a healthy northern latitude: "often consciously erected as a barrier to keep strangers out, and bearing about as much contact with reality as a Blackpool beach picture postcard has with the daily lives… of that other seaside town…" (Richard Cobb).

Rational organization of city growth tends towards erasure of zones of shadow and elision of mystery, at least in France. But this does not appear to have happened in literary perceptions of Marseille, nor does it feature in present experience of this enigmatic town and it might be a cause for mourning if ever the enigma were to be reasoned away. Louis XIV's embellishments left the old town alone to go on as it was: Marseille, true to itself, needs the shadowy zones, while for the mainland French it has its role as exit and release for refugees escaping the *pensée unique,* that beaten path from which thought and manners are not expected to stray. "You never get up twice running in the same Marseille," said the poet Saint-John Perse, while Blaise Cendrars was more specific:

Marseille… is not a city of architecture, religion, *belles-lettres,* academic art. It is not the product… of political economy, royal or republican… It seems good-natured and laughing, it can look grubby and awful. Nevertheless it is among the most mysterious cities in the world and one of the hardest to decode.

Albert Londres remarked that "When the daylight goes, you always feel more mystery in a port than in a mainland town. In a small town, night time is the signal for rest. In big ones it marks the start of new life. In a port, night has an air of complicity... with what, in the old Marseille?... a little light and music, a bit of alcohol and some flesh, the top-up for a meagre income."

Of these elements, most attention naturally has been focused on the flesh. Of his passage through the more respectable quarters of Marseille, Casanova boasted that "there is no town in France where the licentiousness of the girls is carried so far... not only do they pride themselves on refusing nothing, they are often the first to offer a man what the man doesn't always dare ask." In 1765 James Boswell appears equally to have avoided the brothels of the Panier:

> Since I arrived at five and twenty, I have determined never again to risk my constitution with women. But Drummond having assured me that Mlle. Suzette was honest, safe, and disinterested, and coun-selled me to put in at that port, I went to her after the comedy... I found her a fine little lively girl, with hardly any of the vile cant of prostitutes... She was so little that I had an idea as if she was a child, and had not much inclination for her... Suzette chatted neatly and di-verted me. I sacrificed to the graces. I think I did no harm.

Next day, a Sunday, he reflected further: "I found I was now above being taken in by whores. I viewed with pity the irregularities of humanity. I went to hear mass, but was too late." The poet Suarès, on the other hand, wrote hyperbolically on behalf of all the clientele of the more sordid streets of the Panier down the ages:

> Every house is a hive of sex... black and blind during the day, the houses light up at sundown, flaring with a thousand yellow, white and red lights... and the infernal rhythm of black music... dedicated women everywhere, the *Cagoles*, sad or not, mad, drunk, calm or

> furious… even some who speak softly and with a sort of politeness…
> In summer through open windows you see a bed, a basin… sitting, the
> *Cagoles* open their thighs without seeming to know what they show…
> soon, to my eyes and senses, this whole magnificent district of ob-
> scenity is nothing but an immense gaping sexual organ… the streets
> its folds, the lights its down, quivering with sweat…

The Jamaican poet and novelist Claude McKay's account in
Banjo of the adventures of a group of beach boys in Marseille in
1932—unemployed, but for their musical instruments, and drinking
heavily in the bars of the Panier,—was inevitably stereotype-
reinforcing but his allusion to the life of the brothels is less inflamed
than that of Suarès:

> On both sides of the alley were the dingy cubicles whose only lights
> were the occupants… gesturing and calling in ludicrous tones: "*Viens
> ici, viens ici,*" and repeating pridefully the raw expressions of the low
> love shops that they had learned from English-speaking seamen…
> The hub of low-down proletarian love, stinking, hard, cruel.

McKay lived in Paris until his return to New York in 1933 and
the hand-to-mouth existence of Banjo and others of his cosmopolitan, colonially mixed and footloose band of characters could as easily
be portrayed on the banks of the Seine (where some of them have
come from), while Marseille itself plays little part in the narrative
except as backdrop lit by the ever-present sea:

> The Negro-negroid population of the town divides sharply into groups.
> The Martiniquans and Guadeloupans… make a little aristocracy of
> themselves. The Madagascans… and the North African Negroes,
> whom the pure Arabs despise, fall somewhere between the
> Martiniquans and the Senegalese, who are the savages… The magic
> thing had brought all shades and grades of Negroes together. Money…
> And of all the great ports there was none so appealing to seamen as
> Marseilles in its cruel beauty… It was as if every country of the world
> where Negroes lived had sent representatives drifting in to Marseilles.

In June 1772 the Marquis de Sade made his only visit to Marseille; he and his valet Latour assembled four girls at a house in the Rue des Capucins and fed them Spanish fly embedded in sweetmeats. Some days later the two men were accused of attempted poisoning and homosexual sodomy, tried in their absence by the Marseille court and condemned to execution—Sade as a nobleman by decapitation, Latour by common hanging. They were by then in Italy and continued to live clandestinely until 1777, when Sade was arrested in Paris where he remained imprisoned until the revolution.

The playwright and novelist Jean Genet evidently shared with Sade the sense Genet described as his "native and irrevocable guilt". In Marseille at the age of eighteen he pursued his profession of thief, "robbing by night whichever pederast had picked me up. The whores of the rue Bouterie [the *quartier* had not yet been destroyed] bought the stolen objects from me." Similar though often hilarious workings of guilt appear in the novels of Louis-Ferdinand Céline, whose antihero in *Voyage au bout de la nuit* embarks at Marseille for Bambola-Fort-Gono and soon finds himself abhorred as the only paying passenger among returning functionaries and officers whose passage is covered at the public expense. Céline provides an antidote to the "gate-of-empire" image attached to Marseille:

Our ship was called the *Amiral Bragueton*... held together thanks to its paint. So many coats of accumulated skin had finished by constituting a second hull for the *Amiral Bragueton*, like an onion... If I had had any experience of the colonial milieu, on leaving Marseille I, an unworthy shipboard companion, would have begged forgiveness and mercy on my knees from this colonial infantry officer I met everywhere, capitaine Frémizon... and perhaps humiliated myself further, to be safe, at the feet of the oldest of the colonial functionaries... But ignorant as I was, my unconscious pretention to breathe the same air as them nearly cost me my life...

Céline's hero was travelling in the wrong company, though the right company for fuelling the caustic of his satire. He might have been more in sympathy with the Swiss writer Cendrars and his fellow *légionnaires,* described by Richard Cobb as the honoured freemen of the Vieux Port and certainly recognized as such by the prostitutes: "Cendrars… a man never for long on land… was a particularly well-qualified observer of the small cafés and the tiny restaurants, their dark entrances protected by fringes of green matting, decorated with coloured beads, and of the varied inhabitants of the anarchical Vieux-Port… But his observation does not extend very far inland… and so his work has become very much a period piece, an eloquent but sad monument to yet something else that has been lost: the sunny, salty, peppery, aromatic fraternity of a maritime community…"

But the maritime community in Cendrars' day included criminals among them the Corsican apprentice gangster, Carbone, later infamous as a collaborator with the Gestapo, of whom Cendrars wrote, "In this teeming quarter of the Vieux-Port one could formerly see a handsome boy of eighteen whose vigour, guts and indomitable courage were legendary in all the outlying parts of Marseille." Olivier Boura is critical of the passage: "'Legendary' gives the impression that the whole town was sympathetically interested in this bad boy's exploits, whereas most people were divided between ignorance of them, reproof, and shame. The novelist… associates his hero with the prestige, then intact, of exoticism… the wide open life is the life of a gangster."

Cobb ascribed aromatic characteristics to the community, but the more real aroma of Marseille were remarked on by Charles Dickens: "A compound of vile smells perpetually arising from a great harbour full of stagnant water, and befouled by the refuse of innumerable ships." And in the opening of *Little Dorrit* he evoked Marseille as he had seen it in August 1844:

There was no wind to make a ripple on the foul water within the harbour, or on the beautiful sea without. The line of demarcation between the two colours, black and blue, showed the point which the pure sea would not pass; but it lay as quiet as the abominable pool, with which it never mixed. Boats without awnings were too hot to touch; ships blistered at their moorings; the stones of the quays had not cooled, night or day, for months. Hindoos, Russians, Chinese, Spaniards, Portuguese, Englishmen, Frenchmen, Genoese, Neapolitans, Venetians, Greeks, Turks, descendants from all the builders of Babel, come to trade at Marseilles, sought the shade alike—taking refuge in any hiding-place from a sea too intensely blue to be looked at, and a sky of purple, set with one great flaming jewel of fire.

Pagnol: Myths and Stereotypes

The sea of arrivals and departures may be what is most emblematic of the divide between the Marseillais and the stranger, the writer from other lands, other skies, and the native with a propensity for literary expression. "There is surely some negative significance," Cobb suggests with regard to the gifted dramatist whose work more than any other has formed the twentieth-century stereotype view of a loquacious, ambrosial, superficial Marseille character, "in the fact that, in the four volumes of his childhood memoirs, Marcel Pagnol never once mentioned... the Vieux-Port; and there is nothing to suggest that the bright-eyed, very observant child had ever seen a ship, while the sea is only glimpsed at a great distance, reflecting the midday glare of a superb sunset... What is more, it is always an empty sea." So Pagnol's imagination could admit no intruder to the swell and horizon of boyhood's *mare nostrum.* But the significance must be more than merely subjective: "Perhaps the potential capacity for native literature has always been exhausted in advance—in speech, in the constant fount of conversation," Cobb suggests, and this, of course, is the fount so fluently (and so lucratively) running in Pagnol's plays and films, in which characters are offered as stereotypes of Provençal villagers whose originals would be more complex, sadder, more silent and more secret than can be shown in the two brilliantly drawn dimensions of his stage *personages.* And the very success of this portrayal which depicts so little of the reality has perpetuated the caricature, created in the nineteenth century by the journalist Joseph Méry, of a Marseille in Harrel-Courtès' words famous only for idle cunning and a mentality of heedlessness, a myth brought into being by authors writing to amuse and exploit a Parisian audience and win fame far from home.

"I didn't know I loved Marseille," Pagnol said after the triumph in 1929 at the Théâtre de Paris of his play *Marius*, "but absence often reveals our loves to us."

Méry had been preceded by Stendhal who wrote in *Les Mémoires d'un touriste* that the Marseillais was "frank and even coarse; he says what he thinks, even when what he thinks is a little contrary to politeness." From the time of Méry's *Marseille et les marseillais* which appeared in 1844, it was difficult to present an inhabitant of the town as anything other than a grotesque. Boura suggests that there was a conviction among these writers that the truth of Marseille was to be found in caricature; Borges pointed out that self-parody is the essence of the baroque, and Boura claims that Marseille is far more baroque in this sense than its reputed extravagence suggests. But what room does this leave, he asks, for the taciturn, the hard-working, the legions of modest people? Let alone for melancholy and death. "Marseille," said the musician-poet Léo Ferry, "is Shakespeare with an accent." Edmond Rostand, too, was Marseillais by birth and made his fortune in the Parisian theatre. His Cyrano, though ostensibly Gascon, has an unmistakable Marseillais flamboyance carried to the extreme and is, as Paul Lombard points out, "a mixture of creative energy and destructive doubt, with a refusal to take himself seriously, which are the main components of the Marseille spirit". Lombard cites Antonin Artaud, author of *Le Théatre et son double*, inventor of the "theatre of cruelty", a Marseillais for whom life and theatre were interfused, as the anti-Pagnol, the "crucified figure of the soul of Marseille" whose heredity, however repugnant to him (he was the son and grandson of wealthy shipping owners), not all the water of the Mediterranean could wash away.

In the same year as the publication of *Marseille et les marseillais* the world was presented with *The Count of Monte-Cristo*. Although Marseille is not greatly present in the famous novel, not much described or shown, Alexandre Dumas assumed in every reader a familiarity with the Canebière, the Plage des Catalans and the Château d'If. Until now the literary existence of Marseille was in history books or accounts of sea journeys; with *Monte-Cristo* the city and its surroundings entered the domain of the imagination and henceforth the fictional or journalistic portrayal of Marseille varied between romance, farce and stage villainy with a cast of characters naïve, broadly comic, or dramatically wicked.

Thirty years later Zola's *Les Mystères de Marseille*, drawn in large part from judicial records, pictured a world of shady businessmen and easy women, bankrupts and usurers; but what above all fascinated writers and their public from the nineteenth century until the Second World War was the old town and its population, inevitably poor, reputedly foreign and potentially dangerous, dwelling in a zone enticingly out of reach of the law, part of a maritime city where moral laxity came as naturally as the sea air that brought it. In Pierre Mac Orlan's novel *Quartier réservé* the old town appears as a secret world open only to the initiated. Literature and journalism, writes Boura, constructed for the respectable reader's imagination a replica of the forbidden city at a ten-hour train journey from Paris.

Cahiers du sud

In 1914 a first step was taken away from this gallery of clichés and towards a more convincing literary representation of Marseille and its people which is still developing, and may be seen as part of a process of demythologizing a city that has perhaps hidden too long behind a defensive screen. This move was the founding, by Marcel Pagnol and his companion at the Lycée Thiers, Jean Ballard, of the literary review *Fortunio*. The First World War, in which Pagnol served, intervened and *Fortunio* next appeared in 1920 under his editorship until he departed for a literary career in Paris where he at first hoped to transplant it. In 1925 the review was renamed *Cahiers du sud*, edited by Jean Ballard alone, anchored in Marseille near to the Vieux Port and continuing as a monthly publication of growing national and international fame until 1966. Until 1938 Ballard was a pacifist but in that year he visited Germany and Czechoslovakia and was convinced that "it was impossible to get anywhere with gangsters". Lombard claims that *Cahiers du sud* began and ended with the age of surrealism; however, the review showed a strongly liberal and open political choice and covered a wide field with texts on poetry, science, metaphysics, theatre, art and history, and published

District of ill repute: the Panier

(*top*) The perfect natural harbour; (*middle*) Mistral fury

(*below*) Most sumptuous of the *bastides*, the Château Borély

(*top*) Fos-sur-Mer, usurper of Marseille trade;
(*right*) Within *Le Panier*, a city in its third millenium;
(*bottom*) The Bourse, housing the Chamber of Commerce of 1599

(Opposite page) (*top*) The walls stood and contained the city until 1665—a map of 1575;
(*bottom*) The Cours, 'noblest street in Europe'

3

(*above*) Nineteenth-century remodelling: Rue de Breteuil;
(*below*) Fashionable restaurants of the Cours Julien

(*above and below*) The Corniche then (1895) and now

(*Opposite page*) (*top*) The *Porte de l'Orient*; (*middle*) Artist's impression for Euroméditerranée; (*bottom left*) Remnants of the antique port; (*bottom right*) Saint George slaying the dragon above the door of of Saint-Victor
(*This page*) (*above*) Château d'If in the splendour of the gulf; (*below*) Neo-Byzantine cathedral and Tour du Fanal, c.1890

(*top*) … mediaeval Saint-Laurent …;
(*middle*) … baroque Vieille Charité;
(*right*) *Atlantes* of the Hôtel de
Pesciolini

(*top*) The Hôpital Caroline destroyed by bombing at the Liberation; (*middle left*) The château where Comtesse Lily Pastré sheltered refugees in the Occupation; (*middle right*) A Marseille santon;
(*left*) Nôtre-Dame-de-la-Garde—sailor's icon

9

(*above*) The nineteenth-century Quai de La Joliette; (*below*) The water of the Durance brought to the heart of Marseille: the Palais Longchamp; (*inset*) Ex-votos in Notre-Dame-de-la-Garde

(*left*) Modesty around the Fontaine Cantini of 1911;
(*bottom right*) (*detail*) Coin from Greek colony of Massalia;
Pytheas ''The Liar,'' sailor to Ultima Thule
(*bottom left*) Neo-Gothic and Le Corbusier's Cité Radieuse

PYTHEAS

(*left*) Rubens' *The Arrival of Marie de' Medici at Marseille*; (*bottom left*) Michel Serre's depiction of the 1720 plague; (*middle right*) In the great days of the colonial Empire: a colonial exhibition; (*bottom right*) Memorial to Alexander of Yugoslavia, assassinated on the Canebière in Octobe 1934

(*clockwise from top left*) At the Libération; The discovery by Cézanne of the gulf from l'Estaque: "a greater progress than the invention of the steam-engine" – Picasso; Paul Signac, *Notre-Dame-de-la-Garde (La Bonne-Mère), Marseilles* (1905); Pagnol's great gifts reinforced a caricatural view of the *Marseillais*…; The *pont à transbordeur*, icon of the city; Alexandre Dumas *père*, creator of the Count of Monte-Cristo

(*top left*) ... further reinforced by Fernandel, the native son; (top right) football, football...; (*middle left*) Street market Noailles; (*middle right*) Home of the *bouillabaisse*, the Vallon des Auffes and its restaurants; (*below*) A collection of faïence of Marseille and Moustiers can be seen in the Château Pastré

(*left*) Zaha Hadid's Euroméditerranée architecture; (*below*) "A sight so touching in its majesty": The archipelago of Frioul

(*above*) A *calanque* only reached on foot or by water;
(*below*) *Pointus* and launches at Cassis

many celebrated names: Gide, Céline, Breton, Artaud, Valéry, Woolf, Kafka, Faulkner, Sartre, Yourcenar... Among the most famous special numbers was one, appearing in 1935 and reissued after the war, on *Islam and the West*. In particular, *Cahiers du sud* is credited with maintaining and nourishing a vigorous intellectual life in Marseille during the Second World War and the period of the occupation after 1942, helping to support writers and artists in exile. "The office of *Cahiers du sud* was the last place of shelter for people like us," wrote the novelist Anna Seghers who with help in Marseille escaped to Mexico with her interned husband before the German forces arrived.

Cahiers du sud was the leading literary and philosophical journal outside Paris and its career of more than forty years brought to Marseille a consideration as an intellectual and creative centre unknown since the Hellenistic age. No less significant was the eventual appearance of a new strain of fiction in which Marseille, seen with candour, without prejudice and in a less sentimental light, would figure as both setting and as a determinant factor in narrative. In the work of the twentieth-century novelists most famously associated with the city—Pagnol and Jean Giono—Marseille always resembles a distant vision; the complexity of its workings remains out of view as if the writers had no sight of them. Pagnol's four volumes of childhood memories, *Souvenirs d'enfance,* concentrate on the family and a small number of friends, reported with great art and perfect control by a self-centred juvenile imagination, and Marseille itself has little significant part to play.

Giono, who was not Marseillais and fell out of love with the town after spending nine months imprisoned in the Fort Saint-Nicolas for his pacifism in 1939, shows in his *Noé* and *Description de 1939* a narrator who is never more than a passer-through by train, by tram, by car; Marseille is a distant place, close in geographical reality but whose name is only spoken in a murmur because it denotes an entity too different from the rest of Provence. Agostini and Forno analyze the effect of the works of Pagnol, Giono and others including the playwright André Roussin who spent his youth in the outlying village of Saint-Barnabé, now enveloped by the town and with a community of families of Armenian origin: "These writers recreate a *quartier*, a mother, a promenade in the hills. The sentimental intensity of their work does nothing to reduce the distance from an elusive Marseille... so separate that a sense of it can only be reached intuitively."

With this reservation, the work of twentieth-century writers slowly created a new and more serious image of Marseille within which the chief fictional development towards the end of the century and afterwards could grow—the image of a dangerous but agreeable city, latitudinarian, if not lax. The genre in which this was and is deployed has naturally been the novel of suspense, the literary thriller whether of police detection or of psychological drama, and in either case with a Marseille more realistic than imaginary in a leading role. Some of the writers have come from outside—the town willingly naturalizes its authors, Lombard claims—such as J.-M. G. Le Clézio and Yann Quéfelec; others are Marseillais by origin, their love, often ambivalent, is already formed and needs no inaugural period of romance yet, in the words of one of them, Yann de l'Ecotais who became editor of *l'Express*, "Marseille is a town that you have to learn." The ambivalence can be seen in the work of Tahar Ben Jelloun who describes Marseille as "a migraine awakened by mistral and exodus". The caustic humour of Philippe Carrese is proof that the Marseillais *roman noir* is never without irony, sometimes tragic, and this is even more fully and effectively demonstrated in the novels of Jean-Claude Izzo, the most admired and best-known among the native writers of the end of the millennium.

Izzo more than any other features Marseille in his work as an entire living character, and perhaps the principal: "Marseille is familiar, from the first sight... Europe is full of beautiful towns with fine monuments, the world is full of beautiful bays, magnificent ports... but Marseille is beautiful in its humanity, its familiarity like bread to be shared by all." His highly successful trilogy, *Total Khéops*, *Chourmo* and *Solea*, is prefaced with the words: "The story you are about to read is totally imaginary... only the town is real, Marseille and all those who live there with that passion which is theirs alone." The themes of the novels—racism in *Khéops*, fanatical Islamism in *Chourmo*, the mafia in *Solea*—might seem to bear out the assertion of sociologists that Marseille is the ideal terrain for confrontations between communities, but Izzo's admirer Paul Lombard claims that these themes serve the novels' intrigues rather than the reality, since Marseille has become a laboratory of peaceful cohabitation. Nevertheless, many Marseillais feel that Izzo spoke for them, they are moved, they recognize their homeland in his pages and themselves, gratefully, in his characters. After his death in 2000, his biographer wrote, "He had one fixed point in reality: Marseille and its biotope, the epicentre of his personal and literary destiny."

Unlike most other great cities, Marseille has never bred a composite fictional synthesis, Dickensian or Balzacian, of which it is the centre and by which it is explained, explored, brought to life, suffering and delight alike. Izzo perhaps came nearest and unfortunately died while still in his prime at the age of fifty-five. Between 1649 and 1653 Madeleine de Scudéry published, under her brother's name, something approaching a global portrait, the epic romance *Le Grand Cyrus* in ten volumes which transposes to Persia her discovery of the legends of the founding of Marseille by the Phocaeans, with shipwrecks, seductions, duels, secret idylls. The tedium of *Le Grand Cyrus'* extreme length was not felt by readers of romances in the seventeenth century. Elizabeth Pepys is recorded in December 1660 as continuing her reading of the fashionable and interminable novel until midnight, and six years later was still recounting tales from it, to her husband's displeasure:

> At noon home, where I find my wife troubled still at my checking her last night in the coach her long stories out of *Grand Cyrus*, which she would tell, though nothing to the purpose nor in any good manner. This she took unkindly, and I think I was to blame indeed [sic]... however, very good friends by and by, and to dinner...

The cubes of Georges Braque

6 | **Visual Images**
Art, Drama and Cinema

Lines parallel to the horizon give extent… those perpendicular to the horizon give depth. For man, nature is more in depth than in surface, hence the necessity to introduce into our vibrations of light, represented by reds and yellows, enough bluish tint to give the feeling of air.

Cézanne

Start with something… Afterwards you can remove all trace of reality. There's no danger then… because the idea of the object will have left an indelible mark.

Picasso

Climate change, which at the end of the Ice Age left the entrance to the Grotte Cosquer (near Cap Morgiou in the *calanques*), 37 metres underwater may in time drown the cave itself and its Palaeolithic wall paintings once and for all, with another and fatal rise in sea level. The municipality, more solicitous of the Marseille inheritance than formerly and watched by a vigilant wider world, intends to create a life-size facsimile of this unique site by 2013, using the same laser 3D imaging technique as at Lascaux, in the Fort d'Entrecasteaux, a part of the Fort Saint-Nicolas at the mouth of the Vieux Port. Verisimilitude will be aided by the fact that the Entrecasteaux, like the crypt of Saint-Victor higher on the hillside, is cut into the rock on which Saint-Nicolas stands, and the reproduced cave, sixty metres in diameter, will lie underground. The wall paintings to be minutely reconstituted were created between 27,000 and 19,000 BC, number almost five hundred and include, together with representations of horses, bison, deer, ibex and auroch, the first known images of marine animals—penguins, seals, fish and shellfish—and, from the most ancient period, more than sixty human handprints, red or black, produced by positive hand transfer of colour or in some cases by a technique of stencilling to leave a negative.

There are also many geometrical figures and some male and female sexual symbols. The cave was not inhabited but used, it is believed, as a sanctuary; the handprints are found near a 24 metre-deep well whose fearsome opening only would have been visible by the shifting light of flames, and the presence at the height of a man's shoulder of childrens' handprints is taken as suggestive of initiation ceremonies. The existence of this ritual and perhaps sacred art of the Grotte Cosquer, which like a secret temple was entered through the cliff face some way above the level steppe leading to the shore, seems to show how the beauty of the site—mountain, bay and islands— has inspired human creative awe from the time of its first known manifestation.

Visible artistic creativity is, however, notably absent from the remains and records of Marseille during the many centuries of its early existence. No major Greek or Roman masterpieces are to be seen in the comparatively modest collection of the History Museum, no great Romanesque or gothic sculptures guard or give witness in the surviving churches; it is as if in the depth of the sea the creative life which would emerge in so extraordinary an outburst at the end of the nineteenth and in the early twentieth century was preparing itself and made little stir. Through the penumbra of this long dormancy some lesser or anecdotal signs of life appear. In the Musée du Vieux Marseille is the first pictorial representation of the town, a painting on wood of 1513 showing Mary Magdalene, patron saint of Provence, preaching to the Marseillais on the shore of the Vieux Port with the unchanging Tour Saint-Jean and the sea beyond. Incidents and horrors of the great plague of 1720 were vividly, not to say gruesomely, recorded in scenes painted in 1723 by Michel Serre, exhibited at the time in Holland and England and now in the Musée des Beaux-Arts. The approach to the harbour, the view from within it and a scene of dancers on the promontary of the Pharo were represented in 1754 in a series of famous works, now in the Louvre and the Musée Maritime in Paris, by the Avignonnais painter Claude-Joseph Vernet who had studied in Rome and is often considered the greatest of European marine artists of the eighteenth century. The best-known of native painters before the revolution was Françoise Duparc, daughter of a Marseille artist, whose female portraits, of which several are now in the Musée des Beaux-Arts, give both a vivid and a touching record of *Marseillaises* at work in the second half of the eighteenth century.

In 1828 J. M. W. Turner passed through on his journey from Paris to Rome, made a number of rapid sketches and at least one brilliant watercolour, visible on the Tate website, of the tower and lighthouse at the mouth of the Vieux Port with shipping in the wind and an agitated sea. The staircase of the Musée des Beaux-Arts is decorated with two imaginary-historical frescoes by Puvis de Chavannes of 1869; *Marseille, colonie grecque* and *Marseille porte de l'orient*, both in a style of motionless, timeless limpidity which effectively stirs the sleeping fantasy while gently numbing the critical sense. In 1824 the artist Adolphe Monticelli, possibly of Venetian origin, was born in the Provençal Alps but his working life was spent in Marseille where he died in 1886, supposedly from abuse of absinthe. His work was unconventional particularly in his choice of supports, often discarded pieces of carpentry, doors or shutters; in the treatment of light, diffused by intentional thickening of pigment and in his non-naturalistic colouring which was admired by Van Gogh (whom it is thought to have influenced). A collection of his work can be seen at the Fondation Monticelli housed in a restored fort above the sea, the Fortin des Corbières at l'Estaque. Although perhaps an underrated artist of the late nineteenth century, Monticelli's place in history is secured by the story of his companionship with the great figure, junior to him by sixteen years, whose arrival and first sight of the Gulf of Marseille would change the temper and direction of pictorial art for ever.

Cézanne at l'Estaque

In the summer of 1864, Elizabeth the mother of Paul Cézanne rented a small house, perhaps a fisherman's home, in the village of l'Estaque which lies in the 16th *arrondissement* of Marseille and from the northern side overlooks the bay, the hill of la Garde, and the mountain of Marseilleveyre as backdrop. It is not known why Elizabeth, wife of a prosperous banker of Aix-en-Provence, should have chosen a working-class village with no *bourgeois* society to pass the summer away from home. Some have suggested sea-baths; others a lover, though this seems unlikely or at least uneasy with a 24-year-old son about the house, surly and preoccupied, his clothing smeared with half-dried paint. Cézanne searched the surrounding valleys and hills for viewpoints, discarding on the spot, it is said, dozens of unfinished sketches and failed beginnings as he marched on, easel on his back, disliked by the village population for the usual reasons—eccentricity, suspected aloofness, taciturnity. "If the people here could throw murderous looks," he wrote to his friend Camille Pissarro, "I would have been done for long ago. They don't like the look of me."

This first visit was not long and no work dating from it has survived. L'Estaque was then a little village at the end of the world. The railway line had been built, with a viaduct later made famous in paintings, and the Tunnel de la Nerthe had recently opened, but there was no station until 1877. The houses came down to the water's edge. The horse-drawn omnibus took two and a half hours to reach the centre of Marseille, wandering around other villages of the *commune* on its way. There were many brick and tile factories in the valleys running down from the hills behind, and the population of workers was growing. Within a few years cement works and chemical industry brought still more labour and by the time of Cézanne's second visit in 1870 there were lines of flimsy housing for immigrant workers, mostly Italian or Greek, and the village boasted three brothels one of which, on the road following the curve of the coast, is now the harbour pilots' office.

The Franco-Prussian War broke out on 18 July 1870. Cézanne, dispensed from military service by the intervention of his father, was at l'Estaque with his mother in a house on the Place de l'Eglise, accompanied by Hortense Fiquet whom he later married; although accused of desertion and called on by gendarmes who found him not at home, the painter's avoidance of the war was quite proper, though it added to his unpopularity, and he remained until March 1871. Zola visited him in September. During this period, according to his cataloguer Venturi, Cézanne produced "baroque compositions with an erotic tendency", and the only finished landscapes, executed in an unusually harsh winter, were *La neige fondue à l'Estaque* and *Village de pêcheurs à l'Estaque*. Nevertheless, from the Place de l'Eglise as described by the historian Félix Vérany in 1874 "the eye falls naturally on a hundred little paths striped with red and grey... one leaves behind one an entire band of blue, the Mediterranean where Marseille bathes...", and this vision would draw Cézanne back on other long visits. He returned in June 1876 by which time he and Hortense had a son and she was installed in Marseille. Following one or other of the hundred little paths with the bay behind and below, moving from point to point in sunlight "so fearsome," as he wrote to Pissarro, "that objects take off in silhouette, not black and white, but in blue, red, brown, violet...", Cézanne created the works that mark the period as that in which he "became Cézanne", learned to "deal with nature through the cylinder, the sphere, the cone, all placed in perspective" as he would later write to Emile Bernard, and concentrated his attention increasingly on the "motif" or structural principle that these forms expressed.

The process of industrialization at l'Estaque and in its surroundings continued; tile, brick and cement works often left a fine layer of white or red dust over the streets and houses, more chimneys rose towards the skyline and Cézanne, despite a well-documented dislike of progress ("just the invasion of the biped," he wrote) was one of the first to introduce the industrial world into art by the place he gave to these chimneys in many of the l'Estaque paintings, of the bay, the village and the shoreline, which in the Venturi catalogue number 53 representations between 1870 and 1889.

For Cézanne the "motif" meant the elements of a landscape combined with the intellectual response and emotion that it aroused, leading inevitably to an increasing abstraction evident, for example, in *Rochers à l'Estaque*, the only site of a painting by him at l'Estaque still intact and unchanged, in which the bay and distant mountains are dwarfed by the huge forms of rock and valley slope in the foreground; while some of the great broader views, such as *L'Estaque, vue du golfe de Marseille* are analyzable in geometric terms. In *La mer à l'Estaque*, which Picasso kept close by him for more than forty years, the mountains have disappeared, the sea is a haze, the chimney stack and house roofs and interlacing trees framing them are stripped of every external element to allow, in Venturi's words, "the representation of light and shadow by which, thanks to a growing simplification, Cézanne succeeds in releasing the very essence of things ..." The low wall in the foreground is less wall than painting, the subject of painting become painting itself, as Jean Boissieu has pointed out. Between 1882 and 1885 Cézanne lived between Aix, Marseille and l'Estaque. In 1886 both his father and his friend Monticelli died, he quarrelled with Zola and thereafter came no more to l'Estaque as though he knew that his work there, built during nine visits spread over sixteen or more years and prefiguring that of the young artists who followed, was completed, and history made. He wrote to Emile Bernard, "I remain the primitive on the road I discovered."

Both Renoir and Monet visited Cézanne at l'Estaque, Renoir remaining several months in 1882 and leaving at least two works of Impressionism with no hint of the Cubist vision to come. In 1897 Paul Signac, working in the pointillist style of Seurat, created a series of variations on the view of the Vieux Port and another on Notre-Dame-de-la-Garde. In 1905 Signac acquired a painting of the Rue Bouterie, most famous of the streets of the old town given over largely to prostitution, by the Marseillais artist Charles Camoin whose master work was a series of three paintings of *Le Vieux Port et Notre-Dame-de-la-Garde* in 1904. Camoin, during his military service at Aix in 1900, had obtained a written introduction and presented himself to Cézanne at home; the young soldier and the venerated artist of uncertain temper formed a friendship, and Camoin became for posterity the vehicle, through conversations and correspondence, of Cézanne's spoken message until his death.

The period of great artistic activity before the First World War brought painters to Marseille and particularly to l'Estaque in the footsteps of Cézanne though not, at first, in the "road of his discovery". Fauvism is held to date from the Salon of autumn 1905 though it was naturally already in existence, and with the exception of Van Dongen all the artists associated with the movement came to Marseille: Matisse, Marquet, Friesz, Derain, Vlaminck, Dufy. Fernand Léger said that the sight of dockworkers diving into the water of the Vieux Port in their breaks "inspired everything that followed in my paintings... my style became more supple, less rigid." Derain in particular worked at l'Estaque in an arbitrary range of colours owing nothing to Cézanne, and he was followed after Cézanne's death in his studio on 23 October 1906 by Georges Braque, perhaps creatively liberated by that event, who painted a series of vivid Fauvist scenes at l'Estaque where he installed himself in the Hôtel Maurin, still in existence though uninhabited, at the foot of the valley of Riaux. It was Braque's first visit to the south of which he later said, "it was in the Midi that I felt the exaltation rise in me."

Braque's Fauvist period was brilliant but brief; he turned from the construction of space by sensual colour to become "the inventor of forms" under the incontestable influence of Cézanne. "It was more than an influence, it was an initiation," Braque declared. "Cézanne was the first to break away from learned, mechanical, perspective..." In May 1907 Braque came to l'Estaque for his second visit. In Marseille he had been joined by Camoin who had returned with Albert Marquet and Othon Friesz from London where they had seen the Turners and the primitive African and Oceanic sculptures at the Victoria and Albert Museum (Boissieu). At l'Estaque that summer Braque opened the history of Cubism with the first of two paintings of the *Viaduc de l'Estaque,* carrying the railway line on its emergence from the Tunnel de la Nerthe. If the painting of 1906 is still Fauvist in its colouring though structured and abstracted in the manner of Cézanne, the second version, of the following year, is reduced to a palette of ochres and greens and the volumes—of buildings, trees, the viaduct itself—carry the principles of Cézanne to their limit. Or nearly so: in *Maisons à l'Estaque* of 1908 the buildings are windowless, the roofs ochre as the walls, the forms cubes (Matisse, a jury member at the Salon d'automne, which rejected Braque's paintings, pointed this out and the term "Cubism" was born), the trees conical; and in the last of Braque's works at l'Estaque, *Les usines du Rio Tinto à l'Estaque* of 1910, the abstraction is almost complete; only the bluish forms in the upper part of the canvas give, in Cezanne's phrase, "the feeling of air" above the ochre cubes and vegetal green triangles. A single relatively realistic chimney stack, itself a perfect geometrical form, rises from the geometry of the whole to indicate the industrial cement and chemical-making character of the site, heavily polluting and destructive of the scenery. Picasso's dictum that "the idea of the object will have left an indelible mark", and the Canadian art historian Claude Jasmin's description of l'Estaque as "the eternal landscape originating from the Mediterranean Eden, along with the most modern image of industrial Europe", find here their demonstration and proof.

Picasso said of Cézanne that what he had done with reality "constituted a far greater progress than the invention of the steam engine", but not every follower on the discovered road went all the way to Cubism. Marseille continued as the scene of work in the years of the First World War and afterwards by a distinguished group of artists linked to Camoin and associated with Matisse, who wrote to Camoin from l'Estaque in January 1916: "I have begun here... a drawing of leaning trees, pine trees... you may know them... on the other side of the road, on the upswing leading to the restaurant on the cliff." Among others of the group were the Marseillais Alfred Lombard whose representations of the town remained in the Fauvist spirit; Albert Marquet who produced aesthetically satisfying paintings in a vein of tempered realism, of the Vieux Port and of the bay from a terrace at l'Estaque where he passed the war in the Grand Hôtel de la Falaise; Henri Manguin with a realism somewhat more pronounced; their friend Albert André whose Bonnard-like female figures (Boissieu) are portrayed in markets and shopping streets; Louis-Mathieu Verdilhan with strong and simplified outlines of views on and around the Vieux Port. In 1925 Oscar Kokoschka brought Viennese expressionism to work in several violent representations of the town, the port, the bay and its shipping. These continue to attract artists using a changing variety of techniques and styles, and students of the many art schools active in Marseille; it

can only be admitted that the sites in a multitude of aspects have
been the scene of so great a creative illumination that later, lesser
lights must be to some degree eclipsed by it.

"The Seventh Art"

Film, or the *7e art*, first appeared in Marseille in February 1896 when
the brothers Lumière presented the work of their *cinématographe* at
the Grand Hôtel du Louvre et de la Paix in the Rue Noailles, with
a queue of eager Marseillais immediately forming up for the next
session. "The cinema," the brothers said, "is an invention without a
future," and they soon returned to their photographic business. But
from the beginning the Marseille public, supporters of the music
hall, the operetta and the popular theatre, was captured, and before
the start of the First World War there were between thirty and forty
cinemas in operation, some of them in former theatres, some smaller
and in halls previously used by lay or religious associations, while
many actors from the music halls were finding work in the new film
business to which they brought their highly developed, extrovert,
broad-toned and popular entertainment techniques and orientation
derived from the French pantomime tradition of which Marseille
was the chief repository. This was to have the long-term effect of representing
Marseille and its people as far coarser in speech and more
elementary in emotional range than any credible reality would bear
out, and cinema, with its propensity for simplification and its leaning
towards cliché (not for nothing the French word for photographic
negative) was the natural vehicle to take on board this entertaining
but delusive impression and carry it, over the years, to the four
corners of the earth.

The light of Marseille and its setting attracted filmmakers from
the beginning; before the First World War the Dumas "roman noir"
had already become *Le Prisonnier du Château d'If,* and by 1917 the
director Pouctal had created a *Monte-Cristo.* In the first year of war
Louis Feuillade assembled the actors and technicians working for
Gaumont in Marseille and produced more than twenty films, including
Scène des Vampires, patriotic dramas and vaudevilles. By the
end of the war a number of independent studios existed in Marseille

and the correspondent of "la Cinématographie française" wrote of "the French Los Angeles" with model open air studios "as in California". However, Feuillade was one of many who continued their work at Nice rather than Marseille because, it has been suggested, Marseille was seen as a predominantly proletarian city where the life of the *grande bourgeoisie* was kept hidden, whereas at Nice it was cosmopolitan, fashionable and paraded in luxury hotels along the sea front in surroundings that met the appetite of the world of film for recognizable society doings. This appears as an example of the preference for a specifically and secretly Marseillais way of life which helped to produce, this time in the context of film, a parodic rather than realistic vision of itself as if the town were saying, "rather a caricature than a portrait".

Nevertheless, in the 1920s a number of traditional films were made—*Capitaine Rascasse* with its images of the Panier as it once was, *le Juif errant, Sainte-Hélène*—before the arrival of avant-garde cineasts whose works such as *Fièvre, Coeur fidèle* and *En rade* emphasized the features seen as being in the tragic nature of Marseille: shipwreck real or sentimental, bars peopled by alcoholics and prostitutes, anti-heroes, themes chosen in the belief that the port of Marseille expressed at the same time the poetry of far-off landfalls and of an *exotisme intérieur* which in the age of depression spoke to a world of victims of fatality.

An emblematic feature of the Vieux Port until its demolition in 1945 was the *pont à transbordeur* (transporter bridge such as that still operating in Newport over the River Usk). Inaugurated in 1905, it carried pedestrians and vehicles across the mouth of the port and stood, a monster of iron architecture, statuesque but disfiguring to the ancient monuments which it dwarfed with its operating platform 52 metres above the water, and appearing from the sea as the *porte de France* below which shipping passed and the town was entered. This construction, often represented in paintings by, among others, Verdilhan, Dufy, Marquet and Kokoschka, also fascinated filmmakers including the Hungarian Moholy-Nagy who in his *Marseille-Vieux-Port* attempted to film it as if with the eye of a sculptor; and later Pagnol, and especially René Allio in his *Transit* where the transbordeur symbolizes the last barrier to exile for refugees from Nazi terror. The iconic bridge was blown up, with much of the rest of the port installation, by the German army on 21 August 1944; one supporting pillar and part of the arm of the transbordeur remained, rusting and dangerous, and were finally demolished with charges of melinite on 1 September 1945, to the nostalgic regret of some of the population but the satisfaction of the ferrymen of the Vieux Port relieved of competition.

The pre-Pagnol silent films had the merit, as well as showing images of ordinary life in streets given over almost entirely to the pedestrian and the tram, of being antecedent to the Marseillais stereotype which was to become universal and enduring. Moholy-Nagy filmed the port in rain, the poverty of the old town, the dirt and the swarming streets, while the muteness of the silent film gave emphasis to gesture rather than to the volubility which was soon to be adopted, exaggerated and then retailed as stock-in-trade. If the superior vitality of Marseille was ignored and the city to some extent bypassed during the silent film era on account of its apparently plebeian character, the arrival of sound quickly led to the exploiting of this very feature.

Speaking films appeared at the moment when Marcel Pagnol's play *Marius* and Vincent Scotto's operetta *Au pays du soleil* were running with huge success in Paris, and though not greatly original but drawing with skill and talent on familiar and well-loved recipes of the Marseille music hall revue, these works created in the capital, and soon in the wider world, the taste by which they and others following would be relished. Pagnol's success in particular, because of the wealth and power it brought him, would have an effect on the representation of the city and its people which still runs and has perhaps become part of their public image, with its emphasis on the Marseille accent as the seal of exoticism, and reliance on the décor of port, sea, Canebière and sun to guarantee the conditioned response. In 1930 Pagnol discovered the talking film on a visit to London where he saw *Broadway Melody,* and immediately understood how his plays could be adapted for the screen; his progressive involvement in the cinematographic activity of Marseille—as author, producer, editor of the review *Cahiers du film*, founder of the production company Films Marcel Pagnol, owner of cinemas and creator and director of his own studios—was the dominant fact in cultural life in the decade before the Second World War.

Pagnol, who filmed several novels by Jean Giono, defined the concept of the "author's cinema" in which the verbal element would be preeminent, and his own best-known films, *Marius, Fanny, César, Topaze, Le schpountz* and *La femme du boulanger*, were figurative, verbal, not reliant on symbolic visual image or echo. His cooperation with a number of powerful actors such as Raimu, Pierre Fresnay and Fernandel helped to create and preserve a cinematic world built on a literary fantasy of Marseille which was probably no more real than any dream of a distant city seen through a distorting haze. And in Pagnol's case it is hard not to suspect a veil of doubtful sincerity or good faith since he knew the reality was not as he showed it, the language at whatever social level was less strident, the feelings more nuanced; and also because he was the child of a landlocked bourgeois family of teachers from Aubagne, none of whom would have set foot more than once or twice in a lifetime on the Vieux Port nor entered any such bar as those where much of his action was set.

Pagnol, according to the Provençal journalist and historian of Marseille Jean Contrucci, was an impenitent liar. The relationship of the music hall revue to life, and the parody that results, are reversed in his work to produce an effect doubly removed from reality; the authors of *Marseille port du 7e art* conclude that the distorting mirror that turns the *galéjade* or tall story of the revues into a poetic form was the hallmark of the Marseillais dramatic comedy which he immortalized, a mythical incubus still haunting the city's reputation. Any visitor to a real-life bar on the Vieux Port will find and hear, not over-emphatic, stentorian volubility, but what has been described as a talkative nonchalance, open and with the easy warmth and consideration that implies.

The literary achievement of Pagnol that cannot be accused of insincerity, though it may be of inaccuracy, is the four-volume autobiography of his childhood and youth which has been adapted for film in four parts, appearing between 1990 and 2006; but these poised and luminous works of self-exploration, written by the Academician that Pagnol became in 1947, show how little of Marseille itself entered into the concerns and memories of the young Marcel, and how when he returned to it from Paris to make films he would be ready to exploit a fantasy version which his great talent rendered classic. In 1935 Pagnol lent his studios and personnel to Jean Renoir to make the film *Toni*, a sociological rather than picturesque view of immigrant elements in Provençal life—Spanish and Italian—and the strains they produced. But the public was disconcerted by the tragic character of the film, preferring to it Pagnol's *La femme du boulanger* with its readily met demand on emotional empathy. In 1938 Renoir's *La Marseillaise*, a drama of the revolution which attempted to offer a different and more authentic vision of Marseille and the Marseillais, ran in Paris for a fortnight to small and unappreciative audiences before being withdrawn.

The dynamiting of the old town in 1943 was the subject of a novel by Rupert Croft-Cooke which attempted to reconstruct the life of Marseille during the occupation from documents in the German army archives, and became in 1957 the film *Les 7 tonnerres* with a cast of mainly British actors including James Robertson Justice and Stephen Boyd. "The story of this film," said the introduction, "is of that moment after which the Vieux-Port was no longer the same and would never again be as it was." The film was missing at the time of the fiftieth anniversary in 1993 of the destruction of 1943 but has since been rediscovered by the Cinémathèque de Marseille; this institution is to be installed in the spectacularly restored Château de la Buzine near La Treille, a nineteenth-century pastiche which Pagnol had bought, where he dreamed of creating a group of film studios as well as his own principal residence, and which was occupied by the German army, then squatted for thirteen years, falling into decay and eventually ruin. Since 1995 Buzine has been a property of the town and will store an archive of more than nine hundred hours of film.

The legacy of Pagnol has been one of those that leave a blessing and a memory of largely benevolent genius but are hard to escape, and inevitably deform the life that comes after. The post-war years have seen the rise and passing of filmmakers in Marseille who have struggled, more or less earnestly, to create work that would express a more complete and less sentimental truth of the city. In the 1950s Paul Carpita, an independent director preoccupied by questions of social justice, produced *Le rendez-vous des quais*, treating the opposition of the Marseille dockers to the war in Indo-China; the film was sequestrated in 1954 and remained invisible for thirty years. Resuscitated in 1989 it won an international renown but had no notable successors.

Henri Verneuil, one of many gifted artists born into the Marseille Armenian community, made popular films including some with Fernandel—*Escale au soleil*, *La vache et le prisonnier*, *Le mouton à cinq pattes*, *Le clan des siciliens*—which were commercially successful but impatiently viewed by critics who condemned their facility and rejection of the "author's cinema". For 25 years the Marseille cinema rested largely on the works of René Allio, particularly those set in Marseille and dealing with aspects of the city's life—*La vieille dame indigne*, described by Richard Cobb as "a charming, perceptive, and compassionate account of the sudden revolt and liberation of an elderly widow previously caged in by the greedy... solicitude of her two sons"; *Retour à Marseille*, a confrontation of past and present; *L'heure exquise*, an attempt at auto-portraiture and family history through use of archives and which is often held to be the best film ever made on the historic reality of Marseille; and *Transit*, based on the novel of Anna Seghers treating the escape to exile of refugees from the Nazi regime.

Bertrand Blier, like many others, was passionately attracted to Marseille and made there *Trop belle pour toi* and *Un, deux, trois soleil* which struggles to extinguish the inherited clichés, while Yves Robert and Claude Berri's filming of Pagnol's autobiographical *Le château de ma mère* and *La gloire de mon père*, as well as his *Manon des Sources* and *Jean de Florette*, seemed a nostalgic return to the mode of the famous legator. Some commentators cite Robert Guédiguian, another Marseillais of Armenian extraction, as the cineast most liberated from stereotype, offering an insight into the Marseille of suburbs and workshops, factories and streets, a world, as such commentators tend to say, of "simple people". But his best-known and loved film, *Marius et Jeannette*, set in l'Estaque and recounting a love story which is as endearing as it is sentimental, lies fully in the Pagnolesque tradition and on an outside view gives little away of the authentic, non-public life of the Marseillais, lived without posture or exploitation of stock responses.

The magnificence of the setting, the extraordinary architecture and the enigmatic character of the inhabitants continue to attract cinema and television producers or would-be producers, and at the Belle de Mai and elsewhere both subsidized and independent workers are many, active and adventurous. To take the place of external focus on inglorious aspects of the town's image—as recently as 1986 the *Figaro Magazine* labelled Marseille the "national capital of fear and violence"—in films such as *Borsalino*, modelled on the pre-war criminal activities of Carbone and Spirito, or *The French Connection* dramatizing the drug trade with Marseille at its centre, it can be hoped that a less stereotyped vision will materialize, grow and earn the respect of the Marseillais who may then feel able (if they wish) to quit the defensive redoubt where so much accepted cliché could understandably have driven them.

Civilization of the *cabanons* ...

7 | Leisure and Pleasure
Popular Culture and Pastimes

> The cabanon!... the cabanon is the touchstone of the Marseille character, it is the most beautiful, the most poetic pastime ever invented by a population of workers... and it is to the fishermen that we owe the creation of the cabanon, as the hide is naturally the work of the hunter.
>
> François Mazuy

The five thousand *bastides marseillaises* of former times (some say eight, some three), chief historic pastime of the vanished nobility and of bourgeois high and low, have mostly gone, taking their way of life with them; but *cabanons* endure and even now proliferate, often rising above the trivia of planning regulations. Although many bastides were handsome, and some grandly imposing, they did not sit at the heart of big domains, hence their great number in a limited territory. And it is this fact that makes the co-existence side by side of bastides and cabanons seem so apt to the basically undivided character of Marseille society. One man had his country house, another, at no great distance, his cabin, shack, lean-to built into the rock, but they were all *résidences secondaires* designed to take families from the heat of the town and out of reach of plagues, cholera epidemics or monotony. While gentlemen in bastides walked their few hectares after partridge or quail, dockers and workmen awaited the passage of these birds from behind a screen of bamboo a few hundred metres away. In 1692 William Bromley, Speaker of the House of Commons, described the habits of the *cabanonniers*:

> About 4 in the afternoon in the Summer-time, when a citizen has done his Days-work, and the Weather grown something moderate, he'll set his Wife on his Ass betwixt a pair of Paniers, in one of which shall be their Child, and in the other a little Wine, Oyl and some Bread, and he himself drives, or follows at some distance to his Country-House; where they are entertained with Roots, Herbs, and Grapes, and their Ass with Vine-leaves till the next Morning that they return back.

However, as Mazuy pointed out, the cabanon was first and foremost a fisherman's creation, and most are built not far from the sea. Many cabanons occupy ground whose rightful ownership is a detail obscured by time and usage. In the early nineteenth century the first working men's associations put up these constructions from random materials and maintained them at the expense of members for Sundays and unpaid holidays; later the taste for exclusive use developed and the cabanons, often more by custom than legal form, came to be seen as belonging to individuals and families. In the largest of the calanques, Sormiou, which is privately owned, nearly two hundred cabanons are held on lease over the generations from father to son and some inhabited all the year, but their origin as recreational outposts for workers whose lives were tied to the sea remains evident in the unchanging aspect of a fishing settlement. The Sunday meal was, and is, brought via the kitchen from the salt water to the table, *bouillabaisse* being its usual form. In the hinterland, the cabanon had the character of a hide though taking a far rarer catch than the generous sea provided. In either case the first cabanon, little more than a shelter in a capricious climate and a shed for tools and fishing gear, was gradually extended to include a kitchen, a bedroom for siestas and a shaded terrace with the same view over hills and sea as that from any bastide. Paul Lombard describes a "civilization of the cabanon, a culture of 'cabanonniers'... Marseille, the most democratic town in France, practised the cult of leisure... to do nothing is to live twice... the cabanon is alive, anchored in the soul of every Marseillais."

The ruling pastime is still the sea. The traditional fishing boats called *pointus*, being sharp fore and aft the better to slice through waves from any quarter in rough weather and carrying a triangular sail rigged with apex downward and a supposedly phallic and pagan protuberance at the bow, are growing fewer but some remain in use or have been restored and are to be seen among the 15,000 vessels—yachts, motor launches, dinghies—tied up in the Vieux Port or moored in coves and on quaysides along the Marseille shoreline. But if sailing round the calanques and islands and all the deep water sports of the Mediterranean are accessible to many, for most of the population the sea means bathing, whether from the rocks outside the Vieux Port, off the seven kilometre-long sea-wall built to shelter shipping in the docks and which, though officially closed to the public since 2001, is still easily reached by rowing-boat or canoe, from the beaches around the Corniche and at the end of the grand Avenue du Prado, or in deep water at the foot of one of the calanques. In the nineteenth century naked sea-bathing became very popular; in 1880 it was said that half the population bathed, watched by the other half.

Marseille may be unique among big Mediterranean towns in having within its limits both a long string of beaches and a National Park as the calanques have recently been constituted. The nearest beach to the Vieux Port is the Plage des Catalans where, after the plague of 1720, Catalan fishermen were permitted to instal themselves, quarantined in the town's ancient infirmaries, and until 1975 this, with the many small inlets, jetties and coves below the corniche, was the most popular access to the water. In that year, Gaston Defferre achieved his ambition of providing a "fine beach for a million Marseillais" at the outlet into the sea of the River Huveaune, by then practically an open sewer. The Huveaune was redirected to the Calanque de Cortiou where the waters are treated before entering the sea, a vast depolluting operation and cleansing system was put in place, sea-walls were built in a semicircle to protect the beaches from the effect of the mistral, the rock and earth excavated from below the centre of Marseille in the digging of the Metro was brought to gain fifty hectares at the expense of the sea, and the surface behind the ten hectares of sand put down to grass. The Plages Gaston Defferre, the great mayor's most spectacular legacy to his town and overlooked by the lifesize copy of Michelangelo's David whose nudity kept the statue for many years in store, stretch for two kilometres and have become the principal playground of Marseille at all times of the year.

The Cult of Football

Between the park of the Château Borély and the beaches is the race-course with a view over the sea, the Hippodrome de Marseille-Borély, created in 1860 and mostly devoted to flat-racing; another racecourse, said to be the most animated and holding 46 meetings a year is the Hippodrome du Pont-de-Vivaux in the eastern part of the town. And not far off on the Boulevard Michelet, a continuation of the Avenue du Prado and the Rue de Rome, is the famous Stade Vélodrome, home of Olympique de Marseille or OM, the city's football team. "What shall I say?" asks the novelist Jean-Paul Delfino, "the Vélodrome is not a stadium: it's a church, a temple, it's the cathedral of the people... it's the dressing-room of paradise." Reconstructed in 1997, the Vélodrome has seating for 60,000 and is full to overflowing at every match under its elliptical dome largely open to the sky.

Commentators and historians agree on the role played by the Vélodrome and the passion for football in the relative social cohesion of Marseille society. "Football is so important at Marseille," says the journalist Yann de l'Ecotais "that... a lecturer at the university of Aix... has published studies to show how spectators belong not only to the popular class but to all classes, and that the stadium reflects the social and geographic structure of the town. The public on the northern side is young and working-class from the northern suburbs... on the south the supporters come from the residential southern quarters, more white than blue-collared... on the east, artisans, shop-keepers, business executives... on the west, officials, members of the liberal professions, industrial and business bosses... all joined in an extraordinary fantasy of fireworks, flags, orchestras, shouting..." For others, the Vélodrome is a great racial blender; Paul Lombard claims that "the passion inspired by the OM is the reflection of the diversity that has been Marseille's originality for two thousand six hundred years. If the Stade Vélodrome can become volcanic, racism has no place there… all communities are dissolved in the two letters repeated a thousand times… OM."

Hooliganism is unknown and it is the more regrettable that the history of OM, rising and falling, has sometimes exemplified the liability to individual corruption—in 1993 OM was deprived of the title of winner of the European Champions League for this reason—of which Marseille is so often accused by media representatives eager enough to be seen and counted under the Vélodrome's elliptical dome in OM's days of glory. And of these there have been plenty; Olympique de Marseille is the oldest football club in France (1899) and has won the French championship more often than any other.

Marseille has been traditionally a city of many *cercles* or clubs, which at their best were aimed at concentrating social interests and energies; in the nineteenth century more than a hundred were counted in the city, ranging from the academies of the arts founded in the eighteenth century, meeting places of like-minded sociability, to the Cercle Artistique created under the Second Empire by the banker Jules Charles-Roux whose membership was from the financial elite, the select Cercle des Nageurs where swimmers have a privileged site near the Palais du Pharo, the Golf Club, the Tennis Club, the Automobile Club, or to a wide flowering of neighbourhood and professional groupings probably intended to get the male population of all classes out of the house on holidays. The select Cercle des Phocéens and the Petit Cercle were both in the Rue Grignan at the heart of the eighteenth- to nineteenth-century bourgeois aggrandisement of the town.

The contemporary club scene appears largely in the associations of *boulistes* and *pétanque* players which can be quite as exclusive and tenacious as any other and serve the same purpose, numbering at least a hundred. The Cercle des Boulomanes (it is claimed that *boules* were introduced to Massilia by the Romans) is the most ancient, founded in 1828 and enjoying a magnificent shaded ground on the Rue Monte-Cristo in the centre of the town, but pétanque can be played anywhere and by anyone. Each year five thousand players, men and women, gather to compete for Le Mondial, sponsored by *La Marseillaise* in the Parc Borély: "Le Mondial," wrote Michel Montana who has presided over the competition for fifty years and like others before and after strives to offer his definition of Marseille, "is very like the city that gave it birth... welcoming, noisy, highly coloured, warm, serious, enthusiastic, generous, pitiless, impassioned, extravert, immoderate, and unique."

Opera and Theatre

Not surprisingly, these qualities have been noted also in the opera house whose audience has always been a popular one. Christian Harrel-Courtès alleges that families of the upper bourgeoisie, although pleased to be noticed at classical concerts, only attended the opera house on gala occasions. With its 1,600 places, it was considered as belonging to the people—"an unruly band of hotheads whistling the tenor or the diva if they missed their note"—but the historians Contrucci and Duchêne declare on the contrary that "at the opera all social classes found themselves, if not mixed, at least joined in a shared enthusiasm. Lyrical art," they say, "is one of the pillars of popular fervour in this town." Italian opera was always more appreciated and performed than any other—*Aïda* was first presented only six years after its original production in Cairo—but the operas of Wagner were introduced to a reluctant public from 1892 onwards and sometimes performed earlier in Marseille than those of Verdi, who, however, is said to have written the parts of Iago in *Otello* and of Falstaff for the *Marseillais* baritone Victor Maurel, their first performer.

Music of all periods and kinds is omnipresent in Marseille, from the Conservatoire to the latest bar in fashion on the Cours Julien, and has always been the leading artistic expression of the town with a tradition of opera, operetta, *chanson-spectacle*, dance and music hall. The Cité de la Musique, a broad-based association of teachers and amateurs with more than two thousand students of music, brings the public a programme of over 120 concerts a year in a wide range of musical styles from classic to contemporary. The churches and theatres of the town are frequent and popular concert venues; the Dôme

Marseille's opera house, 1930s

in the Avenue Saint-Just is the emblematic centre for contemporary music, with 300,000 places taken every year, while the biggest concerts take place in the Stade Vélodrome. There are experimental, improvisation and jazz groups and a computer science music laboratory as part of the cultural policy structured by the city. Rap developed first in the Panier before proliferating: "Get it in your head once and for all that here we are Marseillais long before we're French," were the first words of the hip-hop band IAM in *Marseille contre-attaque,* proof that a familiar refrain, if it strikes a chord, can be indefinitely renewed.

After a period of dormancy, the 1980s saw a resurgence of theatre in Marseille, and there are now more than a dozen theatres active, including the famous Théâtre National de la Criée on the Vieux Port in a reconstructed and extended building previously housing the fish auction market and recently put under the direction of the Marseille-born Macha Makeïeff, a choice imposed by the Ministry of Culture against, it is claimed, declared local preferences but with an ambitious programme which will include literary works, opera, dance, cinema and music, and will aim for an international dimension; the Théâtre des Bernardines in a converted convent chapel, the centre for experimental theatre; the Théâtre du Gymnase offering classical productions, an early nineteenth-century theatre doomed to demolition but rescued and restored by an American patron in memory of his parents who had been made welcome in Marseille during their wartime flight to America; the Théâtre du Merlan, another *théâtre national,* an attempt to create theatre experience in the concrete world of northern Marseille; and many others both evanescent and established. The Ballet National de Marseille was founded in 1972 by Roland Petit who directed it until 1998, and is allied with the Ecole Nationale Supérieure de Danse in its specially designed building between the Prado and the Parc Borély.

The most famous of Marseille's many music halls was the Alcazar, opened in 1857, where stars such as Fernandel, Yves Montand, Tino Rossi and Maurice Chevalier began or pursued their careers before audiences notoriously brutal in their reaction to disappointing performances. The Alcazar finally closed in 1966, was gutted by fire though the entrance front was preserved, and now houses behind it the magnificent municipal and regional library on 18,000 square metres of a luminous modern structure which follows the original pattern of the building consisting of galleries around a deep central atrium. The Alcazar's historic rival and centre of operetta, the Théâtre des Variétés, founded in 1856 and home of the *Folies Marseillaises*, survived the music halls' decline and stayed afloat as a pornographic cinema, but since the 1990s has won new respectability with a theoretically innovative film programme.

In the industrial buildings of the former tobacco factory at Belle de Mai near the Saint-Charles railway station, dating from the 1860s when the state tobacco monopoly set up in 1674 still ran and which finally closed down in 1990, a complex of centres related to patrimony and the arts has been created: the *pôle patrimoine* containing the municipal archives and centres for conservation and restoration of communally owned works whether in museums or public buildings; the *pôle médias* with workshops and film sets for audiovisual and multimedia professionals, communications infrastructure, production offices and set designing and manufacturing studios; and the *pôle auteurs* with the Théâtre Massalia, consecrated to contemporary artistic creation, music, dance and the plastic arts, recording studios, concert and performance spaces, and residential facilities, temporary or permanent, for actors and production teams.

Like most southern French towns, Marseille has its festival, but with the difference that much of what is offered is the work of permanent or semi-permanent groups or organizations present in the city rather than from beyond, and is to that extent perhaps a more authentic and rooted product than some of the others which may, like Avignon, be better known but are essentially metropolitan in make-up. However, the Fiesta des Suds, a carnival manifestation emblematic of southern cultural diversity, calls on talent both local and from outside, while Marsatac, unsupported by municipal funds and therefore independent in both venue and content, is an annual international festival of pop, electronic and African music which at its origin was devoted to hip-hop in its early manifestation. The Festival International des Documentaires is, as the name implies, a competition open to documentary filmmakers world-wide and judged by an international jury, and the Festival Jazz des Cinq Continents is no less international. The Festival de Marseille, designed around an annually chosen theme (in 2011, Afro-American history and culture) and with the declared policy of avoiding excessive elitism, occupies sites throughout the town and often in public spaces, bars or restaurants. The Théâtre du Merlan is among the principal theatrical sites with its concentration on contemporary texts; and at Montévidéo, in the Impasse Montévidéo near the Préfecture, is an extensive layout of studios for new literary productions and studies, for music including the improvised, and art work based largely on videos and photography. Resident artists have freedom to research and to show work in progress to audiences familiar with the style and policy of the organizing associations. The Fiesta des Suds, with two thousand professionals including Massilia Sound System and four consecutive days of concerts, was described by Jean-Claude Izzo as being for music what the *Cahiers du sud* were for literature. It is held every autumn at the Dock des Suds in a street behind the docks at Arenc, known as the finest musical landing stage in the south, a medina of five thousand square metres with a hall, studios, cabarets, bars and restaurants.

Open Spaces

It may be in the conviviality and commercial atmosphere of markets that the relative secrecy of life in Marseille is most relaxed. The largest of the many Marseille markets is that held daily on the Avenue du Prado between the Place Castellane and the Boulevard Périer, for vegetables, fruit, clothing and on Fridays for plants and flowers, but there are markets in every *quartier*. The fish market on the quays of the Vieux Port where cargoes of fish are disembarked is and has always been the most inclined to encourage the famous Marseillais stridency that is superficial, deceptive but animating. The Marché des Capucins beside the Canebière is exotic, reflects the ethnic mixture of the town centre and resembles a souk. A book and antiques market is held on the Cours Julien, while the large neighbouring Place Jean-Jaurès has since 1892 accomodated the vegetable market formerly held on the Cours Julien. In the streets near the Porte d'Aix and the exit from the *autoroute* are informal markets largely patronized by North Africans, West Africans, Chinese and Comorans, many of whom live in this quarter of the town; and this mixture is even more apparent in the weekend markets at the *puces* of Arenc, in a huge assembly of stalls both outside and, since 1987, in disused Alsthom industrial hangars covering an area of four hectares and welcoming more than 100,00 buyers and sellers each week.

The historic cafés of the Canebière—the Café Turc, the Café de l'Univers, the Café Riche—and others, once thought the finest in France and the meeting place of every race and class in the world, have all vanished during the twentieth century. Their place as the social hub both for some Marseillais and all passing visitors has been taken—though with less oceanic flavour since the disappearance of the shipping that produced it—by fashionable bars and restaurants in the Cours Julien and, particularly, in the mass of such establish-ments in the pedestrian streets around the Place Thiars to the south of the Vieux Port which were once the headquarters of the galleys. But it is not to these that informed gastronomes among the popu-lation go; their standard is fair but undistinguished at prices due more to location than quality, while the most highly reputed restau-rants are generally found along the Corniche, at Malmousque or in or near the Vallon des Auffes, specializing in the multitude of fish for which the Gulf of Marseille is famous.

The gradual disappearance during the eighteenth century of the vineyards for which Marseille had been celebrated since Roman times left the hinterland between city and hills as essentially a lightly tilled, uneconomic rural pleasure ground for the owners or occupants of bastides and cabanons. This traditional "cult of the soil", seen as a prolongation of urban life and coexisting with a cult of the sea, is still evident in the popular, familiar use of the hills, the remaining open spaces between villages, such as that of the Chemin des Bellons between La Treille and Allauch made famous by Pagnol in *Le Château de ma mère,* and most of all the calanques, all within the boundaries of the widespread Marseille commune.

Moreover, Gaston Defferre instituted a policy of creation of parks and gardens; the 1980 development plan reserved ten thousand hectares of natural open space, much of it taken from the terrain of former bastides, and there are now 1,100 such areas scattered about the extent of the agglomeration. The most notable are those of the Palais Longchamp which was once the zoological garden; the comparatively little-known Jardin Valmer on the Corniche, with a panorama of sea and islands; the Parc du Pharo, largely for its view over the Vieux Port and the city; the oldest garden in the town, the Jardin Puget, a somewhat neglected and secretive belvedere at the summit of the Cours Puget above the Vieux Port; the parks of the Château Borély and la Magalone with their classic formal layouts and French and "English" gardens and the more natural and wild landscape of the Campagne Pastré at Montredon; and the Parc des Bruyères at Saint-Loup, which is one of the largest publicly owned and naturally wooded spaces of Marseille, leading to the open hills behind it and from there to the calanques themselves.

The calanques of Marseille are in the ninth *arrondissement* of the town. The banal administrative detail both conceals and underlines the topographical circumstance thanks to which a city of a million people, haphazard, piecemeal, turbulent, often aesthetically and historically careless, contains an undestroyed land and seascape of such extraordinary, universally recognized beauty that not even the Romantic poet Lamartine presumed to attempt a description of these Mediterranean fjords. The largest of the calanques, Sormiou and Morgiou, are accessible by narrow roads often closed in the summer, and at their foot are small fishing villages of cabanons. They have no fresh water source, and like the whole of the *forêt domaniale* of the calanques are subject to strict regulation covering hours and modes of access, fire precautions and conservation of the rareties of flora and fauna. When the fire risk is highest, the area is closed to the public though the number of wandering paths threading the hills makes the prohibition difficult if not impossible to enforce. Camping is forbidden at all times. The paths, or those of them not dying out unpredictably in some thicket of kermès oaks, are the best and, along most of the 28 kilometres of coastline, the only approach to the sea, to the ridges and valleys above and to the mountains behind them which can be crossed anywhere between Cap Croisette, a favourite with deep-sea divers at the extremity of the Bay of Marseille, and Cassis. But there are three main starting points, with many others less known and harder to access. The road continuing the Corniche southward around the gulf stops finally at the village of Callelongue, from where the main pathway which ends at Cassis begins, leading the walker the full length of the crests on a ten-hour foot journey; the Calanque de Sugiton, the paths to east and west, and the ascent of Mont Puget, the highest of the Marseille hills, are reached on foot from the Parc de Luminy, developed by the science and fine arts faculties and situated behind the crest; further east the cliffs favoured by rock-climbers rise more and more steeply from the track, culminating in the vertiginous Falaises de Devenson mounting from the calanque of that name while the sea, its inlets, and the small offshore islands are spread out far below; Devenson, the northern slopes and gullies of Mont Puget and the remote Calanque d'En Vau, sometimes considered the most dramatically beautiful of all, can be reached on foot from a forestry track that leaves the Marseille-Casssis road to end three kilometres nearer the coast at La Gardiole. There are three further kilometres of footpath leading to the summit of the cliffs and the sheer drop to the sea 350 metres below. In good weather the calanques are never deserted but the long walk to the sea and the steep climb back keep the rocks and small shingle beaches uncrowded, while the great space of hills, valleys and crests, though not lonely, survives as an emblem, fiercely defended by the Marseillais of today, of the idyllic, unpeopled land discovered by the Phocaean adventurers 2,600 years ago.

... and culture of markets

8 | Changing Faces
Immigration, Race, and Faith

All French people are the children of immigrants.

Fernand Braudel

The distinction between migrant and refugee is a fine one; in either case, hope for a better life has brought a constant stream, sometimes a tide, of populations in movement to Marseille at least since the decline of the Roman Empire. Paul Lombard asks, "How could Massalia, a city of exile, not always give welcome to the uprooted, the displaced?"; and in reference to the intellectual flowering that coincided with the dismemberment of the Roman Empire in Gaul, Jean Guyon points out in *Marseille antique* that Marseille was then a safe haven for intellectuals as it would be again in the early part of the Second World War until the Nazi invasion of the Free Zone in 1942. Such migrants were mostly, in material terms, among the world's fortunate and for them the haven could be transitory; but over the centuries much of the human tide has come from perturbed Mediterranean lands and Marseille was the destination where their children would become *Marseillais*, part of a breed whose polymorphous (and sometimes polychrome) variety has often been the cause of its rejection by Frenchmen ignorant of Fernand Braudel's aphorism.

Despite occasional outbreaks of unreason, rejection by the Marseillais themselves of the incoming element has not generally been a character of the mutations of the city. Although the law did not admit Jews until the end of the eighteenth century, hundreds if not thousands were already long established and living on terms of tacit, relative tolerance; while many of the "merchant aristocracy", which if it did not govern the town still ruled its fate between the seventeenth and twentieth centuries, were of foreign origin and often not naturalized. The cosmopolitanism of Marseille has always to a varying degree been accepted and always renewed; it is as inherent as the sea water of the Vieux Port.

Before the Big Battalions

In the foreground of Claude-Joseph Vernet's painting in the Louvre, *L'Entrée du port de Marseille*, is a group of Ottoman merchants on business by the quayside. Braudel alleges their presence in numbers from the sixteenth century. Commerce with the *Echelles* of the Levant had been continuous and growing since the twelfth century; an edict of 1669 established Marseille as a free port enjoying a monopoly of French trade with the Echelles and accorded Levantine merchants in Marseille the same privileges as the Marseillais. The human traffic along the resulting network of trade routes contributed to a fifty per cent increase of population of the town in the course of the eighteenth century, a growth far more rapid than before. Until the seventeenth century the numbers, varying with conditions of peace or war, prosperity or want, health or plague, are estimated at a maximum of 20,000; in 1650 the estimate is 50,000, by 1831, 132,000. Other contributing sources of population growth, particularly after the great loss of life in the plague of 1720, were the Alpine valleys of Provence and further north, the Piedmont, Genoa and of permanent significance, Corsica. These migrations were largely of workmen and their families—masons, farm labourers, dockers and seamen—drawn in by the growing prosperity and physical expansion of the town. Fernand Braudel's assertion that the most typical immigrant to Marseille was Corsican, and that the town in the sixteenth century was "almost half Corsican" must be weighed with the estimate of other historians that Genoese and Piedmontese then made up the principal foreign minority in the city, and the fact that their regular if fluctuating arrival would continue for several hundred years.

Although open both to the Mediterranean world and to the mainland, Marseille, ostensibly if not in practice, was hostile to the religions of minorities. The most striking instance was the refusal to implement the Edict of Nantes of 1598, which by granting freedom of worship to the Huguenots placed France, for a time, among the most religiously tolerant of European countries. In 1562 the Huguenot community of Marseille was officially though probably not effectively expelled, in 1585 the consuls ruled that no one who was not of the "Catholic, apostolic and Roman" religion could take any office in the city, and this ban continued until the revolution.

A similar attitude of contrasting principle and practice was taken towards Jews after their expulsion from Spain in 1492; a series of interdictions coexisted with the continuing presence, illegal and precarious, of a considerable unbaptized population which increased after 1670 with the arrival of Jewish merchants from Italy. Commercial jealousy led to new orders of expulsion between 1682 and 1703 but these too were no more than sporadically enforced. The Armenian merchant community dealing in the silk trade from Smyrna was preferentially treated by the central power from the sixteenth century; but Marseillais antagonism, due more to commercial rivalry than to any religious objection, and to the well-founded suspicion that much of the resulting wealth was taken away from Marseille where it had been created, led to the temporary disappearance of the Armenian colony by 1658. It was renewed after the edict of 1669, became permanent, and the massive arrival of Armenians in the early twentieth century was to be one of the most significant immigrant phenomena in the history of the city.

It is believed that at the end of the eighteenth century five per cent of the 100,000 people of the town were *étrangers*, of whom the majority were Italian and much of the remainder Jewish, particularly from North Africa. Of the leading merchant class, estimated at 750 of whom over 400 were foreign to the city, 25 per cent were Swiss and 15 per cent German, often owing their integration in Marseille society either to marriage into one of the long-established Protestant families whose wealth had accumulated discreetly, as it did in Nîmes, during the years of public interdiction and tacit acceptance, or to Masonic associations. This class, whose power and influence in the reign of Louis XIV and under the rule of Colbert had replaced that of the old Marseille aristocracy, was notably cosmopolitan in origin, including Greeks and Levantines as well as Scandinavians and, at least until the Napoleonic wars, some English, and this fact is an indication of the practical religious tolerance which continued to operate in Marseille despite the revocation of the Edict of Nantes in 1685, the frequent, virulent anti-Huguenot exhortations from the pulpit, the theoretical Jewish exclusion and the ban on religious observance in the town other than Catholic. A document of 1771 proclaims that "It is only too true that the diverse nations attracted to Marseille for commercial reasons have introduced a mixture of religions which can degenerate into tolerationism. The Jews, present in large numbers, have their synagogues; the Protestants, even more numerous, their temples..."

By 1791 the Jews had achieved official recognition and their integration is thought to have been more rapid in Marseille, with its constant power of absorption and fusion, than in any other French city, although even after the decrees of 1808, which fixed the status of French Jews, discriminatory regulations continued. And beside the revolutionary proclamations of equality and tolerance there appeared texts denouncing foreign participation in counter-revolutionary violence—"the criminal scum issuing from the prisons of Genoa, of Sicily, of all Italy, of Spain, of Barbary..."—while in practice peaceful coexistence continued as before in quarters of the town where the population was mixed. The ambiguities are underlined by the fact that from 1792 the state subsidized the Protestant cult equally with the Catholic.

The revolutionary and Napoleonic wars were the occasion of new population movements, largely but not solely in the Mediterranean, many of which passed through or settled in Marseille. From 1791 the French colonists of Saint-Domingue were driven out, either by the English or by slave revolts, and their return continued until 1796; in 1794 the English took control of Corsica, and in 1800 of Malta, and the republicans of these islands departed to exile on the mainland; in 1801 the evacuation by the French armies of Egypt following Nelson's victory at the Battle of the Nile and the return of Turkish domination brought to Marseille a flood of refugee soldiers of many nationalities—Greek, Syrian, Albanian and Copt—who had collaborated with the French as auxiliaries in the Greek and Copt Legions and became known as the Mamelukes, though there were few Muslims among them. Some of these, skilled horsemen but unruly, "not used to the discipline of European armies and speaking only Arabic", were enrolled in a battalion of Chasseurs d'Orient and sent to fight with the Napoleonic armies; others, with their families, lived in huts on the outskirts of the town and were increasingly unwelcome as their numbers grew. "Please consider," wrote the mayor in 1806, "that Marseille, already full of Mamelukes, Jewish refugees from Algiers, and Egyptian negresses [a euphemism for former slaves fallen into prostitution] watches with alarm as these foreigners arrive in ever larger numbers." The situation was unchanged in 1815, and during the Hundred Days the Mamelukes became more visible and were suspected of preparing a jubilant welcome for the returning Emperor in a city with no love for him. After Waterloo a crowd of townspeople descended on the "Egyptian" quarter and a massacre followed, the principal victims being the prostitutes who were herded into the sea and fired on from the shore. Of the survivors, some found refuge elsewhere in Provence, many were arrested and deported and others melted into Marseille to leave descendants who remain a component of the population.

Although xenophobia, which has appeared sporadically in Marseille as elsewhere in France, was certainly an element in the massacre of the Mamelukes, it has been pointed out that the victims were semi-destitute in a time when the impact of war on trade had impoverished the town and that refugees of means, including many who came to Marseille at the same time and aboard the same ships (in particular the English frigate *Pallas*), were in general tolerated if not warmly accepted in the first generation of their presence. By the second, following a process repeated again and again and which not only the custom of society but even the geography of bay and gulf seemed to impose, they were swallowed, digested and had become Marseillais themselves. The same process led to the social integration of families of the Greek merchants and Jewish intermediaries in trade between France and the Ottoman Empire, come to fill the gap left during the wars by departing English, Dutch and Swiss business houses, and who ensured the survival of sea traffic through Marseille even if the growing English naval command of the Mediterranean might send some of it to the bottom.

Although the religious practices of these minorities continued to arouse opposition in the closed Catholic community in the early nineteenth century, a sign of openness to come was the renewed influence of Freemasonry recruited among the "oriental" groups—Jewish, Greek, Levantine, Egyptian, Syrian—which brought them into closer contact with Swiss and German Protestants, Italian musicians and painters and the indigenous and prosperous Protestant minority whose Masonic connection dated from the eighteenth century. By 1822 and the Turkish massacres on the island of Chios in which 25,000 people died and 50,000 were enslaved, the Greek mercantile community of Marseille, like the Jewish, was sufficiently prosperous and established to receive those Greek refugees from Chios who were lucky enough to escape. The growth in the population by 30,000 to 40,000 between 1812 and 1830, clearly not accounted for by any natural increase, was dominantly Italian, largely from Piedmont and Genoa, and included some, such as the Borelli family (not to be confused with the Borély installed since the sixteenth century and ennobled in the eighteenth), who by gradual enrichment and social promotion were to join the prominent Marseille bourgeoisie. From 1806 to 1879 the excess of births over deaths was 11,285 while the population increased by 219,500; two thirds of the population was therefore in the end not native.

It is a truism that the first step towards recognition of religious minorities is the granting of cemeteries well in advance of permission to build places of worship; in Marseille the process began, for Protestants and Jews, before the revolution which in principle gave equal rights to every cult. In 1804 the Jewish cemetery was enlarged, followed in 1806 by the Protestant. In 1820 the Protestant community acquired a site in the Rue Grignan and began the construction of the magnificent *temple*, the first non-Catholic edifice in the city, with financial help from both state and town, which was inaugurated in 1825. Adjoining it was a building rented by the Jewish Consistory as school, assembly hall and place of worship which remained in use until the Second Empire when the Grande Synagogue of the Rue Breteuil was built. In 1821 the oldest Orthodox or Melchite church in Western Europe was constructed in the Rue Edmond-Rostand and remains as the most striking evidence of Marseille's Levantine past. Despite occasionally virulent opposition, both Jewish and Protestant minorities were allowed to live and sometimes prosper in semi-legality in Marseille during the centuries in which French unity was created and enforced through submission to the monarchy and above all to the Catholic Church. Tolerated minorities left their mark on the life of the town not least through the process of familial integration by intermarriage. An Armenian printing works was active in Marseille in the seventeenth century; the conviviality of café life introduced from the orient appeared earlier here than anywhere else; Tuscan potters and porcelain makers, Italian lutenists, Carrara marble craftsmen were part of the diversity and constant renewal of the migratory flux which made Marseille an exemplary city in its own way, giving more rapid acceptance to the less advantaged minorities than in any other part of France.

Italian Invasion

The 1830 population of 130,000 grew to 600,000 on the eve of the 1914 war; this fivefold increase went with a tenfold increase in the numbers of foreigners, from 10,000 to 110,000 without including those whom the law of 1889 automatically naturalized as born in France. It is thought that if all were counted at least a quarter of the population of Marseille was comprised of *étrangers,* spread around the former villages and in the territory of bastides, or accumulating in the Panier and in streets of the quartier of Belsunce abandoned by the retreating bourgeoisie to leave a zone which became progressively proletarianized and condemned as a ghetto for an as yet unassimilated immigrant mass, the bulk of which was Italian.

The expansion and growth of wealth of nineteenth-century century Marseille was to a notable extent built on imported cheap labour in which Spanish, Greeks, Syrians and Lebanese contributed, with the Italians, to make Marseille a mirror of the Mediterranean world; and which created, in the economy of the enterprises employing it, a dependence considered by some commentators as having impeded modernization. "Marseille," wrote Hippolyte Taine, "is a potent sucker which draws in life and spreads it about... like a Liverpool of the Midi." Migration is said to nourish migration—in the 1880s regular convoys set out from Constantinople, Beirut and Alexandria—and by the end of the century what were once minorities, and were often still without fixed abode or settled work, had become a permanent part of the population as a whole.

Census figures show the numbers of Italians keeping pace with the accelerating growth of immigration: the 16,000 of 1851 represented 86 per cent of the foreign population; in 1881, 57,000 made up 87 per cent; in 1901 they were 90,000 for 91 per cent, constituting more than 18 per cent of the population as a whole. These workers were largely concentrated in the northern part of the spreading town or in the vicinity of Lacydon. The relatively better off foreigners, whether Protestant, Jewish or Greek, were found south of the Vieux Port. In 1863 almost half the 500 Greek houses of business in Western Europe were in Marseille, while English, Swiss and German merchants and industrialists continually increased in number and influence through the century.

The most notable of the English colony, whose children would become naturalized French, was the engineer Philip Taylor, born in Norwich in 1786. Taylor founded a steamship building company in his name which acquired the naval shipyards at La Seyne, by 1853 employed 1,500 men and by the end of the decade 2,500 including English and German mechanics. The later history of the company in which it was taken over by the Parisian group of the Messageries Impériales is seen as illustrating the growing influence of Paris in Marseillais enterprise and on the direction it was to take. The ancient Swiss community, chiefly Protestant and self-renewing from the Alpine valleys, can be traced to the sixteenth century; as well as merchant families rising steadily in the social hierarchy there were artisans and tradespeople and, in the second half of the nineteenth century, an army of domestic servants in hotels and private houses. The Cercle Helvétique was an elite business club whose president was usually the Swiss consul, and marriages between members of the Swiss community, many of whose antecedents included Huguenot refugees from the Languedoc, and members of the French Protestant families of Marseille, were frequent.

These presences, however, were nothing to the tidal wave of Italians which in a few years altered the demography and image of Marseille by introducing a Mediterranean underclass without money or skills. By the end of the century the Neapolitans, mostly illiterate, penniless and concentrated near the Vieux Port, had taken the place of the Piedmontese on the scale of contempt in which Italian immigrants of the first generation were often held. In 1896 Italians made up 23 per cent of the population in the densely overcrowded streets of the Panier, did the most unhealthy and arduous of the factory work and were regularly relied on by employers as strike-breakers. Many women were in domestic service or, particularly, employed as children's nurses. Perhaps because of the harsh conditions of life they had left behind, Italians of the second and later generations were more completely integrated into the Marseille population than, for example, the Swiss who maintained a connection with their towns and villages.

A few among the Italians rose in the social scale; in 1891 Georges Borelli of the third generation of a family arrived in 1816 became vice-president of the chamber of commerce and founder of the Banque Populaire, and the painter Monticelli who accompanied Cézanne on his walks in the hills above l'Estaque was also third generation. But successful or not, almost all Italians were famous for frugality: "The whole life of the Italian worker," wrote Pierre Milza in *Français et italiens*, "is dominated by the concern for saving"; and the hardness of existence perhaps accounted for a contemporary report that "there were many more drunkards among the immigrants than the French". The process of migration and industrial employment of a previously peasant population would seem to have led to a degree of secularization; the Italian presence was dominant in anarchist groups and free-thinking associations and was said to have been notably missing in religious ceremonies. However, toward the end of the century religious charitable institutions appeared, aimed at protecting women and young girls from the demand for prostitution which for the most defenceless was often the only resource.

At the end of the nineteenth century a permanent, massive immigrant population grew simultaneously with the potentially violent xenophobia of which Marseille was far from having a monopoly, although the size of the Italian colony made it a manifest example. The presence of anarchist groups and political refugees from both Spain and Italy created an image of foreign terrorists in a period of rising nationalism which in France was especially strong after the defeat of 1870, and at the same time elements of the Parisian press promoted a notion of the "fundamental inferiority [due to economic backwardness] of the men of the Midi" against which the Marseillais might react by turning on minority groups seen as "foreign" and too conspicuous. In 1886 the bilingual journal *L'International anarchiste* was published in Marseille, and in 1890 an Italian language publication, *L'Anarchia*, while Italian socialism was propagated by the journalist Luigi Campolonghi in his newsletter *L'Emigrato socialista*. The aim of the young socialists was to foster approaches between Italian and French workers—"Never use a knife… if you have an enemy, embrace him… don't heed the voice of false patriotism…"— in order to counter the xenophobic current. A letter of the *préfet* of the Bouches-du-Rhône in 1881 spoke of the "treacherous knife of the Italian", used not only for cutting bread but for defence and attack, and put into play alternately with the accordion.

Accusations of criminality against the Italians seem to have little foundation, even if there was already a form of Neapolitan *camorra* living from the profits of prostitution and gaming; it has been shown that delinquency was mostly minor and the belief that any crime involving bloodshed must involve Italians was false. Nevertheless, the belief took hold and joined with that which imputed drunkenness, lack of hygiene, contamination and cholera outbreaks to the inhabitants of the poor and immigrant quarters of the town, "the great turbulent crowd of the Italian invasion", or the "swarm of locusts". The xenophobic periodicals of the time such as *La Patrie* also showed the clearest anti-Semitism, evidence of the ultra-nationalist racism that reached its height in the Dreyfus case and its expression in the

Ligue des Patriotes supported by the Catholic bourgeoisie. At the same time and despite the tradition of Marseille for relative religious tolerance, the local edition of the Catholic periodical *La Croix*, founded in 1880, could denounce the "enemy to attack" as the Freemasons, the Protestants and "cosmopolitan foreigners" in general; and even the respected writer Horace Bertin in *Les Marseillais, moeurs et paysages* accused the Italians of remaining "foreigners in the country that made them welcome".

The episode known as the "Marseille Vespers" had both industrial and nationalist contexts in the aftermath of the war of 1870 and the consequent fall in employment. The Italians were charged with taking work by accepting lower wages, with strike-breaking and with not having paid the "tax of blood" by evading conscription in the war. The occasion of the outbreak in June 1881 was political. French intervention had won for France a dominant position in Tunisia and tension followed between French and Italian governments. The return of troops from Tunisia to Marseille was enthusiastically greeted by the population with the exception of some in the Italian national club on the Vieux Port, from whose open windows a sound of derisive whistles was thought to have been heard. Thousands of angry Marseillais gathered and the préfet ordered the club to close; for four days Italians were systematically attacked in the street, a large number wounded and three killed. *Le Gaulois* demanded the suppression of the Italian colony of Marseille while in the *Gazetta di Torino* the writer and parliamentarian Petrucelli della Gattina claimed that "the moral capital of the Latin race is Rome and we, not the Gaulois, are its true representatives". If the Marseille Vespers seem comparatively mild in the scale of riots, they offered an argument to the adversaries of France in Italy and to the partisans of a closer association with Germany; although with no relation of cause and effect, a few months later the treaty creating the Triple Alliance between Germany, Austria-Hungary and Italy was signed.

The blame for the massacre of Aigues-Mortes in 1893 in which eight Italians were killed and at least fifty wounded, and for other violent manifestations in southern towns, was more realistically attributed by socialists to employers like those in Marseille who "speculate on the hunger of foreign workers to increase their profits, and make use of them... to starve French workers and break strikes". Nevertheless, in the port strike of 1883 it was said that solidarity (possibly out of fear of reprisals) between immigrant and indigenous workers was complete, and by 1900 the Italian colony was seen to be dissolving by degrees into the melting pot of Marseille: the Italian consul Rossi reported that "little by little they lose interest in anything to do with their home country... and undergo an insistent pressure from the local authority... the family, the school... to change nationality."

In the early years of the twentieth century a change in population movements appeared. Between 1910 and 1913 the foreign population grew from 104,000 to 122,000, still predominantly Italian. But Corsican migration was increasing; that from Algeria and Tunisia was accompanied by arrivals from the Ottoman Empire, referred to as "Turks" whether Muslim, Armenian or Jewish; and the numbers of Spanish grew from 2,500 in 1910 to 6,000 in 1913, a rate of increase far higher than in any other group including the Italian. The image of the Italian worker as blackleg was being lost as industrial solidarity grew and more Italians, or those of Italian stock, became involved in social action to the point of being considered less as the breakers than the instigators of strikes. From that point the natural reaction of the employers was to bring in a more docile workforce, whether from Spain as had long happened in the agricultural Languedoc, or from North Africa. In 1909 the *Domenica Italiana* denounced the "shameful operation mounted by the syndicate of Marseille bosses" to break a strike by importing untrained Algerians at derisory wages; in 1912 brawls occurred between Italians and Algerians.

The entry of Italy into the war in 1915 and the subsequent mobilization of a proportion of the Italian as well as the French workforce created a labour shortage which was met in part by refugees among whom Serbs were at first preponderant. Prisoners of war also were put to work and many employed in the shipping tunnel under l'Estaque. For the rest, new foreign workers were largely Greek, Spanish, and others repatriated from the eastern Mediterranean.

When the Spanish began to strike more men were imported from North Africa, particularly Algeria, to form an "army of reserves" for breaking strikes, and they tended to live far more separated from the Marseillais than European immigrants had ever done. Between 1915 and 1918 at least 130,000 North African workers arrived in Marseille, and if after the war some went home, many remained and others are believed to have returned to make up an important part of the immigrant population. Loss of life in the war, a falling birth rate, the Russian Revolution and upheaval in the structure of the Ottoman Empire brought in new migratory waves: "The Russians brought... their iconoclastic fury, the intrepidity of their ignorance and their heroic thirst for martyrdom..." The foreigner was seen not only as of "another nature" but after 1917 as the enemy of society, and to the extent that migrants, underpaid and under-qualified, a menace to employment in times of crisis and a supposed source of delinquency and subversion were progressively integrated into the population, Marseille came to accept and even assume the noxious image of itself reflected back from the exaggerations of the national press.

Inter War

The significant characteristics of this period were the increase of arrivals from Corsica following a fall in agricultural income in the island, and of refugees after the disintegration of the former Ottoman Empire, neither migration being in response to a demand for labour. The Corsicans, French citizens and therefore less easily distinguished by census, tended to bring with them the social structure of their origins and to recreate in Marseille and impose around them a semblance of familiar conditions, relationships and customs including those which by the start of the Second World War contributed heavily to the reputation of parts of Marseille such as the Panier as lawless enclaves. The refugees, of whom the majority were Armenian following genocidal massacres in Turkey, represented an unforeseen and sudden migration of poverty and distress creating problems slow to resolve. The illusion of prosperity given by an active port in an age of exultant imperial expansion and worldwide shipping—the *mirage colonial*—was contrasted with the close vicinity of stinking alleys, wretched yards in which "a people from everywhere and nowhere" foundered, existing in wooden huts without amenity, "vandals and communists", according to André Suarès in the hyperbolic pages of *Marsiho*. The foreign population in 1931 is estimated at 150,000, nearly 25 per cent of the total of 793,248. Of these, 128,000 were Italian and 20,000 Armenian. With Russian émigrés after the revolution and the return of Greeks, Turks and a number of British, the cosmopolitanism of Marseille was even more marked than before the First World War. But the growth of immigrant poverty in a city where neither employment nor housing could keep pace with new arrivals led to a decline in social conditions, and in the image of the town.

The growth of the Armenian community of Marseille followed the genocide in which two million Armenians were deported to the deserts of Syria and Mesopotamia from all parts of Turkey except the capital; of this number it is estimated that a tenth survived. The defeat of the Greek army by the Turkish in 1922 forced the majority of these into definitive exile and more than 100,000 entered France through Marseille between 1922 and 1928. The honour, dignity and industriousness of these refugees have come to be generally recognized but first reactions against their arrival were sometimes extreme: the mayor Siméon Flaissières wrote of their "resigned indolence" and described them as "passive, ancestral". The Camp Oddo through which many of them passed, situated north of the docks in the district of La Cabucelle and formerly used by the army, was designed to accommodate temporarily a few hundred men. More than 3,000 Armenians, including many children left orphaned by the massacres, were permanently installed; the men were reproached with refusing casual work in the distant countryside because these people in distress feared isolation. By 1927 when the camp was finally closed it was said that "these foreigners decidedly have succeeded in transforming a few skeletal huts into a true Asia Minor village", and the head of the Red Cross, protesting against the closure, wrote "We will embitter these refugees who were grateful and ready to give themselves to us; it is not the best way to assimilate them."

By 1935 approximately 5,000 Greeks remained in Marseille and 30,000 Armenians, many of them settling together in villages such as Beaumont, Saint-Jérôme or Saint-Antoine, others in streets near the Porte d'Aix, and achieving integration more rapidly than Spanish or Italian migrants since for the Armenians there was no hope of return to a land of origin, however mythical. This particularity applied equally to the number of Italian refugees from the fascist regime arriving between 1927 and 1930 and for whom exile became permanent. The singer and actor Yves Montand, who as Ivo Livi, of Italian descent, grew up in Marseille among Armenian children, learned to speak their language and kept his Armenian friends all his life. The marked cosmopolitanism of Marseille in the years to 1939 and the presence of refugee groups and populations of the forcibly displaced linked the idea of the city in the collective imagination to fears and fantasies of insecurity and terrorism, greatly increased by the assassination on the Canebière in 1934 of Alexander of Yugoslavia (see p.21) and, as often before, of contagion: foreigners, said Suarès, "will end by building a hospital for the scabies-infected proletariat of all nations on the ruins of the Château Borély". Yet scrutiny of population figures in 1936 for the most ancient part of the town, the Panier, with its dark and unhealthy streets of neglected houses, shows that eighty per cent were French and the rest largely Italian with a Corsican minority and a scattering of other nationalities. The Armenians were by now for the most part established in peripheral villages and many of the integrated Italian families in the quarter of Endoume whose streets, lanes and staircases wind down almost to sea-level on the Corniche. During the Second World War many Armenians worked in the Resistance although their historian Stephan Boghossian does not exclude the possibility of a small number of informers among them. One, a café owner, was summarily tried at the Liberation and executed.

Associations of mutual aid among immigrants existed in Marseille from the eighteenth century, with Genoese and Catalans congregating near the port and points of maritime employment. Later, religious solidarity helped keep together Sephardic Jews, and

Greek Orthodox communities. Church attendance was often more interested than devoted: "They are Christians for practical reasons," said one writer of the Armenians, "even if non-practising", and this is thought to be true of other groups. Religious feasts celebrated in the Eglise de Saint-Laurent by Neapolitans or Corsicans went with more mundane, and lengthier festivities organized by associations; Muslims gathered to celebrate the Feast of Sacrifice in rituals of solidarity attended by the poorest. The Armenian benevolent associations, the three Armenian churches, evangelical, Catholic and Apostolic, occupied the same building as the central council of the Armenian communities whose aims were political. The most numerous of the friendly associations were the Corsican, prone to clan rivalries and apt for the creation of networks of clients, informers and enforcers. Political *clientélisme*, the system of votes for services including financial, came to a head after 1929 and the election of Simon Sabiani as strong man of the municipal council, and led to a state of affairs by the start of the Second World War in which protection of the interests of the client immigrant group was not distinguishable from a sort of gangsterism culminating, after 1942, in an alliance between gang leaders and Gestapo.

Work in the port attracted immigrants of every nationality; at the time of the effective cessation of activity in 1942, less than half the 5,000 workers were French. "The entire Mediterranean can be found on the quays of Marseille, a Babel whose populace often has great difficulty in making itself understood or getting intelligible words from the next man (Témime)." Marseille's industry was very largely manned by Italians; 75 per cent of the labour force in 1925 was foreign, with Armenians, who were considered good workers, overtaking the Italians and the number of North Africans increasing in the context of unqualified, unreliable and sometimes occasional work which disappeared in times of financial crisis. The relatively low unemployment figures for Marseille in 1933 are taken as signifying only that many immigrants had been repatriated, or found the means to repatriate themselves. This, however, was not an escape available to the Armenians from whom appeals for help were increasingly heard until 1939 when mobilization began, bringing a solution to unemployment as it did for those North Africans present in Marseille—4,000 out of 15,000—who were without means of support.

The German occupation brought fugitives in large numbers— "hundreds of thousands" according to the novelist Roland Dorgelès though the figure is contested—in search of escape through the port. "A large part of France fell back on the Vieux-Port of the Phocaeans," wrote the resistant Henri Frenay. The entry of Italy into the war on the side of Germany created at first a problem for the Italian colony of Marseille, whose men were called on to declare loyalty to France and in the great majority did so. Fugitive German Jews, at first interned, were authorized to leave by sea from 1939. The exodus continued, with the Vichy government encouraging the repatriation of Italians, Spaniards and North Africans, until the occupation of the Free Zone in 1942 when the recorded numbers of foreigners in Marseille fell drastically. Yet of the 18,000 Jews believed to have been resident in July 1942 not more than 1,500 were known to have been deported, suggesting widespread support among Marseillais shocked by the arrests. Nevertheless, for many fugitives still left in Marseille after November 1942 when the activity of the port ceased, the refuge became a trap which shut with the explosion of the Panier in January 1943 (see p.21) draining the town of part of its population. "Marseille is a lair of international bandits," declared the German General Oberg, "it is the canker of Europe and Europe cannot live until Marseille is purified."

The Resistance found support in the Armenian community and among Spanish, Polish, Greek and other Balkan migrants, and at the end of the war many of the militant opponents of fascism returned home. This movement, however, seems not enough to account for the fall in the immigrant population to 53,000 in 1946, less than half the figure for Italians alone in 1926, the proportion of foreigners falling in the same period from almost 25 to 8 per cent of the total; the decline of the port economy and industry and in the flux of migrants to and from the European former colonial empires in the immediate aftermath of the war are put forward as explanations.

Decolonization

> "Marseille is a happy city through which a lot of unhappy people pass."
>
> Albert Londres

Between 1954 and 1975 new movements caused the population to grow from 650,000 to 950,000. The great semi-rural spaces surrounding the villages that formed the *couronne des saints* and made Marseille unique among French urban areas, shrank or were submerged under a flood of concrete to house the hundreds of thousands out of more than two million repatriated French colonials, principally from Algeria, who passed through Marseille. "Let them go and readapt elsewhere," said Gaston Defferre in 1962, but enough remained, most of them fiercely attached to the ideal of "l'Algérie française", to alter the appearance and social climate of the town and the structure of its population more, and more lastingly, than any previous migratory movement. At the same time, growing industrial production and the surge in housing construction after 1954 attracted a new wave of unqualified workers, largely North African, into an ageing population, a considerable part of which had departed in haste and in danger from the very countries these new immigrants belonged to by birth. In 1954 the number of Algerians was officially put at 210,000, mostly working in the building trade, and this was probably an underestimate since in each year between 1950 and 1956, 200,000 Algerian Muslims are known to have passed through the port or airport of Marseille. Following the end of the Algerian war and the despair of French Algerians, the exodus and the arrivals in Marseille reached levels never seen before; on 25 June 1962, 10,437 passengers disembarked, both French and Algerian *harkis*, men who had served in the French army and faced persecution if they remained in Algeria, while the average daily figure of disembarkations for the month was 3,500.

The resulting tensions, almost wholly non-violent, are accepted as still partially unresolved, and the necessary adjustments of mentality continuing. Apart from the Red Cross, many religious organizations—the Secours Protestant, the Jewish Fonds Social, the Salvation Army, the Secours Catholique—joined with the authorities in attempting to meet the crisis in a town where reconstruction since 1957 had been to remedy neglect rather than accommodate immigrants, and many Marseillais on public housing waiting lists found their places taken by strangers from the other shore of the Mediterranean. The naturally "happy city" has needed time to temper the unhappiness of this huge post-colonial movement of people. The years of growing prosperity in the French economy after 1961 attracted once again a low-qualified immigrant workforce, mostly from North African countries, especially Algeria, but also in increasing numbers from parts of black Africa; in Marseille this population was largely concentrated in the centre and nourished the fantasy of a city "delivered to Maghrebian migration". A comparatively rare outbreak of violence occurred in 1973 after the murder of a bus driver by a mentally disturbed Algerian; "We have had enough," wrote an editorialist, "of this uncontrolled immigration bringing into our country all the rabble from beyond the Mediterranean," and while racial disturbances were also widespread in other French cities, over the next two years in Marseille at least thirteen immigrant workmen were killed in incidents which went unresolved and unpunished.

In the early 1950s no quarter of Marseille was without a *bidonville*, a shanty town whether on an abandoned site or in ruined buildings, some of which had been in existence since before the war, inhabited by Arabs, gipsies, Armenians and without running water or sewerage. The slow process of destruction of the bidonvilles and demolition of some streets in the centre such as the Rue des Chapeliers, symbolic of all the poverty-stricken immigrant settlements, swelled, with the flow of repatriated colonists, the current of population movement outward from the centre toward the ever-expanding periphery and beyond it. Some streets near the Gare Saint-Charles and the Porte d'Aix still testify, with their population of variously immigrant origins and obviously low income, to the flux of the period of decolonization and afterwards; but the new urban landscape, improvised and incomplete, remodelling and often effacing the nineteenth-century town, is evidence of the city's attempt to solve the problem imposed on it by history and to reclassify in coexistence the various components of the population. The jurist Paul Lombard claims that France, blaming itself for its own immigration policy, attempted to set up Marseille—the city that had most resisted the national Jacobinism—as a scarecrow in ethnic matters. But in vain; Marseille, once again defying stereotypes, saw nothing of the racial community riots of 2005 which inflamed the suburbs of many French towns. Xenophobic declarations in the press accusing "Arabs" of delinquency and infection and the rise of irrational Front National rhetoric are considered as minority manifestations in a town with centuries of experience of the immigrant presence and reliance on it for the manifold enrichment it has often brought.

Co-existence

The Stade Vélodrome, as Paul Lombard has said, is perhaps the principal meeting place of the races as it is of classes. Olivier Boura claims that at Marseille football has something of the character of a religion, "if behind that word one can see both the fervour of belief and the rejection of those who don't share it". He could have added idol worship, in the form of the adulation of the Marseille-born international player Zinédine Zidane. Boura was a teacher in the northern *quartiers*: "My pupils were not rich… their childhood was not pretty to see… Some were Arabs, others not. There was much separating them… But on match days they arrived, Christians, Muslims… with their scarves and T-shirts in the colours of the town… and at that moment something, at least, united them."

No one denies the existence of discrimination or the cruelty of impoverishment. The Franco-Algerian documentary film-maker Bania Medjibar has, among others, analyzed the social aspects of a segregation which circumstances impose even where policy is designed against it: "The danger is more a social segregation than an ethnic one… But if a young graduate gives his address to a possible employer and lives in one of the *cités* of the northern part of the town, he isn't taken on. If he looks for an apartment and has a name like mine, he doesn't get it. There are codes. It's a reality… in which it is easy to turn out badly." Yet after trying out Paris with its stress and condescension towards the provinces she says "I understood how much I love Marseille, I'm passionate about it." And she describes that other meeting place of the races, the flea market as "the belly of popular Marseille where all the communities are side by side... a gigantic Sunday bazaar, colourful and noisy".

Even as an unyieldingly Catholic city, Marseille was always an arena of different religions with tolerated communities of heretics and Jews; since the end of the nineteenth century new religious allegiances have been introduced, but paradoxically the identification of minority religious practices with foreign minorities is less marked than elsewhere. The Greek Orthodox continue to maintain their church but the most prominent of them have been French and Marseillais for generations; the North African Jews and those of the Levant were easily absorbed into the old Jewish presence; the Protestants are distinguishable if at all only by political sobriety and the financial rectitude they are believed to stand for; Islam is essentially represented by North Africans of French nationality. In fact, religious practice is in decline, has been so since the middle of the nineteenth century, and no estimate is possible of, for example, the proportion among the recognized Jewish population of practising or even believing Jews in relation to the whole. The total congregation of the numerous synagogues at the feast of Yom Kippur is calculated at 25,000 out of a Jewish population far higher, and at other times the congregation is much more modest. And the designation of Muslim, in a city of such heterogeneous origins as Marseille, is at least as ambiguous as that of Jew. Nonetheless, religious influence, and especially the tradition of religious tolerance, are taken as contributing to the relatively peaceful coexistence of a great diversity of social, economic and national components in a town where the rest of France expects to see violent disorder.

The presence in the forefront at the funeral of Gaston Defferre of the heads of all the religious communities, side by side and standing before the massed congregations they led, symbolized this coexistence and, many believe, reinforced it with the stamp of a memorable image.

Shipping, as on Tyneside, was one of the main interests of the Marseille industrial dynasties

9 | **Dynasties**
Industry, Finance and Wealth

> Constrained by the meagreness of their territory to exploit the sea
> rather than the land, the Phocaeans sought their means of existence
> in commerce and piracy... as was usual.
>
> Marcus Justinus

Justin's remark was made in the second or third century AD. By the sixteenth century the Marseille nobility was largely composed of enriched families that had long ago risen into it from below, and until 1660 these families continued to rule the town as consuls, through their ramifications in the Church or by ownership of the trade-carrying fleet. From 1561 French nobles were forbidden to take part in commerce but five years later the Marseille nobility obtained as a special favour an abrogation of this rule for themselves, and were able to continue benefiting by their share in the prosperity of commercial enterprises for another hundred years. However, the reforming edict of Louis XIV after the sedition of 1659 excluded them from the government of the city which was given, subject to increasing supervision by royal officers, to aldermen drawn from the mercantile class in place of elected consuls from the aristocracy. As part of a policy of reducing the power of the nobility, the administration and the principal power were henceforth to be bourgeois, and the social history of Marseille with the place in it of the *grande bourgeoisie* was marked, in contrast with such cities as Lyon and Bordeaux, by the relative absence of a hereditary and closed aristocracy of the old kind, rooted in the town's most distant past.

From the early eighteenth century a distinction between the terms merchant and *négociant* came into being and was sanctioned by separation on the tax rolls. The merchant was a local trader often limited to dealing with a single outlet. The négociant dealt in international wholesale traffic in considerable quantities and added shipping, maritime insurance and banking to the range of his activities; success brought great wealth and with it, and while the wealth lasted, a proportionate rise in the social order. The négociants constituted the aristocracy of commerce and were aware of it, though their town houses in the famous *cours*, and later in the streets to the south of it, remained comparatively modest. Modesty may have been due to the remarkable fact, adduced by Laurence Américi and Xavier Daumalin in their study *Les dynasties marseillaises*, that in a city where the Edict of Tolerance had never been endorsed or applied, the work of capitalism was mainly done, by the time of the revolution, by French Protestant business houses; and some of these continued to play a leading part in the trade and industry of Marseille for two hundred years alongside a growing number of Catholic, Jewish and Orthodox recruits to the ruling class in a network of intermarriages, business associations, partnerships and family relations where, by the end of the nineteenth century, almost everyone was connected to almost everyone else. In the edifice of which they were part the load of each element was borne interdependently by the others; fracture of one could threaten the state of all.

Between 1783 and 1792 the average yearly value of the commerce of Marseille was 138 million *livres*, of which 56 million was in the Levant trade. Many of the two hundred or so family names that would echo under the majestic vaults of the Palais de la Bourse during the next two centuries were already well-known: Roux, Rostand, the Protestants Fraissinet and Rabaud, Régis, Bergasse, Pastré. Between January and March 1794, 745 suspects were guillotined, including a Rostand and a Rabaud, while the ship-owner Fraissinet was imprisoned in the Fort Saint-Jean. The revolutionary and Napoleonic wars for a time ruined the trade of Marseille; English ships, too heavy to dominate the coastal strip as they did the deep water, left inshore navigation as the only resource. But the vigour of the mercantile families was reaffirmed with the return of peace, the arrival of new names—Fabre, Luce, Imer, Straforello, Jacob-Cohen, Schloesing, among others—and the rise to predominance of some of the earlier of which Pastré is a particular example. The founder of the Pastré fortunes, establishing himself in Marseille in 1781 in the treatment of imported wool and later of North African hides, was from a sheep-raising family of the Languedoc. His son Jean-Baptiste was sent to Egypt where he opened offices in Alexandria, was soon among the leading négociants and shippers in the city, and thanks to confidential relations with the Pasha Muhammad Ali to whom the Pastré brothers regularly lent money, won a powerful hold on the cotton trade between Egypt and France. It was said that after Jean-Baptiste's return to Marseille in 1835 he "came to dominate the trade between the Nile and the Rhône to the point where it was almost his private domain", and he was naturally among the financial backers of de Lesseps in the construction of the Suez Canal and a member of the board of the Suez Canal Company created in 1858. From 400,000 francs in 1828 the capital of the company founded by the Pastré brothers rose to 4.5 million in 1869 before its liquidation in 1878 after a period of internal dissension, leaving Jules Pastré as head of the Anglo-Egyptian Bank which had taken over a large part of the Pastré interests.

The Genoese family of Rocca opened offices in Marseille in 1811, dealing at first in olive oil and wheat and before long controlling a fleet of 45 ships and becoming one of the principal economic powers and employers of the town. In the course of the nineteenth century the family was connected through marriage to the families of Fabre and Régis, and through them to the Roux, the Rostand and the Fraissinet. Dispersal of Greek merchant families from within the bounds of the Ottoman Empire after the uprising of 1821 brought an influx to broaden and fortify the Marseille *haute bourgeoisie*— Mavrogordato, Scaramanga, Rodocanachi, Zafiropulo and Zarifi who as Z&Z expanded, as did others, into industry and banking. The Bazin and Fraissinet families, closely connected by marriage and originating in the Languedoc, and the Rostand family installed in Marseille since 1746, specialized in the development of steamship navigation to India through Suez, to Africa and the Black Sea. In 1882 the capital of the Fraissinet company was twelve million francs and their ships in that year transported 100,000 passengers overseas.

By 1880 freight through the port of Marseille had reached 7,235,000 tons. The Fabre and Luce families whose names became joined by marriage as Fabre-Luce, and the Régis family, also closely connected by marriage, shared, like others in different localities of the Marseille hinterland, local territorial interests with a domain at Luminy on which several *bastides* were built, two farms and a forest of pines cultivated; Luminy was an exception among the lands surrounding bastides in its extent, exceeding a thousand hectares and kept together as part of the estates of the Abbey of Saint-Victor until acquired by the Fabre family in 1819.

This trio of families were among the first of those to exploit the colonization of Algeria whose consequences greatly influenced the history of Marseille in the nineteenth and twentieth centuries. The Marseille Committee for Colonization stated: "The Revolution, which lost us the Levant trade has left us with only a few unimportant colonies in India and America... Algeria may reopen the Levant and replace the colonies." The Fabre and Bergasse families were also engaged in shipping to the Americas from 1819 onwards as Marseille came to occupy the fifth place among the world's ports.

The liquidation in 1878 of the house of Pastré was followed in 1883 by that of the Roux de Fraissinet company as a result of imprudent banking loans. The structure of the Marseille business community and dynastic *cousinage* was rocked but not overthrown; apart from companies set up by groups of families to manage their extensive property holdings—those of the de Roux and Rocca families, for example, valued at two million francs in 1917—the dynasties invested more and more in the growing finances of the colonial empire, though without ever favouring the intervention of the state with its ensuing train of civil servants. At the Congress of Berlin in 1878 Great Britain and Germany urged the government of the Third Republic, diplomatically in retreat since the defeat of 1870, to interest itself more actively in Africa and particularly in Tunisia whose trade was largely controlled by the *Marseillais*; the bank Société Marseillaise de Crédit was created to finance the economy of Tunisia and to some extent of Algeria, with a board composed of members of the leading families whether of French, Italian, or Greek origin.

Others such as the Estrine, established as merchants in Marseille since 1741, expanded their activities into East Africa, Morocco and Indo-China, and the Rocca and de Roux families into Ceylon. By the Second World War the traffic of the port had reached ten million tons and by the mid-1950s eighteen million, with over two million passengers. Américi and Daumalin point out that the historic concentration of business in and trade to and from the colonial empire, though not exclusive, would create, for Marseille and the industrial and mercantile families, particular and sometimes insurmountable difficulties with the drama of decolonization and the development of the European single market.

Meanwhile, however, the expansion of shipping, banking and eventually aviation interests, usually on a basis of comparatively modest capital investment, continued without interruption. The Daher family from Aleppo arrived in Marseille in 1847 and combined the creation of a new shipping company with involvement in and finally control of the cement making company Lafarge whose products, with those of the Saint-Louis sugar refinery and of the tile manufacturers of l'Estaque they shipped round the world. "How is it," wrote André Daher in a memoir quoted by Américi and Daumalin, "that despite the pitfalls our businesses have always kept their heads high? Remember that my father [Paul, who finally obtained French nationality in 1922] and I were always influenced by our reading of Jules Verne... that inventive spirit who in our youth took us sailing with Captain Nemo." In 1909 a company was formed with participation of many of the leading families for the construction and exploitation of airships, and in 1930 the Fabre family became the first to combine air with sea transport by the trial and development of hydroplanes on the Etang de Berre. A daughter of the Catholic Fabre family had married the Protestant Jean Fraissinet in 1924, and henceforth the companies of the two dynasties advanced together; by the outbreak of the Second World War Jean Fraissinet was at the head of the three principal shipping and shipbuilding businesses of Marseille, owned two newspapers, *Marseille Matin* and *Marseille Soir* whose politics were markedly right-wing and opposed to the socialist government of Léon Blum, and, an aviator himself, sat on the board of Air France and acquired a majority shareholding in Air Algérie.

The career of perhaps the best-known of Marseille businessmen, Jules Charles-Roux, is emblematic of the variety of enterprise that long characterized the wide group of families he came from. Shipping was the first of his interests but he was vice-president of the Suez Canal Company, president of several banks in Marseille, of railway companies, sugar-refining businesses and companies involved in Franco-African cooperative development particularly colonial, re-publican deputy for Marseille from 1889 to 1898, judge of the *tribunal de commerce* and president of the Geographical Society of Marseille. The ship-broking Barry family which in 1889 sold the yacht *Zingara*, rechristened *Bel Ami*, to Guy de Maupassant after his ruthless haggling over tonnage and equipment, grew in strength to become by 1914 the largest company of its kind in France, dealing with government departments including the Ministry for War, and later acting as brokers for the Union Castle and Lloyd shipping lines. But despite these striking examples it was true that the political influence of the dynasties in a great popular city remained slight and their leaders in the background. When in 1983 Pierre Rastoin allied himself to Gaston Defferre and his common policy with the Communist Party, Rastoin found himself ostracized by his kind as a traitor to his class.

Between 1960 and 1990 a void in the economic fabric of Marseille was created with the taking over by international groups of the leading companies, or their progressive withdrawal into inactivity. The family directors of these concerns have been attacked for the social consequences and criticized for the history of management and failure to modernize that led to them. But the city was made vulnerable firstly by its dependence on the colonial trade which in 1954 made up sixty per cent of the traffic of the port and was drastically reduced by decolonization; and secondly, in consequence of the development outside Marseille and with state backing of Fos-sur-Mer as a terminal for oil tankers, pipelines and the refining process. A new deep water port able to dock tankers of over 100,000 tons was built at Fos in 1968, and in 1988 the nineteenth-century docks of La Joliette were abandoned. The retreat from the primary activity of many firms was in any case neither precipitate nor complete—the gradual redeployment of the famous house of Fraissinet is an example. Withdrawing from naval construction and shipping, the company engaged in air transport including helicopter development and airport infrastructure, and then in real estate dealings, particularly in the vicinity of airports; but these activities were for the most part carried on outside the Marseille sphere and so without direct or calculable benefit to the local population. Similarly, the Daher family, still active in shipping and in aeronautics, has to a great extent spread its commitments abroad though the headquarters remain in Marseille. Moreover, new dynasties have appeared of which the Saadé family is the preeminent example. The Saadé, Orthodox Christians who arrived from Syria in 1978, specialized in container transport and are now, despite a long internal dissension which ended in fusion of the affairs of two branches of the family, fifth among the world's "global carriers" with a combined fleet of 172 vessels, and are the largest private employers in Marseille, occupying a new, largely glass, spire-like office building 147 metres high designed by the Anglo-Iraqi architect Zaha Hadid for the business quarter of Euroméditerranée.

The négociants and shipping families, the banking groups and the brokerage firms were also involved in the industrial history of Marseille from the late eighteenth century onwards. Though the city has been reproached with failure to diversify from its long traditional role of trading station into productive industrial growth, the charge is at least partly undeserved. From the tile and cement factories of l'Estaque to the lead workings of Callelongue with their snake-like chimney built to crawl up the flank of the hill and void pollution into the air above the *calanques*, the gulf and city carry a full share of industrial revolutionary scars, the worse for being to a large extent now disused. A large number of soap and chemical factories, sugar refineries, the production of oil, paints, agricultural fertilizer, flour milling and alcohol distillery with, in particular, the invention of aperitifs such as Noilly-Prat vermouth and the *pastis* of Ricard were among the industrial activities that fostered the spread of the nineteenth-century town and of rapid, sustained population growth. The soap factories producing *savon de marseille*, many of them in the ownership of the Roux and Estrangin families, were the chief employers with a workforce of over five thousand in 1880, while the Bazin and Rostand families were leaders in sugar refining. But industrial inventiveness and adventure were perhaps concentrated in the shipbuilding and steamship groups headed by the Luce and Benet families who sent representatives to England to study engineering methods and discoveries, and to import components. The Benet group worked in association with John Barnes, and Robert son of George Stephenson.

Early petrol refining was the work of the Protestant families Fraissinet, Imer and Leenhardt, all connected by marriage; prospecting was carried out in Russia and a pipeline built from the Caucasus to the Black Sea where the crude oil was embarked on ships owned by the Fraissinet Company to be treated at La Madrague in a refinery of the Compagnie Générale des Pétroles largely controlled by the Leenhardt family, associated in 1923 with the Standard Oil Company and finally taken over by Esso France in 1947, as the petrol interests of the Mante family had passed in the early 1920s to the Consolidated Oil Corporation. In both cases the family directors continued in office and kept their shareholdings. The interconnected Rocca and de Roux families, engaged in comestible oil and soap production, employed almost two thousand workers by 1930 and modelled their management on observations made by Jean-Baptiste Rocca at Port Sunlight: "Can you imagine," he wrote to his father, "anything more beautiful than the work of Sir Lever? He makes a fortune, has the greatest satisfaction to his pride, the love of his population of workers whose happiness he provides, and a good conscience." The influence of English industrial practice and experience was increased by the presence in Marseille capitalism of some of the great Tyneside industrial families, a remarkably similar dynastic network, intermarried, self-perpetuating and ubiquitous; notable among these were the numerous branches of the Cookson family, since 1700 one of the most prominent with businesses that included banking, steel foundry and coal-mining and, in common with others of the Tyneside dynasties, land ownership in the Northumbrian hills on a scale far greater than the more modest holdings of the Marseille plutocracy.

Cheap labour, often immigrant and relatively docile, was one of the foundations of Marseille's industrialization; however, some employers such as Paul Ricard who developed and commercialized the famous aniseed-flavoured (and from 1915 to 1932 prohibited) aperitif and was producing 3.6 million litres of *le vrai pastis de Marseille* by 1939 and 9 million litres by 1950, were benevolently paternalist in labour relations though hostile to union activity. Ricard, who was later involved in the Resistance, was already allowing his employees three weeks of annual holiday in 1936 when the Blum government introduced the fifteen days of *congés payés,* and in 1946 he opened a free holiday centre on the coast at Sausset-les-Pins for the families of his workers. Américi and Daumalin point to another ambiguity in the conduct of their affairs by the local industrialists: "If the dynastic entrepreneurs remained very hostile to any extension of the regulatory role of the state... they did not hesitate to shelter when necessary behind customs protectionism or to demand an increase of public orders..."

The progressive closing down of industries after the 1960s created a sense in Marseille, not yet dissipated, of the end of a golden age which had lasted two hundred years. The most spectacular of these disappearances was the judicial winding-up in 1978 of the thirteen companies constituting the Terrin group of shipbuilding and maintenance yards, with a final loss of nine thousand jobs. According to the regional monthly *Objectif Sud,* this was "worse than losing Algeria". In the same year the group of soap and oil manufacturers Unipol, the work of a number of combined dynasties, disappeared as a result of speculative take-over and dismemberment. The tile makers Tuileries de Marseille et de la Méditerranée similarly passed under control of the cement-making group Lafarge in 1987 and closed in 2006. The Marseille chemical industry declined to vanishing point in the same period. Of the big businesses only Ricard with its pastis sales prospered, and allied with Pernod succeeded in taking over the Canadian wine and spirit firm Seagram.

Many possible explanations are offered for the industrial collapse of the family concerns, from their incapacity to re-form after the loss of protected colonial markets to the influence of divided patrimonial interests in conflict with each other and a hindrance to restructuring. What is certain is that the value of building land and sites and the money to be made from them in a period of rapid urban growth led to property dealings, sale or demolition of former industrial buildings and reinvestment of capital which was often made elsewhere than in Marseille.

Mœurs and Family Values

The social and familial life of the Marseille bourgeoisie was very strongly marked by dynastic concerns. The birth rate in these families was exceptionally high throughout the nineteenth century and into the twentieth, and grief at infantile mortality sometimes continued for half the lifetime of parents in an age when such losses were commonplace at all social levels. Américi and Daumalin cite correspondence showing strength of paternal feeling towards children quite out of the ordinary, and this impression is confirmed in the memoirs of Marcel Pagnol who wrote of a school companion, son of a shipping merchant, adored and pampered by his father but fiercely punished for any bad school report. Education, conventional, methodical, not creatively encouraging but a potent transmitter of values, was as dynastically formative in the families of the Marseille bourgeoisie preparing the ground of their succession as in those of nineteenth-century England, and as in England, boarding-school was often part of this training; Paul-Cyprien Fabre spent four years from the age of fourteen in 1884 at a Jesuit school near Canterbury and was said to still speak with anger about the experience at the end of his life. In the late nineteenth and in the twentieth century, periods spent in England, study of industrial method and learning English were a regular part of the education of future leaders of the Marseille bourgeoisie; yet the historical and geographic reality of Marseille would be so potent that until the final period of decline, and perhaps beyond it, basic Mediterranean identity continued as the chief element in the personal and professional outlook of this caste.

Moreover, many dynasties preserved unity and continuity by a system of endogamy or selective marriage. Through the fecund Fraissinet family, all the Protestant families of the Marseille bourgeoisie were related; among Catholic families there were also frequent intermarriages and cousinly alliances though some married into the aristocracy, particularly of the impoverished kind which in exchange for material security brought a spark of social lustre into the starchy, rather sombre atmosphere of bourgeois salons. Américi and Daumalin quote Marie Bergasse of the wine merchant family established since the eighteenth century, "humble bourgeoise that I am", criticizing the vanity of the aristocracy into which her niece had married "with their dirty carriages and false grand airs". But more usually, marriages served to reinforce, or followed from, business interests. Pierre-Paul Zalio in *Grandes familles* has shown how the Rastoin, Rocca, Tassy and de Roux families, founders of the twentieth-century Marseille domestic oil industry, intermarried in a complex configuration of repeated links. Américi and Daumalin give a striking example of the self-healing process in the dynastic body through marital alliance: in 1865 a dramatic split in the Régis and Fabre families led to legal separations, illegitimate births, evictions, ostracism, disinheritance, exclusion from burial in the family mausoleum and, worst of all, public scandal with each new development given to its readers by the local press. Yet within two generations new intermarriages came to reunite the destinies, the joint fortunes and the future of dynastic interests.

The topography of Marseille and the hybrid origins of its population are as much the keys to comprehension (as far as can be achieved) of the role and way of life of the upper bourgeoisie as of any other group in the city. The physical geography, the horizon of sea and shield of hills, was probably echoed in that characteristic described by Christian Harrel-Courtès in writing of his own caste as "more closed and turned in on itself than any other group of provincial citizens"; yet he noted in Marseille society "a propensity to speak with a touch of English accent, or a shade of Greek pronunciation for those with Hellenic antecedents but who spoke no Greek", suggesting that the closure of this exclusive tribe was more against the mainland than the wider world. Like their neighbours in *cabanons* who might keep a boat, a *pointu* on the shore at Callelongue or Pointe Rouge, the rich owners of bastides tied up their launches or yachts at the same quays. On terrain or water, bourgeois and proletarian were figures in an essentially Mediterranean scene which both understood and all preferred to keep to themselves. René Allio through the narrating voice in *L'Heure exquise* said that in each Marseillais there is a peasant and a seaman, with consequent tension between the two reflecting that between sea and land. In town, Harrel-Courtès claims that receptions, marriages and balls were always attended by the same two or three hundred people who had known one another all their lives and were usually related; he offers a picture of a self-satisfied clique purring with pleasure at living within a social *cordon sanitaire*, impervious to the arts, contemptuous of intellectuals, led by what he calls *le clan des grecs*, immigrants of the late nineteenth century who had injected capital into Marseille businesses. About the reputation for musical appreciation in these families, Courtès is heavily ironic: "One subscribed to the *Concerts classiques*, one had one's box at the opera, one's seat for the chamber music recitals; one yawned, but it was well thought of to be present on these occasions which allowed you to think of something else, or to doze off."

Music was nonetheless part of the usual education and way of life of many rich bourgeois families, notably the Borelli, the Rostand and most of all, perhaps, the Pastré who, combining the fortunes of the house of Pastré and of Noilly-Prat, staged woodland performances of *Midsummer Night's Dream* under the moon at Montredon, in the first year after the fall of France for an audience which included artists, musicians and intellectuals from many parts of occupied Europe. Harrel-Courtès claims that the *grands bourgeois* did not meet these refugees, but in the woods of the Château Pastré they shared on this occasion the experience of hearing "Oberon's invocation to the moon as it floated above the summit of Marseilleveyre".

It has been suggested that for the Marseille bourgeoisie the nineteenth century came to an end in about 1950; and Edmonde Charles-Roux asserts hyperbolically that of the great families "nothing is left". However, Pierre-Paul Zalio shows that many descendants of these families have been reabsorbed into the business fabric of the region without emigrating to Paris; some have become architects, lawyers and members of the professions though few have entered the high ranks of the public service which he explains as an illustration of the continuing separation of Marseille from Paris, and Jean Viard confirms this by pointing out that many of the descendants of the historical elite remain fixed in or near to Marseille in intermediate rather than dominant positions. Although, in addition to the residential enclosures along the Corniche and the Prado, Cassis and its nearby countryside have been adopted as a refuge by many of the rich families who find there echoes of the former life of the bastides, the partial dispersal of the clans, the weakening of clan loyalties or claims and the break with the central life of the city from which their wealth was derived are, says Zalio, a page turned in the history of Marseille.

The effects of the dynasties in action in modern times on the economy, the townscape and the social structure of Marseille cannot be unthreaded from the stuff of historical accident. As the industrial and trading base of Marseille seemed to break up over thirty years, did the dynastic families which had so greatly enriched themselves, and helped bring prosperity to the town in the process for two hundred years, feel a loyalty and a responsibility, or betray them? Were their contributions to a range of charitable and providential organizations in that time, often under the aegis of the churches, enough to acquit? Américi and Daumalin in their conclusion state that "Between the town... and the business dynasties, identity of interest was part of an economic system which did not require any lasting domination, and so the social anchorage of the dynasties proved transitory..."

Much less transitory were the physical consequences for the fabric of the city itself. The dynastic families lived in town houses, usually of restrained elegance, in neighbouring streets and they often owned several such houses for use by different members of the family. In 1860 the Pastré occupied four *hôtels particuliers* in the Rue Saint-Ferréol and with their immediate relations five others in nearby streets. When the new Palais de Justice and the Préfecture were built, the aristocracy of commerce congregated in the streets round about which became until the 1930s what Marcel Roncayolo described as a "West End Marseillais". Later, residential choice shifted south toward the district of Saint-Giniez and after 1914 to the Avenue du Prado and its vicinity where property is now the most expensive in the Marseille commune.

The centre, once home to the various orders of *notables*, was progressively abandoned; Américi and Daumalin argue that "by the choice of their habitat the families of the economic elite brought about changes in property values and imposed their cultural model on the town: it was the wealthy who guided the population," a remark apparently at variance with their claim that dominance by these families was transitory rather than part of a common destiny. And there seems little doubt that property speculation including the break-up and sales of the bastides and their lands in face of, and exploiting, the pressure of urban expansion, and reinvestment of the proceeds outside, particularly at Fos and in the new industrial areas around the Etang de Berre, have in a more or less negative manner prolonged the domination exercised by the class of capitalists, with all their diversity of origins, which over the centuries made auspicious landfall at Marseille.

Bouillabaisse, soupe de poissons, bourride ...

10 | Consuming Interests
Tastes and Trade

Pastis, that cloudy drink, gets a bad press like Marseille whose only speciality it is. Pastis isn't forgiven for being the alcohol of the people.

Olivier Boura

Boura seems to ignore the famous bouillabaisse, which he says everyone talks about though no one eats; this is perhaps an example of local disdain due to an over-exposure by which Thackeray, recalling in The Ballad of Bouillabaisse a Marseillais restaurant in Paris, was not affected:

This Bouillabaisse a noble dish is –
    A sort of soup, or broth, or brew,
Or hotchpotch of all sorts of fishes,
    That Greenwich never could outdo;
Green herbs, red peppers, mussels, saffern
    Soles, onions, garlic, roach, and dace...
All these you eat at Terré's tavern,
    In that one dish of Bouillabaisse.

Lombard states that after Thackeray it was not until 1959 that three Provençal songwriters celebrated the invention again in verse. But bouillabaisse, he claims, is not a mere dish, "it is a whole civilization".

The pastis of Marseille, according to Boura, is a rootless drink, a product not of the soil but of alchemy, not for tasting but for standing rounds, not to be appreciated and consumed in moderation but to bring forgetfulness. When Paul Ricard first commercialized his brand of the product there was to be found a coin of two sous at the bottom of each bottle as a recompense, marking pastis as the drink of the poor likened to gin in England in the eighteenth century. In fact, like gin, pastis is happily drunk by all classes and not only in the Midi; but the name sometimes calls out a tendency to self-denigration among the writers of Marseille, a manoeuvre to distract and disarm.

The concoction, invented to replace the forbidden absinthe produced by Henri-Louis Pernod, is composed principally of aniseed, fennel, liqorice and sugar in alcohol of 45 per cent ABV compared to the 72 per cent of absinthe; it was first legalized at a lower strength in 1920 and is reputed, according to Paul Lombard, to "ease the digestion, cure maladies of the intestine, stomach and liver, stop hiccoughs, and awaken a drowsy libido". Five volumes of water to one of pastis is regarded as the correct starting mixture which serious drinkers will invert measure by measure to parity; purists claim that ice should be in the water jug, not in the glass, and they speak with contempt of the cocktails made by addition of mildly alcoholic syrups or, more lethally, of whisky or cognac.

It is alleged that notable gastronomy in France can only be found where notable wine is made; the wine of Marseille was highly reputed in Roman times and praised by Pliny the Younger in the first century AD; it became the chief agricultural activity of the Abbaye de Saint-Victor and was exported in quantity in the Middle Ages to Syria, Egypt and London. In the nineteenth century it was even drunk in Russia, but the expanding town steadily reduced the area of vineyards and the opening of the Canal de Marseille in 1849, bringing water to the lands of *bastides* and the gardens of *cabanons*, favoured the spread of market gardening at the expense of the vine.

Only one Marseille wine is still produced, near the limits of the *commune* with that of Cassis, and this singularity is mirrored in the historically unchanging gastronomy based on the catch of fish from the abundant shoals in the gulf, some of which are laid out daily for sale on the quayside of the Vieux Port. Bouillabaisse is not the only resulting speciality: *bourride*, similarly prepared but in theory only from the angler-fish, a predator of smaller species, and served with another Marseille speciality, *aïoli* (an ointment, not a paste, the knowledgeable insist) made wih garlic, egg-yolk and olive oil; *soupe de poissons*, of fish netted close inshore off the rocks and in which all depends on the freshness of the catch as it does equally with bouillabaisse itself; and the great range of Mediterranean fish of which *loup de mer* (sea-bass), *daurade* (sea bream*)* and *rouget* (red mullet) are perhaps the best known, grilled on a fire of vine prunings and eaten, like most local dishes, dressed with *aïoli*. The novelist Jean-Claude Izzo, who wrote of Marseille without sentimentality but in entire symbiosis, spoke of its unpretentious *cuisine* accommodating, with art, all ingredients "disdained by the rich", a remark giving substance to Lombard's description of bouillabaisse as a "civilization".

Markets and Marketplaces

As a great port the town has always been the distribution point of exotic ingredients cheap or dear, and its many markets, particularly those of the Place des Capucins and La Plaine are colourful, spicy and rich in imported produce. Nicholas Woodsworth in the *Financial Times* claimed that the daily non-stop Capucins market brings the *cuisine* of the whole world to Provence; efforts sporadically put up by the authorities to move such markets (some of them unofficial) elsewhere as an alleged cause of disturbance always fail, the stalls and their customers return, and this fact is sometimes cited to illustrate the argument that Marseille cannot be governed, though if left alone it will govern itself—tolerant, untidy, disrespectful to the environment but not of the citizen's liberties.

One among the innumerable imported substances was coffee, first brought into France through Marseille from Constantinople in 1644; in 1670 the first of the Marseille cafés—later to be celebrated by Stendhal, Gautier and Conrad, by whose day they numbered 280—was opened by an Armenian near the Hôtel de Ville four years before the opening of the Café Procope in Paris. By 1700 Marseille imported 600,000 kilos of coffee annually from the Levant, and by the end of the eighteenth century seven million kilos from the West Indies of which the greater part was re-exported.

From the sixteenth century the Levant privileges brought to Marseille a great share of the luxury trade passing in both directions across the Mediterranean, in silk, cotton, minerals, spices and coral,

Unloading imports, 1778

in which there was a monopoly and which, with hides and wheat (though these were not within it), was traded in Constantinople, largely against textiles. This trade was the origin of the historical development in Marseille of luxury goods, now greatly prized and generally seen only in museum collections, which belong to the period of the city's past elegance and grace rather than the rougher (if still richer) modern age of industrialization and imperial commercial adventuring. From Bengal, from Persia, from China came printed and embroidered cottons whose dramatically beautiful designs were soon reproduced in Marseille and other towns of Provence on imported white cotton cloth, under the direction of Armenian artisans using engraved wooden moulds, and commercialized as *indiennes* in quantity throughout Europe. Daniel Defoe reported such a taste for these printed cottons that material meant for clothing "children and the people is now used for dressing great ladies". Protectionism led, in 1686, to the prohibition of this import trade, lasting until 1759, and the destruction of the moulds by royal command.

Nevertheless, by a characteristic exception, in 1733 as many as eighty workshops producing printed cottons for export were still active. Equally or still more highly valued was the *faïence* of Moustiers and of the factories on the Marseille outskirts whose output of decorated porcelain was increased by the ban in 1689 on manufacturing table silver and the melting down of great amounts, including much from Versailles, to finance the wars of Louis XIV, with a consequent substitution of porcelain for silver. Italian potters first arrived in Marseille in the sixteenth century and it is claimed that the quality of the sand deposited on beaches near the mouth of Lacydon, and that of the clay found in the valley of the Huveaune were particularly favourable to the production of the most delicate and often elaborate pieces whose enamel and paintwork could be fired consecutively and which could be compared, according to Paul Lombard, with the porcelain of China or Delft. There were many famous makers among the sixty at work by the eighteenth century, of whom the most celebrated was the widow Perrin; but at the revolution the craftsmen and artists, unhappy with new conditions and returns for their work, deserted the Marseille *faïnceries* en masse, took their skills to Genoa, the city's eternal rival, and the classic porcelain making of Marseille was extinguished—though production of copies continues.

Savon de Marseille, soap making, seems a prosaic activity for a site so apparently drawn by nature to startle and waylay; but from the fourteenth to the late twentieth century the soap factories were the leading employers in the city and their output one of the principal elements in its economy. By the First World War Marseille was producing, largely for export, 180,000 tons of soap a year in at least ninety factories. Olive oil was traditionally the chief ingredient, though the arrival of other oils from Africa in the nineteenth century created competition from northern, mainly British, manufacturers which led to the diversifying of material; the various secret formulae for preparing savon de Marseille were never patented and virtually identical products began to appear in different parts of the world, until the use of detergents and washing machines after the Second World War progresssively and finally brought about the closing down of nearly all the *savonneries.* Three of them continue to function with success, producing a range of high quality soaps made with palm oil and coprah for textiles, or, still much appreciated, in toilet soap with the traditional olive oil.

As well as its markets of which there are at least twenty about the town, and the famous flea market (see p.157) there are streets, particularly near the Alcazar which now houses the town library, and in the vicinity of the Porte d'Aix, where the contents of shops spill over from the interior to the pavement, attracting a swarm of customers mainly from among the North and West African communities, and extending into the new and constantly growing commercial centre behind the Bourse. The liveliness of these streets is far from being hemmed in by the invisible but effective social boundaries that in many cities, and above all in Paris, give the sense of compartments defined by the credit limit of those occupying them.

In Marseille the popular current crosses the Canebière or the Place du Général De Gaulle with its merry-go-round opposite the Palais de la Bourse, and flows uninhibitedly back and forth along the Rue Paradis and the Rue Saint-Ferréol, side by side with the fashionable and well-heeled clientele of elegant and expensive shops co-existing, often sharing the same building, with a random mixture of more modest retail outlets, in that kind of democratic variety seemingly imprinted in the nature of Marseille ever since plebs and patricians kept house cheek by jowl in the narrow alleyways of the Panier.

CONSUMING INTERESTS

11 | **The Dark Side**
Vice and Criminality

Marseille as the French Chicago, with its hot streets, brothels, murders, rackets, drugs… all true—and all exaggerated.

Christian Harrel-Courtès

The equation in the public mind between prostitution and criminality and disease is so usual that the inference of some sense of primal guilt seems irresistible. When Marseille was struck by the great plague of 1720 it was presumed to have originated in one of the poorest streets of the Panier, the Rue de l'Echelle, finally destroyed in 1976, a long, narrow, winding alley walled at the end by the Hellenistic rampart and with a dozen brothels working night and day: "With its poverty-stricken people, its beggars, its prostitutes and receivers, it was a virtual source of infection in the eyes of the Marseillais," says the historian Régis Bertrand, "the disease must have been born there."

In fact, the plague came in from a ship, the three-masted *Grand Saint-Antoine* sailing from Smyrna with a cargo of silk and cotton and owned by one of the richest and most powerful of the city aldermen, which was placed in quarantine in the normal way at the Île de Pomègues; declarations of clean health by the captain were falsified or accepted by interested authorities, the cargo, which could have been spoiled by a long delay in sun and wind, was discharged and passengers and some of the crew were allowed to land at the infirmary of Arenc near to the cathedral. Soiled linen passed through the bars of the infirmary is now believed to have been the plague's origin, but blame can only be imputed, if at all, to the bourgeois oligarchy, not the poor occupants or passing clients of the Rue de l'Echelle.

A similar mechanism seems to have been at work at the time of the blowing-up by the Nazis and officials of the Vichy regime of part of the Panier in 1943; a zone of prostitution, though home also to many ordinary families sharing the quarter with women of the streets in "honest complicity" in Harrel-Courtès' phrase, was seen as a focus of crime and destroyed to the eventual profit of well-placed investors, and perhaps with their connivance.

Marseille, according to André Bouyala d'Arnaud in *Evocation du vieux Marseille*, "has in the course of its history always been a temple of prostitution"; similar hyperbole was much indulged in by André Suarès who called the Panier "the great brothel [*lupanar*]... a fortress of gross lust with each house a hive of sexual organs." His and other writers' fascinated descriptions of the squalor of the streets and the women working them can be tempered by Edmond Jaloux's account of "small, modest rooms with small windows through which you glimpse a bed, a water-jug, a pious image..." And it was not unknown for some beautiful girl such as la Ribier in the late seventeenth century to rise in society to the point, in la Ribier's case, that her marriage to Georges de Scudéry, governor of Notre-Dame de la Garde, was only prevented by the intervention of his sister Madeleine.

All the same, the number of prostitutes in the Panier was remarkable; three hundred in 1640, eight hundred in more than a hundred brothels by the mid-nineteenth century. After the defeat of the insurrection of 1793 the vengeful measures taken by the committee of public safety of the national Convention included the restriction of the prostitutes' quarter to streets previously inhabited by the Marseille aristocracy; the brothels were housed henceforth in the former *hôtels particuliers* of the Abbess of Notre-Dame de Sion, of the Marquis de Marignane, the Cardinal de Chatillon, the de Ricci family... In 1878 the Bureau des Mœurs (Office of Public Morals) laid down the conditions and named the streets in which the profession could be practised, with at their centre the Rue Bouterie where "half-naked girls, their legs strapped up in silk stockings, keep up an interminable conversation among themselves... interrupted only to address some gilded word to a passer-by..." (Jaloux). Suarès took particular relish in pointing out that bourgeois merchants of the ninetenth century avenged themselves against the arrogance of the aristocracy by settling the lowest grade of the brothels in houses that were once the mansions of the nobility and still carried their coats-of-arms over the door. There was weekly medical inspection from 1878 onwards after which any prostitute venereally infected was confined for at least forty days in the convent of the Conception, then released if found healthy enough to return to work.

If the *quartier chaud* of the port of Marseille was the most notorious in the world it seems, as with other aspects of its reputation, that at least some of the notoriety was due to the talent of its writers who wilfully and for literary purposes daubed the image of their city with a garish lacquer of the sordid and the miserable. A different idea can be had of the mood and character of the prostitutes from their custom, mentioned by Evelyn Waugh (see p.91), of stealing the hats off the heads of men passing in the narrow street below their windows, in an age when no man walked hatless, and so bring him indoors to reclaim it. The German destruction of a great part of the Panier and the consequent disappearance of the brothels almost completed a project first advocated in 1858 by the industrialist Jules Mirès, who married his only daughter to the Prince de Polignac, of demolishing, levelling and rebuilding the ancient town, with all the speculative profit to the local capitalists that would follow. But the Panier stays alive, still attracts to itself an easy reputation for the shady, the suspicious and the dangerous after dark; and now, Olivier Boura claims, it is no longer the Italians, the Catalans, the descendants of the first Greeks who have a bad name, but the Arabs of North Africa, poor and readily identified by colour.

Marseille's Mafia

Theodore Zeldin has pointed out that in the mid-nineteenth century, with a population of 300,000, Marseille lived in reasonable security with a police force of 213. Conditions changed in the 1920s when the Panier became the headquarters of the Corsican clan—legendary, exaggerated and exploited in films feeding on legend, but real. "There were the right-wing *nervis*," says Richard Cobb, "trigger men, gangsters, the Corsican protectors, including that irresistible duo of Carbone and Spirito, hiding under... hilarious surnames the exceedingly nasty reality of many gangland killings in the quartier of the Panier, the underworld of Marseille... never too far from the waterfront, and, later, torturers and murderers in the service of the French Gestapo in Paris."

Carbone was born in Corsica in 1894 into an illiterate family with cousins in Marseille; he went to sea as cabin boy on a contraband ship and was quickly absorbed into the clan. Spirito, six years younger, was brought from Naples by his parents as a child and in the words of Paul Lombard, "climbed the rungs of crime in great strides". The two men, whose careers were made the subject of the film *Borsalino* produced in 1970 with Alain Delon and Jean-Paul Belmondo, first met in Cairo where they made a small fortune in drugs and prostitution. The film is an example of romanticizing crime; "the wide-open life," says Olivier Boura, "is the mobster's life—beautiful women, true friendship, perpetual holidays..." In Marseille, Carbone and Spirito invested in bars and brothels and set up a laboratory for producing illicit morphine. 1936 the Spanish Civil War brought opportunities for gun-running. For fifteen years, under the political protection of Simon Sabiani who was elected to the municipality in 1929 and dominated it until the end of the occupation, Carbone and Spirito with their army of fixers and the Corsican clan which when not directly involved in their activities was tacitly complicit—all in all a relatively small world of villains and their passive collaborators—brought to Marseille the universal reputation for lawlessness and violence which is still not shaken off from the stereotyped perception of the city. Spirito, during the war, lived much of the time in the Avenue Foch in Paris in an apartment confiscated from a Jewish family where Carbone was a frequent visitor; but the opprobrium attaching to their names was visited on Marseille, not on Paris.

Jean Viard suggests, with imaginative flair, that the shading of near-respectability which at least until the 1970s seemed to shield many of the leading members of the criminal *milieu* in Marseille from social rejection by the property-owning bourgeoisie, and pursuit by the authorities, was possibly due to folk memories of ancestral piracy on the high seas of which these landlocked and unromantic delinquents were seen, however unworthy, as a survival. Moreover some of these men, unlike Carbone, Spirito and Sabiani, had served in the Resistance and so were restored after the war to a kind of "moral virginity" which for a while outlasted their peacetime criminal debauch. And thirdly, it is certain that lawyers and doctors played a predominant role in the governance of Marseille in the twentieth century; both of these professions, Viard shows, had connections with the underworld whether in its dealings with justice or with mortality. The result was that there was a permanent relationship between the politically dominant sector of the community and the redoutable figures controlling the milieu; this beating between shores of lawlessness and impunity, which can happen in any great port where "ferrymen" rule, is taken as specially the case of Marseille. Beyond its borders, talk of crime in the *cité phocéenne* can show at once by the reaction of any interlocutor how the city is used as scapegoat for national shortcomings. The self-image of France requires a proxy to answer for imperfections—Marseille is cast in the role, can expect no redemption, and almost certainly wants none.

Nevertheless, it remains true that for a long time Marseille was a destination and an objective for gangsters. "The dream of every international criminal," wrote Albert Londres in the 1920s, "is to become *patron* of a bar in Marseille" where all transgression is allowed for and "trials behind closed doors are followed by executions in the open air". The Marseille gangsters, claims Olivier Boura, "remained faithful for a long time to the flamboyant style of the matador. They knew how to spend, to kill and to die… and sometimes even with a kind of elegance… but their prestige… only lasted as long as the belief in a clear separation between the underworld and the world of honest people… transforming part of the town into a ghetto." In other words, the Second World War was a turning point after which, by degrees, civic reality began to reclaim the city from the Corsican and Neapolitan network which had ruled for too long.

But it was a slow process and may not yet be complete, calm as the formerly most shady streets such as the Rue Thubaneau now appear. Antoine Guérini was born at Colanzana in Corsica in 1902; at twenty-one he bought the Bar de l'Etoile in the Rue Thubaneau where prostitution was the main activity and the police were among the most regular clients. After a good war (and the multitude of sins which that covered) in the Resistance, Guérini gathered up a string of bars and nightclubs owned by former collaborators—le Perroquet Bleu, le Méditerranée, le Paradou—and from his residence on the Corniche reigned over the world of prostitution and drugs and to an extent that many Marseillais would be reluctant to admit, over much of the life of the town until June 1967 when he was assassinated at a petrol-filling station in the Avenue de Saint-Julien by two never-identifed riders of a mobylette. The matador, the resistant, the survivor from the brave corsair days died without elegance on the concrete forecourt beside the pumps.

This gangland regicide triggered a long-running factional war in which urban guerrillas of various allegiances—sometimes allied, at others murderously opposed—followed Guérini to their last rest. The eventual ruler of the underworld to emerge was Gaëtan Zampa, a stammerer born in the Panier in 1933 to parents of Neapolitan origin, and who at twenty was one of Gaston Defferre's bodyguards. He followed his career of crime in Paris and returned to Marseille in 1964, surrounding himself with hard men who progressively came to rule in certain Marseille streets. Zampa was ruthless, violent and feared, and never hesitated to eliminate whoever got in his way including his half-brother. From investment in prostitution and nightclubs he passed to dealing in heroin. Though he was in prison at the date of Guérini's execution it was believed to have been carried out on his orders. In the 1970s Zampa expanded into international, cross-border arms trafficking and in his absence his authority was challenged by Francis "le Belge" Vanverberghe, formerly his chief lieutenant, with consequent multiple murders on both sides. In 1973 le Belge was condemned to fourteen years of imprisonment and hostilites were suspended though other rivals surfaced and assassinations, notably and infamously that in 1981 of the judge Pierre Michel who had been in the front line in dismantling the drug ring known as the "French Connection", continued sporadically. In the event, this murder was proved to have been the work of the Mafia, not of Zampa who was finally arrested in 1983 for a bombing in Aix-en-Provence where he owned the largest nightclub in the region, 'Le Krypton.' In 1984 while awaiting trial Zampa, said to be affected by dementia and practically silenced by his stammer, made two unsuccessful suicide attempts and at last hanged himself in his cell with a skipping-rope. Some of his colleagues, still at large though diminished by this loss in the hierarchy and keeping a relatively low profile, persevered in less spectacular but sometimes lethal crimes until the last of them was assassinated in 1997. Francis le Belge, for long a Parisian resident, was assassinated there in 2000.

The decline from the 1970s onwards of what French journalists call, with a shade of envy, *le grand banditisme*, coincided with the decline of the importance of Marseille as a port of entry. Pimping and drug dealing began to lose "the romanticism of the bazaar" (Boura). Or it might be supposed that this happened as part of a historical cycle often repeated during twenty-six centuries, in which the nature of the city reasserted itself after a time of turbulence and disorder that Aristotle would not have recognized as natural to the self-governing folk of Marseille. The present mayor, a politician of the centre, was a teacher not a lawyer by profession, and teachers have as a rule no particular constituency to favour in the underworld; a locality in any case where the Marseillais welcome no intruders. Richard Cobb points out that Simenon, a perceptive writer, never attempted to send Inspector Maigret any nearer to Marseille than Cannes.

Criminality on a more modest scale certainly continues as in any big town; recently an exploiter of pinball and fruit machines called Joel le Turc, an ex-lieutenant of Francis le Belge, was shot down in a bar in the town centre. But this settlement of accounts in the book-keeping of one-armed banditry seems a little tame compared to the sanguinary record of the serious villains who, fortunately, have not been replaced; and almost effete in the perspective of that long line, not wholly imaginary, of ancestral pirates braving the capricious Mediterranean in their light, rapid vessels out of Lacydon.

The territory of the Marseille *commune* enjoys 57 kilometres of coastline and 10,000 hectares of open space

12 | Escape
Suburbs and Surroundings

> At once wild and easy of access, nature around Marseille offers us its glittering secrets...
>
> Simone de Beauvoir

Offered secrets can be taken in the knowledge that others are withheld, but in the case of Marseille what is accessible may be enough to show how the people use the legacy of their surroundings to vary and swell the heritage of the city to which most of them—as writers often claim—remain passionately loyal. Only some families of the *grande bourgeoisie,* and by no means all, have migrated to Paris and loosened, to their loss as the *Marseillais* think, their Mediterranean ties. For the mass of others of all kinds it is enough to see the coast road and villages of the delightful Côte Bleue between l'Estaque and Martigues to understand that this has become what the *bastides* and *cabanons* used to be, the playground and haven of citizens, far removed from any tourist trail or fashionable resort. The rich, the famous, the actors, politicians, stars and television crews shadowing them stay well away from here and a low profile is kept in the hope that the circus will pass on the other side. The unique Fernandel, who built a family house at Carry-le-Rouet, was an exception, but he was a native son.

The Islands and *Calanques*
Apart from the southern *calanques* the nearest escape from the beloved city is to the archipelago of Frioul, principally made up of the islands of Ratonneau, Pomègues and Château d'If. The last of these with its fortress is the only one much visited by tourists setting out on one of the ferries from the Vieux Port. The others, in practice, are

mainly a Marseillais preserve and an anchorage for yachts and fishing boats. From the day when Caesar installed his galleys the islands were a military zone, and from the sixteenth century a port of quarantine with a garrison relieved at irregular intervals. In 1765 a guard, probably left too long alone, declared himself king of the island and fired with cannon and musket on those sent to carry him away peacefully to the Invalides. American bombing at the end of the Second World War destroyed the fortifications and the Hôpital Caroline, and from 1970 the town progressively reclaimed the islands for the people from the Ministry of Defence. Legend has it that François I hunted stags on the Île de Pomègues but the animals could only have been imported and released for the king's pleasure. Another passing immigrant was the original of the rhinoceros immortalized by Dürer's woodcut of 1515 whose details he took, never having seen the animal, from a description: "Brought from India to the great and powerful King Emanuel of Portugal… has the colour of a speckled tortoise and is covered with thick scales. It is like an elephant in size, but lower on its legs and almost invulnerable… fast, lively and cunning." The king sent the rhinoceros as a gift to the pope but, according to certain historians, the ship carrying it sank in a storm off La Spezia and the animal, being chained to the deck, was drowned. The Marseille story is slightly different and may be an early example of the *galéjade*, those elaborations allegedly characteristic of the Marseillais spirit. The rhinoceros, in this version, made a long stay on Pomègues in 1516, was visited on the island by François I and by admiring and amazed groups of local nobles and naturalists but fell ill, died, and after being skilfully stuffed by local taxidermists was forwarded on to the pope with respects from the city.

The island conditions are governed by the wind; without shelter, the *mistral* flattens the vegetation so that wild olive trees grow horizontally to the ground and plants normally upright spread like a carpet. There are more than three hundred rare plant species with many not found on the mainland and a bird population, migratory and native, including many rarities. Ratonneau has a long beach but for the most part the shore of the islands consists of cliffs giving safe nesting-places to birds and rocky inlets accessible only by steep paths or from the water; in still weather the translucent, teeming sea, its bottom littered with the hulls of shipwrecks of the ages, is a paradise for divers as the arid, open land above is for walkers.

Port-Frioul, formerly the quarantine harbour, seems, apart from its landing-stage and yacht moorings, an unfinished village of small houses and studios built in the 1970s; Gaston Deferre launched a project, mercifully aborted, for the construction on Ratonneau of a town of 2,300 apartments, a hotel, a high-rise block of subsidized housing and moorings for 1,500 boats. The necessary services were never brought and the project was abandoned in 1978. Ratonneau and Pomègues, like the other, smaller islands dotted about the Gulf of Marseille, were left in the care of nature and of preservation bodies, though how long these good offices will protect them nobody can be sure. Their position in the bay and the fierce beauty of the islands are a lure to the imagination of developers, but the very complete and loving protection afforded to the great natural site of the calanques between Marseille and Cassis gives ground for optimism.

There are also calanques along the 25-kilometre coast from l'Estaque to Cap Couronne, though both less protected and less spectacularly beautiful, and many of these too are only accessible on foot. Near Cap Couronne at the extremity of the Côte Bleue, Carro is a fishing village which has spread, and is spreading, in a comparatively discreet way by the addition of small villas built by Marseillais, often for themselves in the style called *artisanal,* a euphemism translatable as "home-made". Between Carro and Cap Couronne the pink limestone rock shelves down to the sea, the distant gulf is visible across the water, and in places the smooth vertical face of the stone can be seen where the Greeks, and after them the medieval builders of the city, cut the materials for their walls, houses and temples before transporting the stone on vessels across the bay. The road winding back towards Marseille passes by Sausset-les-Pins and Carry-le-Rouet, both a little but not much more chic than Carro, but nowhere on this coast is there a sense of any alien presence and very little sign of insensitive development; the only tower block of ten storeys is at Carry-le-Rouet, hidden among trees. The road down to the calanque de Niolon passes between savage limestone cliffs and a vegetation of dwarf holm oak growing from cracks in the rock, waterless and impoverished, but where the soil is deeper there are pine woods tragically vulnerable to fire and now protected, in many places too late, by draconian regulation.

Do the Marseillais in their recreation and escape stray far from the sea? It would seem, given their history and the maritime passage by which most of them arrived, that as land is to a farmer, so the sea is their fundamental element and it claims them back. Cassis, a favourite resort for those with money to spend, and surrounded by vineyards producing a well-known dry white wine, is at the south-eastern end of the calanques of which some of the most beautiful can be reached from there on foot; in the centre is a seventeenth-century town hall and a Mediterranean museum of archaeological finds. Nearby La Ciotat, formerly a ship-building centre, is still a fishing and sailing village, and even Martigues with its pervasive odour of oil refining on the Etang de Berre provides an access to the sea for many Marseillais with boats. From the hills around Cassis and La Ciotat, above the building line for farms and villas, the tremendous panorama, like everything else in or near the territory of Marseille, is oriented toward the sea as if benevolently planned to spare an elect people any need ever to feel exiled from their element.

To the north-west the Camargue and the Rhône delta, with international fame and star ranking on tourist itineraries, are probably less visited by the Marseillais than those coastal neighbourhoods where a sense of feeling local can reign undisturbed, and intrusion from the mainland is at a minimum. However, this largest of European wetlands with its black bulls and flamingos and expanses of sandy beach forms, like the national parks of the Cévennes and the Provençal Alps, part of a wide hinterland of Mediterranean regions within reach of Marseille, countries where the olive tree grows, the sea is on or over the horizon and natives of the city know that they can quickly get back to it. It was along the west-east route crossing this territory that their ancestors harrassed the intruder Hannibal, forcing him to travel the Alpine passes and earning the gratitude of Rome; even if few Marseillais know the history it must be laid, together with other historical exploits and as happens with the exploits of other peoples, like sediment in rock fixing a stratum of identity and a tint of character.

Rivalries and Affinities

The French Mediterranean arc and the Golfe du Lion are especially remarkable for the number of historic cities, mostly created by the Roman world, that stand about them, and although the Marseillais tend to give the impression of visiting these places from another country, they are in a profound sense part of the Mediterranean context to which Marseille belongs, and where it should by right of fame, antiquity and historical and numerical pre-eminence, play the leading role which a largely factitious reputation dating from the disaster of the burning of the Nouvelles Galeries (see p.84) and the reaction of the pre-war government has denied it. That the Marseillais themselves, with their propensity for self-mockery and literary exploitation of their own caricature, have had a hand in this denigration is undeniable but question-begging. It is felt in the south that too much in France emanates too despotically and with too little empathy from Paris, and Paris, at least since Louis XIV, views Marseille with a jaundiced eye—Marseille, primate city of all France but centrifugal by essence.

The town which has most benefited in the eyes of the *bien-pensant*, the conventional, by the long fall from grace of Marseille is its ancient rival Aix-en-Provence, Aquae Sextiae of its Roman founders, capital of the Kings of Provence with its mansions, unlike those of Marseille, superbly preserved. But for some time now Aix shows the stigmata, not of economic decline but of the embarrassment which Marseille has so far been spared, an international blandness of wealthy housing investment and presence. Aix has become incorrigibly bourgeois. This has not yet happened to Arles which though it has built a greatly admired and rich museum of Roman antiquities remains a market town, the centre of the Camargue and the rail-head for its farmers and stock breeders. Avignon is perhaps too medieval, too preserved, too Catholic for most Marseillais to feel at home there. These cities are among the architectural and environmental wonders of France, though subject to the risk of outrage, but

Marseille does not aspire and has never aspired to this category; the sea which washes away outrage at the first storm is, as Caesar said, almost all its environment.

Protestant Nîmes has, perhaps unexpectedly, a long connection with Marseille, not only on account of the shipping lines by which the *Nimois* textiles, notably denim, were exported to Genoa or the New World. The Protestant presence among the leading mercantile families was strong, ancient and came largely from the Languedoc Huguenots whose historic centre was, and is, Nîmes; it seems no accidental coincidence that two of the most celebrated twentieth-century mayors of Marseille, Siméon Flaissières and Gaston Defferre, were of Languedoc Protestant origin, nor that the architect Espérandieu who left so powerful a mark on the Marseille townscape was a Nîmois. Without its Protestants, France would seem monolithic; with their reputation for integrity in business and in personal life they have given variety to the French perspective and kept alive for themselves a sense of apartness and independence which would account for an evident affinity between the Nîmois and the Marseillais.

A very strong affinity naturally exists between Corsica, the "isle of beauty", and the great number of Marseille families with Corsican origins, however distant, Corsicans being noted for the endurance and fidelity of family ties. The ferry crossings to Bastia or Ajaccio are cheap, fast, frequent and crowded. The island's mountains and forests and often wild coastline are certainly among the most favoured of the escape outlets for those Marseillais looking to stray beyond their own coast, and the Corsican reputation for clandestinity in remote mountain country and sheltering in hiding of outlaws finds a resonance among the people of a city which has lived so great a part of its history in a state of relative disaffection from the ruling culture and the central power.

The bounds that constitute Marseille are sea and hills. Between them, turned towards each, it follows its evolving tri-millennial life. If the sea is dominant, the hills with *garrigue* and game and great walking spaces make the freedom of the citizen ashore, as portrayed for all time by Marcel Pagnol in *La gloire de mon père*. Beyond the nearest range is the Massif de la Sainte-Baume where the Huveaune rises, with a network of paths and tracks and from its summit immense views over the intervening hills and the Mediterranean. Yet further away are the pre-Alps of Provence, the homeland of the novelist Jean Giono who somewhat lyrically described the orientation of this territory towards the distant maritime city—alluring, negligent, adventurous, refusing all claims on it: "Over an area a hundred kilometres square of valleys, mountains, plateaux, forests and moors, in every town and village house, in every farm, each evening above every bed when the lamps are out, there's a kind of mist in which a golden town appears, like a king's crown, a great crown of the elect—that is Marseille."

Further Reading

Apart from Richard Cobb, references to Marseille in English works are chiefly found in guides and histories of Provence, to and from which the city is historically antecedent, geographically separate and culturally quite different. Otherwise allusions and brief accounts like those of Boswell, Dickens and Conrad are merely casual.

Some works of the great historian Fernand Braudel exist in English translation, and of these *The Identity of France* (London: HarperCollins, 1989) and *The Mediterranean and the Mediterranean World in the Age of Philip II* (Berkeley: University of California Press, 1996) are of the greatest interest.

There is naturally a mass of works in French on Marseille and its past and present problems. These tend to show a character of critical puzzlement on the part of authors who are not *Marseillais,* and of elusive defensiveness in those who are. In either case, the astute and affectionate detachment of Cobb is lacking though in Paul Lombard and Christian Harrel-Courtès the love of Marseille is as touchingly evident as the huge panorama of the city and its history deserve.

The following is a selection of works in French that have most contributed to this study and seem the most accessible and rewarding.

Américi, Laurence and Xavier Daumalin, *Les dynasties marseillaises de la Révolution à nos jours.* Paris: Perrin, 2010

Baratier, Edouard, *Histoire de Marseille.* Toulouse: Privat, 1973

Bertrand, Régis, *Le patrimoine de Marseille.* Marseille, Jeanne Lafitte, 2001

Bonillo, Jean-Lucien, *Marseille, ville et port.* Marseille: Parenthèses, 1996

Duchêne, Roger and Jean Contrucci, *Marseille, 2600 ans d'histoire.* Paris: Fayard, 1988

Langevin, Philippe and Jean-Claude Juan, *Marseille: une métropole entre Europe et Méditerranée*. Paris: La Documentation Française, 2007

Roncayolo, Marcel, *Marseille: les territoires du temps*. Paris: Editions locales de France, 1996

Témime, Emile, *Migrance, histoire des migrations à Marseille*. Aix-en-Provence: Edisud, 1989

Viard, Jean, *Marseille, une ville impossible*. Paris: Payot, 1995

Zalio, Pierre-Paul, *Grandes familles de Marseille au XXe siècle: enquête sur l'identité économique d'un territoire portuaire*. Paris: Belin, 1999

Writers of memoirs, fictions, journalistic or non-specialist analyses can seem closer to the truth of such a great cosmopolitan city as Marseille, if less detached, than historians and academics. The following works are especially valuable.

Agostini, Julie and Yannick Forno, *Les écrivains et Marseille: anthologie commentée de textes littéraires sur Marseille du Ve siècle avant J.-C. à nos jours*. Marseille: Jeanne Lafitte, 1999

Boura, Olivier, *Marseille, ou la mauvaise reputation*. Paris: Arléa, 1998

de l'Ecotais, Yann, *Marseille, la porte de la Méditerranée*. Monaco: Alphée-Jean-Paul Bertrand, 2009

Harrel-Courtès, Christian, *Marseille nostalgie*. Paris: L'Harmattan, 1994

Langlade, Isabelle and Sylvie Masson, *Marseille et ses quartiers, I & II*. Collection des Archives Municipales de Marseille, Alan Sutton, 2002

Lombard, Paul, *Dictionnaire amoureux de Marseille*. Paris: Plon, 2008

Londres, Albert, *Marseille porte du sud*. Marseille: Jeanne Lafitte, 1980

Suarès, André, *Marsiho*. Marseille: Jeanne Lafitte, 1990.

Useful websites

www.marseille-tourisme.com
www.marseille.fr
www.marseille.com
www.laprovence.com
www.marseillecityofculture.eu

Index